The ACOA's Guide to
Raising Healthy Children

The ACOA's Guide to Raising Healthy Children

❖

A Parenting Handbook for Adult Children of Alcoholics

❖

DR. JIM MASTRICH
with BILL BIRNES

COLLIER BOOKS
Macmillan Publishing Company • New York
Collier Macmillan Publishers • London

Collier Books
Macmillan Publishing Company
866 Third Avenue, New York, NY 10022
Collier Macmillan Canada, Inc.

Library of Congress Cataloging-in-Publication Data
Mastrich, Jim.
  The ACOA's guide to raising healthy children: a parenting handbook for adult children of alcoholics/Jim Mastrich with Bill Birnes.
  p. cm.
  Bibliography: p.
  Includes index.
  ISBN 0-02-040581-2
  1. Adult children of alcoholics. 2. Parenting. 3. Alcoholics—Family relationships. I. Birnes, William J. II. Title.
  HV5132.M365 1988
  362.2'92—dc19   88-23445
                                                        CIP

Macmillan books are available at special discounts for bulk purchases for sales promotions, premiums, fund-raising, or educational use. For details contact:

  Special Sales Director
  Macmillan Publishing Company
  866 Third Avenue
  New York, NY 10022

10 9 8 7 6 5 4 3 2 1

Printed in the United States of America

Contents

Preface: The Big Zero

Several years ago I began noticing an interesting pattern in the stories that my clients at the Community Mental Health Center at Rutgers Medical School were telling me. As a psychologist, family therapist, and substance-abuse specialist, I spoke to many clients who came in for all sorts of reasons: chronic depression, marital discord, parenting difficulties, anxiety, and dissatisfaction with their career choices. Very rarely did any of them voluntarily identify themselves as having alcoholic parents. Many still were not even aware that their parents were alcoholics. Yet, over the course of getting to know them, I realized that over 60 to 70 percent of my clients were adult children of alcoholics. Most came for counseling, assuming that their current problems had no connection with their past. And most were not ready to admit that they came from alcoholic families.

With the discovery that their past had been compromised by the physical and emotional abuse that oftentimes takes place in alcoholic families and the realization that many of the conflicts they faced in the present were the result of their experiences in alcoholic families, many of my adult children of alcoholic clients came to new realizations. Most ultimately realized that they were not only the victims of abusive parents but also the victims of an extended campaign to deny the truth, to hide it not only from the outside world but also from the children in the family. When we shared our feelings about the implications of this discovery during therapy sessions, most of my clients were able to realize, of course, that nothing was wrong with them; they had lived under "the big lie" for twenty, thirty, sometimes even forty years. As a result many had developed a personal view of the world that was particular to their own situation. Having grown up in an environment of distorted reality, they had developed equally distorted views of the world around them. Now, however, as adults and parents, they had to adjust their perceptions to a world interpreted by people who had not grown up in alcoholic or dysfunctional families. And this was one of the major sources of conflict.

I began conducting an informal survey among my clients who were adult children of alcoholics and found that the overwhelming majority of them—men and women alike— were prototypical survivors: assertive, strong-willed, self-reliant, success-oriented, focused, and intense. Many were classic Type A personalities who were more unforgiving of their own shortcomings and mistakes than those of others. If left undisturbed by the turbulence caused by intimate relationships and child rearing, most of my clients would have pushed forward into their middle years, chalking up success after success, packaging the fears and nightmares of their childhood into smaller and smaller boxes in the most remote corners of their consciousness.

However, in my survey I found that the singular most sensitive trigger in the lives of almost all of my clients was raising children or the prospect thereof. Taken as a matter of course by most non-ACOAs, for ACOAs raising children threatens to raise the specter of their deepest fears of insecurity, worthlessness, and abandonment. As a biological imperative, most physiological and many psychological aspects of children's lives are prepackaged almost from the moment of conception and are beyond their parents' control. I found that those ACOAs who had tucked away their memories of childhood into neatly wrapped parcels were most afraid that their own children not only would open the parcels but, in malicious abandonment, would spread the contents all over the living room floor for all the world to see. Those ACOAs eventually found out, as you will too, that this is *not* going to be the case.

It was obvious to me, however, that whether perceived or real my clients' fears about children or even having children were seriously disrupting their lives and threatening to destroy their relationships with their spouses or lovers. The more we explored these problems, the more we kept confronting one simple, basic truth: most of my ACOA clients had never experienced normal childhoods. Purely and simply, they did not know how a normal, functional child was supposed to grow up. Many of my clients watched "The Cosby Show" or "Family Ties" on television and reported that it was like watching life on another planet. It all boiled down to one question: What goes on in a normal family?

Had most of my clients been able to experience functional family lives, they would not have looked upon the prospect of raising children with such trepidation. Without the benefit of memories of a normal childhood, my clients had no basis for understanding how children should be cared for, how they should be nurtured, how they should be raised, what parents were supposed to do, and what parents' expectations of children should be. As one of my clients expressed it, her childhood was "a big zero, a giant black hole that sucked everything in." She complained that she could not pull a memory out even if she wanted to. So, she asked, how was she supposed to figure out what to do with her own children?

All of this told me that if ACOAs who were parents or thinking about it had a map of the terrain of raising children, a road map that would tell them which way to go, with a compass always pointing to normal, then they could find their own way without needing to serve eighteen years in a normal family setting. They would have greater confidence as parents. They might not have to ferret out their worst memories of parental mistrust just to keep their own eighteen-month-old from sticking a fork in the wall socket.

Many of my clients came into therapy sessions fully armed with baby- and child-care books, but, they explained, it was like reading a foreign language. Because most of them did not share the same basic assumptions as the authors—the world is healthy, the world is full of trust, your parents loved you, so you can love your baby—my ACOA clients were lost. What if your parents did not love you? some asked. What if you could not even remember most of what your parents said and did? Without those memories, without those assumptions, much of the standard advice in child-care books simply fell on uncomprehending ears. It was not the reader's fault that the author was not speaking the same language.

Therefore, I decided to write a book for adult children of alcoholics about how to raise healthy children when you did not come from a healthy family yourself. My clients told me that if they could have a manual or reference guide that spoke directly to them about what they were supposed to feel, they would at least have a set of instructions to help them. No book could replace the warm feelings that being raised in a loving family environment can create, but it might help readers provide that kind of environment for their own children.

Actually, I wrote this book with as well as for my clients. You will hear their own stories, experience their memories, and work with them to solve their problems. Most of all, you will see how you yourself can raise your own child to be healthy and happy even if you were not raised that way by your parents. I have changed names, of course, as well as details here and there, to protect confidentiality, but all the stories are true.

The book is organized chronologically like a standard child-care guide, from birth through adolescence to adulthood. However, I have included chapters early on for ACOAs who are new to parenting, then later chapters on talking about alcoholism and substance abuse with a child or teenager, alcoholism in your child, the empty-nest syndrome, dealing with an aged or infirmed alcoholic parent, and grandparenting your child's child, especially when alcoholism or substance abuse appears in the family. These are topics most of my ACOA clients wanted to see included in a book because they can be found nowhere else addressed to the needs of ACOAs.

I would like to start all of my readers off on the same foot. I realize that most of you understand what it means to be an

ACOA and have come to grips with some of the feelings surrounding your childhood and early family life. This book is not a primer for ACOAs, it is about raising healthy children. However, if we can agree on some of the shared goals that most ACOAs adopt when they consider having children and then understand what alcoholism is, we can all move forward at our own pace, at least we will be speaking mutually intelligible dialects.

Goals

1. *Rewrite the script.* Most ACOAs I speak to want to rewrite the script so that they do not carry the dysfunctions of their families of origin into their children's generation. They want to rewrite their personal scripts and the scripts of the family so that their children and grandchildren do not become alcoholics and can live without the fears and insecurities that plagued the lives of the ACOAs who are their parents.

2. *Break the cycle.* Of utmost importance to most ACOAs is breaking the cycle of alcoholism. The behavior that resulted in alcohol abuse or drug abuse is oftentimes carried from one generation to the next. Physical infirmities, the nature of the disease of alcoholism, and genetic predisposition toward substance abuse must be fully understood and appreciated by children so that they do not trick themselves into "just one drink" or "just one puff."

3. *Eliminate denial behavior.* Most ACOAs report that one of the most troubling aspects of their families of origin was denial behavior, pretending that something that was apparent was not really there. "Dad's just sick, he's not drunk"; "Mom's having 'girl' problems today"; or "Outsiders don't understand." By denying the truth in their families, ACOAs can become very sensitized to the truth and the absence of truth. They can be vulnerable to and victims of the social games and nuances, many of which involve a level of dissembling or downright dishonesty, that weave the pattern of everyday dis-

course at work and at home. Denial can become a cancer in families and relationships, and understanding what denial is should be a goal not only for ACOAs but for all people who have grown up in dysfunctional families.

4. *Our children are not ourselves.* Children should be allowed to live out their own lives and write their own scripts. Our job as parents is to do our best to raise healthy, happy, honest, positive, independent, and productive children. They should not be forced to live out their parents' lives or their parents' deepest emotional aspirations. Children are not the material to repair the damage in the ACOA's own childhood. Do not use your child; raise your child. If you have nagging problems that still reach into your present family from your own family background, you should consider working with a mental health professional who is a specialist in working with ACOA-related issues. Do not force your children to solve the problems for you or to live in such a way that your problems are solved vicariously. Let your children be children.

Origins and Types of Alcoholism

You probably already know that alcohol is one of the oldest mood-altering substances known to man and that alcoholism has been a problem since the dawn of recorded history. In virtually every society alcoholic beverages are produced from such raw materials as grains, fruits, vegetables, and flowers, and they are consumed for many reasons, ceremonial and otherwise.

Alcohol works in your body chemically by depressing your central nervous system, although depending upon the dosage, social setting, expectations of the individual, and phase of the drinking cycle, there are a variety of seemingly contradictory physiological effects. Alcohol may depress, stimulate, tranquilize, or agitate; it may release one drinker's inhibitions while sedating another's. Some people become mellow, others bellicose and even pugnacious. In almost all drinkers there are some mood swings, impairment of judgment, and impairment of perception and muscular coordination. The greater the amount of alcohol, the greater the impairment. Too much alcohol will inevitably induce stupor. A repeatedly high intake of alcohol inevitably produces some degree of permanent brain and neurological damage, deterioration of the kidneys and liver, ulcerations of the intestinal and stomach lining, and may ultimately result in muscular paralysis, coma, and death.

Alcohol is also classified as a toxin. For chemically sensitive or genetically predisposed individuals—and you or your child may fall into this category—alcohol can be a deadly poison. For such an individual, one drink is all it takes to trigger a chemical mechanism that can make that person profoundly sick. If you have an allergy to alcohol or a serious physiological reaction to the substance, avoid drinking at all costs. If you are an ACOA, you should avoid drinking as a rule because you may have a latent allergic predisposition that can be triggered at any time. You may not be allergic at all, but you are playing Russian roulette with your metabolism. I ask my clients who are ACOAs to follow a simple rule: Don't drink!

All ACOAs should understand that alcoholism is recognized as a disease by both the American Medical Association and the World Health Organization. The disease may be manifested differently according to the individual, but it is nevertheless a disease that can reach through two or three generations and snatch the unsuspecting descendant. It should be no surprise to you that many ACOAs have struggled with alcoholism themselves.

Despite the common stereotype of the Bowery drunk, only about 5 percent of all alcoholics are skid-row types. The vast majority are employed, married, and hold positions of responsibility in their communities. Alcoholism is often masked behind likable, even affable people with good jobs, seemingly stable family relationships, and pleasant demeanors. Alcoholism recognizes no racial or social barriers and cuts across all economic classes. Succinctly stated, alcoholism is a physical or psychological dependence or involvement with alcohol to the point of its interfering with the individual's adequate or healthy functioning in employment or in relationships with spouse or children.

At this point, having understood what alcoholism is and what our initial goals should be in raising healthy children and breaking the cycle of substance abuse, you should not be afraid of your own emotions. You may not understand them, but you have the ability and the power to control them. Allow yourself to be emotionally intimate with your spouse or mate. Give trust a chance to work. Build cautiously, but progressively, and you will soon see that you can raise healthy and productive children.

As I indicated earlier, *The ACOA's Guide to Raising Healthy Children* is the result of the aspirations of the hundreds of ACOAs I have spoken with about raising children and the problems they have confronted. I wish to thank all of my ACOA clients for helping me to assemble the material for this book. I dedicate this book to them, the many ACOAs I have had the honor to know over the years. I am particularly indebted to the members of the ACOA groups I work with for their willingness to share, and their courage to face themselves and grow.

The ACOA's Guide to
Raising Healthy Children

ACOA Parents in Crisis

Susan's son flinched instinctively. He drew back from the refrigerator as if he'd received an electric shock. The moment he caught his mother's angry glare out of the corner of his eye he knew he was in trouble. "I didn't hit him. I didn't have to. He was already afraid and beat his retreat through the living room without even looking back." Susan followed him through the living room, preparing to unleash the verbal barrage that had welled up in her from the moment she heard his footsteps coming down the first-floor landing. Yet angry as she was at her son, she felt a tremendous surge of guilt—and then anger at herself. Finally, she was overwhelmed by a feeling of remorse. By the time she confronted her ten-year-old son in his room, she was so disconcerted by her own conflicting emotions that what she told him made as little sense to her as it did to him. "I knew all the time that I was completely out of control, but there was nothing I could do about it. I only prayed that I wouldn't hurt him."

Many months later, Susan still couldn't explain the anger she felt toward her son. She knew that she was overreacting. "I have a hair-trigger temper that makes me lash out at him for even the most minor infractions of rules I set." In therapy she explained that when she was most out of control, she could see herself only as a little girl who had failed yet again to please her father. And she was angry at her failure, full of a child's rage that respected no boundaries.

Susan complained that she did not know how to discipline her son.

I don't know. Whatever other parents understand about the balance between correcting a kid's behavior and allowing him the freedom to explore completely eludes me. When he disobeys, I can only perceive it as his disapproval of me as a parent. It's like he's saying, "You fail!"

She took his natural assertion of his own will—what every parent ultimately wants his or her child to achieve—as a fundamental personal challenge. And she responded as if she had to prove her power as a parent over and over again. Her child's willfulness touched strings in her that resonated deep into her past and kept her from dealing with the reassuring logic of the present.

This was a far cry from the successes that highlighted the rest of her life. Susan was a special education teacher who had won praise from her department head and the school principal. She was an overachiever, a statuesque "all-American beauty" who seemed reassuringly calm and competent in the face of any challenge. She was a perfectionist in her professional life as well as at home.

Susan had married a man who was also confident of his own abilities and of Susan's. He depended on her to work around the house with the same level of commitment that she gave to her elementary school students. He, too, worked around the house, and planned to teach their two boys to be as handy with tools as he was. Yet for all his self-confidence, he was unresponsive. Assuming that Susan was as capable of handling her own problems as she was of handling the problems of others, he did not support her in what he considered "domestic" chores. Nor did he initiate conversations on his own. She was forced to prod him for attention or throw a temper tantrum when she felt she could no longer cope. Consequently, Susan was left to solve her problems on her own in the solitude of the night after the rest of the family had gone to bed. And as the tensions in the family grew,

Susan's tantrums became more frequent and pushed their relationship closer and closer to the edge.

By the time Susan entered therapy, she was in crisis. Her realization that she was losing control was not the result of any identifiable single event; rather, it had developed gradually from a long series of minor events that had stretched her coping abilities beyond their resiliency. As hard as she worked to maintain an outward semblance of normalcy, the energy required to cope with new circumstances demanded she work even harder. Eventually, her hair-trigger temper began to make her fear her own capacity for violence.

When I'm mad I just get confused. I don't know what normal anger is. When I get mad I don't stop. It seems to all pour out or be forcing itself to the surface. I know this isn't right, but I can't help feeling it.

Susan found that she was replicating the behavior of her alcoholic father. His violent temper and his inability to cope with the slightest of obstacles were always directed at his children. Even though Susan was not herself an alcoholic, she nevertheless was living out a script written for her years before when she grew up as one of seven children in a dysfunctional alcoholic family. As she grew up, the survival mechanism that she had developed in her family helped her become an overachiever. She overcompensated for her father's weakness by becoming strong. And she was able to succeed because she had a rigid determination driven by the image of her father chastising her throughout her childhood.

When she married, however, Susan found she had to work harder. She relied on her husband for support, and in the early years of marriage the support was always there. But when she became a parent, dormant memories of her own childhood began to surface and dictate her responses to her husband and sons. She panicked as she realized she did not know how to parent. No one had taught her. She had not grown up in a functional family and therefore had not seen how normal parents played out their roles. For the very first time in her adult life, Susan found herself alone and frightened that she could not do the job. Her response was to become a rigid disciplinarian just as her father had been. And the more her husband failed to support her in this role, the more she turned on him, as if he, like her two boys, were baiting her and threatening to expose the deep secrets of her past. Her family had become the "them" she had envied throughout her life, the normal people who navigated through life's obstacles with an insouciance that defied all reason. And now she, even within the confines of her own home, was standing alone against the enemy.

Bill's own personal crisis was less dramatic than Susan's, but it was no less poignant. It came later in his life—in his forties—as he watched his fifteen-year-old daughter glide into her first significant relationship with an older boy. He had watched from a distance for years as Kristin matured, guided through her adolescence by her mother, whom she seemed to emulate in every way. She was reserved, an unlikely quality for a teenager, studious, and a varsity athlete in two sports. To the world of her peers and teachers, Bill's daughter was a tribute to the strength of his marriage, a child that any parent would have been proud to have raised. Yet to Bill, there was a disquieting undertone to all of this.

Unlike most of the children in her age group, Kristin showed no signs of rebellion or true expressions of joy. Her ebullience at winning a field hockey game or an event at a swim meet was always paced according to the emotions of her teammates. She was happy at being on the honor roll, but that was enough. There was no drive to be first in her class or even to slack off and be "bad" as many of the other girls in her honors classes had done from time to time. Kristin was a follower, a loyal assistant manager who carried out her instructions with diligence and dedication, but stopped the moment she had fulfilled her responsibility.

Now, in her relationship with her boyfriend, Kristin was again a loyal follower. She was displaying attributes that reminded Bill all too painfully of his own disdain for sticking his neck out.

We were becoming exactly alike. We both had this uncanny ability that I learned as a child to adopt the camouflage of my surroundings. It wasn't the worst attribute in the world; in fact it got me through some pretty difficult times when I was growing up. But over the years I came to hate it about myself because it seemed sneaky and weak.

As a child, Bill had learned to adapt to whatever changing situation overtook his family. He had learned to agree with those around him, even when he knew they were wrong. He had accepted every lie his mother told him about his father's problems, learning to ignore the obvious.

She would always say, "Your father is sick again," or "I just don't know what to do about your father's illness. Lord knows, I've been to doctor after doctor, but none of them can help. We'll just have to live with the problem ourselves." Time and again she would say, "You're such a helpful little boy," as if I really had a choice. Other fathers would go to picnics, play in school softball games, drive a group of us home on a Saturday afternoon. But my dad was always sick. There were times when he would just sleep on the couch for hours, so that if my friends wanted to come over, they couldn't. "People wouldn't understand," my mother would say. And I went along. I went along with everything. I didn't really buy her story. I just didn't argue. You couldn't argue with her because she kept on saying the same thing over and over again as if she didn't hear what you said. I learned that you get along by going along. That's the way I've lived my whole life. And now I'm forty and my daughter will grow up to be just like me.

The only thing is that sometimes I get so mad, I don't know where to put my anger. I learned long ago never to hit out at anyone, so I never fight. But still I get mad when I acquiesce to something I don't want to do, and it happens much more now than it used to. There are times when I feel like I'm chewing myself up from the inside out. And I don't even drink.

Bill found that in the process of learning to accept whatever his mother told him as the truth, he had become just like one of the courtiers in the tale of *The Emperor's New Clothes*. Now, he sadly realized, his daughter had learned the trait from him. He wondered whether the same anger that knotted up his stomach at nights burned within his daughter as well, but he was too frightened at first even to involve her in his therapy program.

Children of Alcoholics as Adults and Parents

Susan and Bill were both adult children of alcoholics who faced crises in their relationships with their own children. Even though they had come to accept their parents' problems with alcohol abuse, they were not prepared for the problems they faced as parents. This, unfortunately, is an all too common occurrence in the life patterns of adult children of alcoholics (ACOAs) who marry and raise families of their own. As mental health professionals trained in the treatment of addiction have come to find out, alcohol abuse not only affects the parent who drinks but can affect his or her children and grandchildren as well.

For Susan and Bill and the hundreds of thousands of ACOAs like you who have grown up in families affected by the presence of alcoholism, the scars left by alcoholic parents run very deep. Parental dependence on alcohol creates an unhealthy family environment characterized by

1. Psychological and even physical abuse;
2. Forced denial of reality, creating self-doubt in children's minds;
3. Loss of childhood happiness;
4. Contorted or reversed child/parent relationships;
5. Inconsistent or fluctuating child/parent relationships;
6. Extreme childhood frustration and anxiety;
7. A profound sense of disappointment on the part of the children;
8. Lack of role models;
9. Fear of the outside world;
10. Distrust of authorities and institutions.

Given these circumstances of the prototypical ACOA's upbringing, it would be virtually impossible for the ACOA not to become a fearful parent. This is a fact that most adult children of alcoholics fail to realize until after they have had children and discovered that their parent/child relationships are crippled by the past. Sometimes, the damage to the ACOA parents can be so pervasive that its effects can reach forward in time through their children into the next generation of family members.

Therefore, ACOAs like you who are parents or who are considering the prospect of starting a family must learn how to raise children within the context of your own background. You have to understand that your reactions to the normal events of child raising will be colored by the unhappiness in your past. You may overreact to your children's problems. You may be a rigid disciplinarian. You may find yourself engaging in abusive behavior patterns. Or you may be so bound by memories of growing up in a dysfunctional alcoholic family that you find yourself incapable of dealing with your children's legitimate problems. In short, you must learn how to be a normal parent who relates to his or her children and to other parents in the community. And that is the purpose of this book: to teach you and other adult children of alcoholics how to raise healthy children who will not be burdened by the guilt, anger, and fears from your past.

The Personality Conflicts of ACOAs as Parents

The very conflicts that troubled you as a young child growing up in a dysfunctional family don't simply vanish when you become an adult. The coping mechanisms that you used to deal with the outside, or normal, world still operate as you navigate through school, college, the business world, and into relationships. The ACOA makes deals with the past, learns to forget or screen out the most painful moments of growing up, and adopts a veneer of positive dynamism toward solving life's challenges. However, because the overwhelming majority of parents see little versions of themselves and their parents in their children, the child of an ACOA can trigger an emotional time bomb by bringing back to the surface those same fears and conflicts that had become manageable over the years. Thus, parenting can too often become an elephant trap, a pit of unresolvable conflicts into which the otherwise successful ACOA can tumble just because he or she does not know that being an ACOA parent should involve ongoing processes of *self-discovery* as well as healthy child raising.

As you, as an ACOA, examine the emotional conflicts that you confront in your relationships with your children, you will realize that the problems began long before you became a parent. They began in the early years of your own childhood when you internalized certain axioms endemic to alcoholic families. These axioms, unless consciously rejected, will always remain and define the relationships you develop with your children, spouse, and grandchildren.

Damaged Goods

Most ACOAs consider themselves to be "damaged goods." This is not surprising because the very fact of growing up in a dysfunctional family can result in severe emotional and often physical damage. If you are an ACOA and feel as if you are somehow unworthy because you are damaged, you are not alone. Moreover, your fears and feelings about the outside world are quite normal considering your childhood.

You can break this cycle of inferiority by recognizing your childhood for what it was. Your feelings of inferiority are as much a part of you as anything else. You can go forward by accepting them as part of you and acknowledging that they were created by your own childhood family situation. You can change how you feel by first becoming aware of what you feel, understanding why you feel that way, and deciphering the messages the child in you tells your present-day adult self. This is not as easy as it sounds. I have observed that for most ACOAs, accepting oneself and the difficulties of one's past is one of the most difficult tasks to accomplish. However, once it is accomplished, many other obstacles on the road to dealing with one's own children are easier to surmount.

Personal Forgiveness

Most ACOAs find child raising especially difficult because they are constantly blaming themselves for the "sins" of their parents they have visited upon their children. ACOAs are in the middle. When Susan lashes out at her son, Bobby, for his real or perceived mischievousness, she is actually striking back at the years of pent-up anger she feels toward herself for failing her father. She has not learned to forgive herself, and, hence, is unable to forgive anyone around her. Because her son is the most immediate object in her environment, he receives the brunt of her anger.

If you are an ACOA, you must understand that how you were raised and how you have to come to see yourself are not your fault. They are merely the hand of cards you were dealt. Yet many ACOAs blame and continue to punish themselves as if they, and not the situation, are the cause of the problem. When ACOAs raise their own families, they oftentimes inadvertently attend to the needs of their spouse and their child at the expense of their own. Thus, when their needs are not met, they are prone to carry blame and resentment into this new family.

If you find yourself falling into this pattern, try to accept that the anger is not your fault. You have the right to be angry just as anyone else would in your situation. It is your responsibility, however, to take control of your life. Doing this means that you will be able to establish meaningful relationships with other family members and structure a healthy and functional home environment. This need to accept responsibility is particularly important for ACOAs considering having children, because the sooner you come to terms with your past, the better able you will be to cope with the normal and predictable strains of parenthood. Indeed, your honest awareness of your emotions, thoughts, and personal beliefs is your greatest asset in breaking the negative cycle.

A Pervading Sense of Fear

Adult children of alcoholics in all walks of life often speak of having a generalized sense of fear that accompanies all of their activities. For ACOAs who are parents, this fear penetrates the family unit and colors the relationships they have with their children. ACOA parents can easily transmit this fear to their children, as Susan has done in her relationship with Bobby, and cause them to be afraid and insecure. Sometimes this sense of fear leads the ACOA parent to become hypervigilant, ever scanning the horizon for the next impending disaster. Consequently, ACOA parents are uncertain of their ability to provide a safe environment for their families. Even though the ACOA parents are no longer children themselves and not subject to the unpredictabilities of life in a dysfunctional family, they still feel vulnerable because of their experiences and carry this vulnerability into their own families.

The most striking characteristic of this fear is the apprehension and distrust of the feeling itself. In other words, ACOAs can be afraid of being afraid. They are afraid of situations that have caused them to be fearful in the past and they are afraid of relationships that remind them of the fears they experienced as children. But because most children learn to deal with fear, ACOAs learned as children to cut off the fear and deny the apprehension. This often has very devastating side effects because emotions are much like the opposite ends of a pendulum. Cutting off fear and sorrow on one side often means cutting off joy and exhilaration on the other so as to balance the emotional load. In this way, many ACOAs deaden themselves to emotions in general by the time they have reached early adolescence.

This was part of Bill's problem and the personality characteristics he exemplified to his daughter. By trying to cut off all his emotions and simply accept whatever his mother told him, he managed to alleviate the most crippling effects of pervasive fear, but only at the cost of amputating part of his emotional response to perfectly normal stimulation. As a result, by the time he had reached middle age and looked forward to enjoying the success his daughter was about to have, he found himself fearing that she, like he, was trapped within an emotional "dead zone." At the end of a full circle, Bill realized that he had his appointment with fear after all, only this time it was a fear for his daughter's future.

Like many ACOAs, Bill expended tremendous amounts of energy suppressing his intense feelings because he was afraid of them. He most feared the anger that he felt for his parents. Again, this is natural. Most children fear the anger they feel toward their parents. But because in normal circumstances their anger is also reasonably mitigated by childhood happiness, children learn to socialize anger, to control it, and to channel it into acceptable modes of expression. Children in

alcoholic families rarely learn to channel their anger. Therefore, because they can't manage it effectively, they are afraid
of it controlling them and consequently grow up to fear it.

Nowhere is the fear of rage more evident than in an ACOA
parent's attempt to deal with his or her own children. The
fear of overreacting to the specific situation or the terror of
misplacing anger can be so great that many ACOA parents
simply do not react until they have already lost control and
lashed out at the most minor of provocations. This causes
some children of ACOA parents to become very shy and
tentative when faced with new situations. It can also result in
spoiling a child—when ACOA parents are afraid of disciplin-
ing, children can learn to take advantage of their parents'
conflicts at a very early age.

The ACOA's fear of feelings is really a paradoxical problem.
On the one hand, ACOAs fear what they might be compelled
to do if they revealed their true feelings, yet they are also
afraid of what others might do to them. The adult child of an
alcoholic flips back and forth between the fear of being
abandoned and the fear of being engulfed by someone else.
The deep longing to be connected with another person is
fueled by an apprehension of being left alone. Thus, there is
always a concurrent worry about being swallowed up by a
spouse or sexual partner. In an ACOA's family, this fear
creates a tension between the parents that makes the children
feel insecure. The child of an ACOA often feels as if his or her
parents are always pulling in two different directions or that
the family home is not as secure as those of other families. In
other words, the very fears that disrupted the ACOA's home
life during childhood often reemerge in the ACOA's life after
he or she has become a parent and disrupt the lives of his or
her children.

Perpetual Guilt

During the course of my clinical practice, only on rare
occasions have I encountered a child who was raised in an
alcoholic family who did not feel guilt, and plenty of it. Guilt
is a tremendous burden, and ACOAs live and breathe it every
day of their lives and long after they leave their alcoholic
parents. Guilt is often accompanied by intense feelings of

shame. Children of alcoholics are embarrassed by the behavior of their parents and at the same time feel responsible for it. The responsibility they shoulder is unfair and unhealthy, it is also unjustified, but it is a fact that the ACOA must accept before he or she can go forward. Susan, for example, felt that she was the cause of her father's drinking problem.

Whenever he was disappointed or angry, I knew I was the cause of that, too. Even as a mother of my own two boys, I know better than to feel blame for his death. I know I'm crazy to feel guilty about it, but I blame myself every day for what happened to my father. I might have just as well pulled the trigger, because that's how I feel.

The guilt that Susan feels is directly connected to an exaggerated sense of responsibility. It is a manifestation of a perceived need to exert control in an attempt to cope with the fear that dominates the life of an ACOA. This scenario creates a myth in the mind of a young child of an alcoholic (COA) that he or she is omnipotent. In alcoholic families, the child's omnipotence in the face of situations he or she can't possibly control gives rise to an unrealistic notion that he or she has the power to fix the problems of the family, but has failed at the job. If only Susan could have helped out around the house more or had loved her father more, then everything would have been all right in the family. And now that she is a mother she can tap into that same guilt when dealing with her own two boys. It makes her angry, therefore, when her omnipotence fails. Her son has made her look bad; he has pointed out another one of her glaring weaknesses as a human being. Because he disobeys, he shows the world that Susan is flawed. Thus she feels like lashing out at him for almost the slightest infractions to keep the world from finding out that she is a failed child of an alcoholic and a failed mother.

Pat, whose alcoholic father continually abused her physically and sexually when she was growing up, feels ultimately responsible for the shame and anger she carries with her.

I would greet my father at the door every night thinking I could calm him down or make him happy. Sometimes I think that I did have the power. I felt very responsible.

Pat has not been able to have children. She has been barely able to establish a functional relationship for any extended period. The guilt, anger, and fear that dog her footsteps every day interfere with her adult life each time she finds herself attracted to someone. She is in despair because she feels that by establishing her own family, she can erase some of the guilt she bore during the years of sexual abuse by her father. She is incorrect in that notion because she still can't accept her childhood feelings as facts without assuming that it was all her fault.

In Susan's case, without an honest understanding and awareness of the feelings of guilt and the attempts to control others—because of her perceived sense of responsibility and power—she trips up her relationship with her sons. It also keeps her from helping her children develop a sense of personal responsibility of their own. Thus, the cycle of "damaged goods" is carried forward into the next generation even though Susan's children are not COAs.

A Sense of Worthlessness

As destructive as all the feelings we have discussed up to now—anger, fear, and guilt—can be, the sense of worthlessness is potentially the most damaging. People who feel totally worthless, those who believe that they do not belong in society, are the most likely to commit crimes against other people. In families, parents who feel worthless—and this includes the vast majority of alcoholic parents and many ACOAs who are parents—are in the highest risk group for child or spouse abuse. In clinical therapy, therefore, one of my first objectives in any crisis intervention situation is to convince a potentially violent person that he or she has worth as a human being. If the person accepts that, then all of his or her other feelings can be addressed. For a person who does not accept a sense of worth, violence or self-destructiveness is only two steps away. It is no mystery that the overwhelming majority of violent felons are people who have no sense of worth.

Children of alcoholics grow into their adulthood with a generalized sense of worthlessness, of just not being good enough. They were not the architects of their dysfunctional family system: the stresses and strains were already at work tearing their parents' lives apart. The children did not have the overall responsibility to insure a sound and healthy structure even though their parents might have told them, as Pat's mother told her: "We had hoped when we had you that you would keep us all together." As a child, of course, Pat did not have the physical or emotional maturity to understand what that meant. She wasn't even old enough to evaluate the nature of the responsibility that had been placed upon her. Yet, like Pat and Susan, children of alcoholics often assume the blame for the emotional instability and/or the collapse of the family. They feel that they have failed and are worthless. These feelings are all the more insidious because they are not consciously acknowledged.

When they become parents, ACOAs who have not addressed their feelings of worthlessness are in a very high-risk group for the emotional or physical abuse of their children. Often they see their children as the cause of their feelings of worthlessness. Many times they transfer the complete responsibility they had to bear as children onto the shoulders of their children. If the marriage is failing, it is the children's fault; if the ACOA can't earn enough money to support the life-style he or she wants, the children's selfish needs are to blame; and if the ACOA parent is not able to make friends or establish social ties in the neighborhood, it is because the children have made him or her look bad.

As the years pass, the problems only get worse. If the ACOA parent isn't worthy, then why worry about the child's needs at all. The parent can slip into profound depressions during which the children are neglected or abused. During periods of near fury, the children, who are the physical embodiment of the parent's worthlessness, are the victims of physical or emotional violence. And if the cycle of dysfunction is allowed to continue into the next generation, the very types of abuse the child of an alcoholic experienced may be committed upon his or her own children. The propensity for violence is directly proportional to the level of worthlessness the ACOA feels. And the level of worthlessness the ACOA perceives is directly proportional to the level of dysfunction in the family when he or she was a child.

The sense of worthlessness which many children of alcoholics carry into their own families and inflict upon their children is also the result of a fear of being abandoned. This is one of the most desperate fears that can afflict any child. In even moderately dysfunctional families, the child of an alcoholic is often left alone without the basic nutrients of physical intimacy with a parent, the comfort of the parent's voice or presence. The absence of the physical presence of the parent translates itself into a sense of having been abandoned. The newborn actually feels anxiety and separation. As the child grows, so does this sense of having been left alone. Anxiety increases as the children in this situation realize that they must care for themselves while at the same time they feel helpless and dependent upon others. The reality, however, is that the child is forced into a form of isolation because of the parent's preoccupation with alcohol. Given the egocentric nature of early childhood, the child cannot know this. Rather, the child justifies it by deciding that he or she is responsible for it.

The feelings of abandonment typically evolve into unarticulated feelings of worthlessness: "No one care for me; no one cares about me; I am not worth anyone's attention; I am all alone!" For ACOAs who are parents or who are about to become parents, the abandonment/worthlessness syndrome must be addressed as early as possible so as to break the cycle. This is even more important in cases where the ACOA is about to have an unplanned-for or unwanted child. Bobby, a nineteen-year-old college freshman, was in that situation when he came in for "last resort" therapy. In one of his many serial relationships with girlfriends, to whom he was unable to commit himself emotionally, the unthinkable had happened: they had conceived a child. They were both Catholics, and abortion was out of the question for them and their respective sets of parents.

Bobby was an ACOA who was suffering from a sense of abandonment and worthlessness that had largely gone unnoticed by his mother. His natural father was an alcoholic who left the family shortly after Bobby was born, and his mother remarried years later. Now, because his stepfather had money and they lived in affluent Princeton, New Jersey,

Bobby had had the opportunity to attend good schools. He was always able to satisfy his immediate surface needs by "running with the pack," but he never developed close relationships. He made surface contact with people, shallow acquaintances which satisfied his need for companionship but never resolved the need he had to reach out and trust that someone might find him worthwhile. After he reached adolescence, Bobby became very active sexually, but all of his relationships were unsatisfactory because he felt that none of them were based on any truth.

I really never knew who I was. That is, I know who I am, but I was never able to explain myself thoroughly to someone else, so no one ever got to know me. I feel all alone and worthless even now. I have got so much going on in my head, but I don't like what I look like and don't even know how to dress in a way that's me. I want a girlfriend, even a wife, but I can't respect any girl who would like me back.

But now Bobby found himself about to be married to a woman he didn't like and about to have a child he neither wanted nor felt able to care for. Part of him wanted to flee but he could only see himself repeating the pattern his father put into motion before he ever knew him. His father not only abandoned him when he was young but kept his distance as Bobby grew older. Bobby still longs for the meaningful contact from his father that he will never receive. Now his child might face the same future that Bobby experienced. That, he said, and nothing else, drove him into therapy. He had to address the deep sense of deprivation he felt about others and his concrete belief he was completely worthless.

I just feel bad. It's like I can do nothing right with anybody. I feel bad that *he* doesn't want anything to do with me. I can't contact him directly. He won't even tell me where he is. So if I want to write him, I have to send it to my uncle and he will send it to my dad. I wanted to write him just to talk to him, especially now. But I just can't do it.

If Bobby does abandon his wife and child, the danger is that the child will grow up with the same sense of deprivation and worthlessness that Bobby faced. It he stays but remains as emotionally distant as he has for all of his life, he might inflict even worse damage on the child. Bobby's only hope is to confront the past and determine just how to rewrite the script that was handed to him. This is what all ACOAs have to do, even those who are not about to become parents.

The challenge for you as an ACOA who is raising your own children is to understand how your past, chronic feelings of worthlessness may affect your present self-image. You have to use this awareness to make and keep the distinction between yourself and your children. This is a constant task, even for ACOAs who have been through therapy and claim to have straightened themselves out. In moments of stress or during crises, it is too easy for ACOAs to fuzz the border between the present and past, as, for example, Susan does, and overlay their own self-image upon their children. As parents, ACOAs must be mindful of their tendency to want to control their children's feelings and behavior, and it is the deep and often subtle sense of worthlessness that fuels the perceived need to control or to be extravigilant.

You must also be aware that you serve as a constant role model for your children. Children observe their parents every waking moment, including words said and those left unsaid. If children sense worthlessness in their role models, they will learn to approach the world in a cautious and defensive manner. They are also learning to devalue themselves. This is especially true if the same-sexed parent has low self-esteem. Why should children feel any different than their parents if that is all they see? This is all the more reason for you as an ACOA parent to be aware of yourself and the signals you send to your children.

Either/Or Thinking

Another characteristic learned by children of alcoholics is a style of perceiving the world in which people or objects are seen as all of one thing and none of another. This is sometimes called "two-valued thinking" and typically shows up when making judgments about others. Someone is either good or bad, right or wrong, us or them. It reminds me of the statement "I know what I believe: don't confuse me with facts."

It is not a coincidence that this inflexible approach to the world is one of the typical characteristics of an ACOA. It is also one of the prime bases of confrontations between ACOAs and their own children. ACOAs are threatened very early in their lives with the fact that the behavior of others is beyond their control. They rely on their own sense of omnipotence, but see it collapse time after time in the face of the drinking, physical or sexual abuse, emotional trauma, and violence that predominate in many dysfunctional families. Thus, the child of the alcoholic clings to those things he or she feels can be controlled and is rigid in his or her defense of them

Within the context of his or her own adult family, the ACOA has the potential to become an out-and-out tyrant. When flexibility and understanding are called for to resolve conflicts with children, the ACOA parent tends to put his or her foot down and refuses to budge—"No, you can't have any more dessert"; "You can't use the car under any circumstances"; "I absolutely refuse to take you and your friends to the mall"; "You can't leave the house and that's final." He or she can be unrelenting in conceding anything to the children. This, in turn, often creates tensions with the non-bases for the ACOA's refusal to even consider the reality of the issues. The problem, of course, is that the ACOA is not acting rationally. He or she is falling back into a rigid two-value stance that was learned as a child and will not be given up until it can be accepted, understood for what it is, and replaced with another navigational coping mechanism.

To make matters even more complicated for ACOAs, as children they see not only that they can't control the thoughts and feelings of others but that they can't even control their own thoughts. Thus, they block out any contradictory information, clapping their hands over their eyes and ears so to speak, in an effort to keep their own mental processes as uncluttered as possible. They want to control themselves and control others. Their two-valued thinking is often a direct result of their ability to accomplish neither goal. Whatever they try to do, they cannot make the world safe or count on others to do so for them.

Accordingly, ACOAs are left "holding the bag" if one of their parents abandons the family. These feelings of being deserted can generate powerful surges of hurt and anger throughout childhood and well into one's adult years. Sometimes the hurt and anger never dissipate. These feelings are so powerful in a young child that the children of alcoholics are often out of balance and risk falling headlong into one feeling or another. If they admit they trust someone and the person is not 100 percent perfect or infallible, the person becomes the enemy and a critical threat to their existence. If the nonalcoholic parent marries again, the stepparent is either the family savior or the monster who had driven out the alcoholic parent. There are no balance and no ability to judge, only the complete rightness or wrongness of any given situation.

For the ACOA parent who has not given up two-valued approaches to situations, the results can be disastrous. This is all the more true because many successful ACOAs sometimes train for adversarial professions in which two-valued thinking is the way one keeps one's "edge." For a public prosecutor, an advertising executive, an independent sales representative, or an aggressive administrative manager, the difference between what's right and what's wrong has to be rigidly defined.

On one side is company policy, and on the other side is the enemy. Let the other side in, and you've lost the battle. It worked for me when I was a kid and it works for me now. The only problem is that it doesn't work for my kids.

When Ron, one of my professionally successful clients, said this to me, I didn't believe him at first. But when I realized that his job as quality control manager for a large retail store chain in New Jersey forced him to think in either/or terms, I understood how well he had been trained for the job. He learned to think in these terms because he was a child of an alcoholic parent who saw the world from an us/them perspective. You were either on Ron's father's side or against him. Ron rigidly defended his father even though the man floated from job to job until he abandoned the family altogether. Then Ron learned to adopt his mother's they're-all-out-to-get-us approach to the world. By the time he was a senior in high school, his aggressive-adversarial approach to any challenge made him the ideal student advocate. He was a sought-after management candidate after he was graduated from business school and moved up quickly in the retail organization. In his case, two-valued thinking was not an impediment to a successful career. It was a critical advantage that he, as an ACOA, had over more balanced thinkers, who may seem too wishy-washy for potential employers. However, when applied to child raising, a two-valued approach almost always polarizes a situation and alienates children and other family members. In Ron's situation, it drove his wife and children away from him and was threatening to break up his second marriage as well. "When you've failed twice for the same reasons," he told me, "then you know it's not *her* fault."

In their attempts to maintain an emotional balance in the face of a chaotic family life, ACOAs tend to chose one feeling or another and hold on tight to it. As in Ron's and Susan's situations, the feeling may be adhered to regardless of any evidence to the contrary and will often lead individuals to force issues in their relationships to justify the self-fulfilling image they have of themselves. Bobby's insistence that he was just not worth any woman's friendship is an example of this, as is Susan's insistence that her son confronts her out of his perception of her weakness and vacillation.

In many cases the feelings are sex-typed. Generally, men tend to choose anger and visual displays of rage, while women are more likely to become victims, feel hurt and abused, or remain passive and weepy, although Susan was an exception to this rule. This is especially the case when the child has been victimized by the parent or when the alcoholic parent is the same sex as the child. When ACOAs become parents, even though the impetus for the behavior is no longer present, the patterns have become habit. Thus, they have a propensity to teach their children to adopt the same roles.

Control

The flip side of either/or thinking is the ACOA's compulsive need to control any and all situations. You may attempt to keep tight control of your feelings at all times because you have to deny the inherent chaos in the world. You might do this because on an unconscious level you know that your unchecked feelings can be very disruptive. Accordingly, you might try to act only in certain familiar or tried-and-true ways and deny any contradictory thoughts and emotions. As you can imagine, this can be very unhealthy because it splits off part of the personality from reality. At best, the effort required to keep real feelings in check drains you to the point where you may be unable to relate effectively to other people. In parent/child encounters, this makes the child of the ACOA very panicky because he or she does not know where the parent is. As Susan's eldest son told me in family therapy: "I never knew whether she was angry or not. She had a mad look and would turn real red, but then she would speak real soft and slow-like. It was scarier than when she would hit me."

The issue of control on all levels pervades the personality style of adult children of alcoholics. They perceive the need to give order to their environment whether it be a structured situation, such as a work setting, or one as unstructured as a dynamic interpersonal relationship. This need to exert control is generally an attempt to compensate for a lifelong history of unpredictability in persons or situations. Like all forms of compensatory behavior, the tendency to exert control is suitable only over the short term. Over the longer period, the ACOA's need for control usually strains his or her relationships with others and eventually destroys them.

ACOAs who exert control over others may also develop manipulative techniques in order to satisfy their needs. They are skilled at eliciting desired behavior from their partners. Both ACOA men and women are able to use feigned weakness, sexuality, guilt, or the threat of retaliation in order to lock their partners into unhealthy relationships. They usually get their way, but the satisfaction is short-lived because even the most gullible partner is soon able to figure a way out of the maze. When a manipulative ACOA finds his or her partner close to escape, the person simply changes the rules of the game and closes another emotional trapdoor.

For ACOA parents who indulge in this behavior there are very few rewards. The children usually turn out to be just as manipulative as their parents, primarily because the ACOA parents are good role models. This often results in a form of emotional one-upmanship in which parent and child engage in years of standoffs until one or the other gives up or goes away. Children of ACOAs who have graduated from these relationships report that their lives are often filled with turmoil as they try to sort out the strategies that they and their parents have used against each other. In the worst case scenario, both spouse and children abandon the manipulative ACOA parent, repeating the very pattern that the ACOA was guarding against in the first place. In short, manipulation as a form of control simply doesn't work and almost always backfires against the ACOA.

Compulsive Behavior Patterns

Many ACOAs also adopt a pattern of compulsive thinking and behavior. Compulsive thinking, unfortunately, leads to difficulties in decision making because one can never be too sure about whether the right choice has been made. This form of thinking often leads many to continual crises: due to apprehensiveness about making a decision, the ACOA puts off taking any action until his or her back is against the wall.

For ACOA parents who must plan some of their children's activities, this kind of crisis situation leads to unresolvable family tensions and constant battles. The children learn never to trust their parent's plans and decisions because they can be unmade as easily as they are made. Moreover, because the ACOA parent is usually less prepared for activities than other parents are, his or her own children come to rely on their friends' parents rather than their own. In an ACOA family where the parent already has a problem with self-doubt and low self-esteem, seeing his or her children turning elsewhere for competent leadership further undermines the parent/child relationship.

In this sort of situation, relationships, even marital relationships, can decay over the long term because the ACOA partner is always focused on putting things together while the other partner can't understand why his or her spouse simply didn't plan more effectively. When both parents share responsibility for a child, the tensions increase even more because one parent always seems to be lagging behind. This seems backward at first glance because most compulsive people plan events down to the last detail. However, the compulsion I have seen is so extreme that the person becomes afraid of planning because he or she is afraid of making a mistake that can't be undone. When the event is near enough that such a crisis occurs, the worry about making a mistake is obliterated by the need to "just do anything." Thus, the compulsive is able to force him- or herself into acting without worrying about the consequences.

This form of compulsiveness is also accompanied by addictive behaviors that are so masked the ACOA doesn't even realize that he or she is repeating a pattern established by the alcoholic parent. For example, ACOAs may believe that deviating from a specific route to work or to school brings with it dire consequences. They may rely on specific items of clothing in times of great stress or a particular briefcase or book bag in order to take an important exam. Their compulsive behavior may evolve into a series of activities centered around sets of events that have to be performed just so in order to be successful.

When I was eleven or twelve, I began taking a fountain pen with me to school for days when we had citywide reading or math exams. In high school, I designated a special "test pen" that would always bring me good luck. I also had special test shirts and good luck socks or other articles that I carried or wore to school. It got so that by the time I was in college, I had entire uniforms that I had to wear to tests. I began to realize one day after my wife broke my pen and tore the pocket on my good luck shirt—which by that time had become a rag—that I had evolved an external skeleton to replace the internal one I never had. Both my parents taught me to be this way, I guess, because their lives were simply collections of rabbits' feet.

Parents may have to dress their children in just the right way in order for them to feel confident. Their children may be forced to adopt rigid and repetitive behaviors just to please grandparents or friends. Deviation from the compulsive's preset schema is tantamount to extreme disobedience and invokes a severe punishment from the parent. These compulsive activities may become so emotionally debilitating for the ACOA's child that he or she may become extremely passive, unwilling to exert any energy because he or she is too afraid of punishment.

The most extreme and self-destructive forms of disorder that ACOA compulsives develop involve alcohol abuse, drug abuse, and a variety of eating and nutritional disorders. The tragedy is that the ACOA has become addicted to a pattern of behavior that by itself resembles the addictive behavior of the alcoholic parent. In the ACOA's case, however, the addiction is actually a form of compulsive behavior, although it may also be a chemical sensitivity as it is with most true alcoholics. Should the ACOA be a parent at the same time, he or she will almost surely inflict abusive behavior upon the family similar to the way his or her alcoholic parent did.

Perfectionism

A very common tendency among ACOAs is to be a perfectionist. In fact, the majority of ACOA professional people who attend therapy sessions are superachievers who routinely surpass their peers. They are tough competitors who don't like to give in and rarely compromise when they feel they can attain victory. Perfectionism is not without its victims, however, as any child of an ACOA will readily attest. Most of the ACOA parents in my therapy groups regret that in their drive to become perfect parents, unlike their own alcoholic parents, they sometimes inflict painful damage upon their children. Like their own parents, they tend to view the world outside the family as a hostile place and fear their children will compare them to "normal" parents and find them lacking. In trying to outdo other parents, ACOAs require that their children also be perfect. Any crack in the veneer of their life-style is a sign of imperfection that ACOA parents feel can't be tolerated.

I routinely facilitate ACOA group therapy sessions which contain superteachers, supercops, super-computer-programmers, superstudents, and supermothers. The drive to excel is so strong that any obstacles—even children—may be plowed under in the onslaught. Many of these superachievers share common physical ailments as well. The majority of them have been diagnosed as hypertensive. Many have been treated for ulcers or other gastrointestinal disorders. Some admit that they are overstressed and have sought group therapy to relieve the strains of having to perform. And finally, many ACOAs freely admit to sexual inadequacies or other dysfunctions.

Perfectionist ACOAs are typically the most rule-bound of parents. They impose a rigid sense of discipline, even though the rules may be masked by a false illusion of flexibility. They are prepared to compromise with their children on minor issues, but behind their rules is the need to generate an illusion of perfect competence in the face of an imperfect world. If the child challenges his ACOA parent's need to be perfect, the parent's response may well be irrational and inappropriate. The challenge goes to the very heart of the ACOA's fears: that he or she is a blemished person and inferior to the rest of the community.

Loss of Identity

It is a commonly held belief that the most effective parents are individuals who are sure of their own identities. In order to help a child discover his or her identity, the thinking goes, the parent should have no conflicts about his or her own identity so that the child will not get mixed signals in using his or her parent as an early role model. As reasonable as this adage sounds, it is purely and simply a myth. There is no written or unwritten law that states that in order for parents to raise healthy children they must be absolutely confident and beyond insecurity in their identities. However, as false as this belief is, many ACOAs not only adhere to it but berate themselves because they believe it's their fault that they are unsure of their identities.

It sounds corny, but the expression "I don't know who I am" routinely turns up as a form of self-description in many ACOA therapy groups. This problem is one of the core characteristics of most adult children of alcoholics. It is often compounded after the ACOA becomes a parent because there are then at least two major conflicts impairing his or her role in the family.

1. Because the ACOA lacked a fundamental understanding of who he or she was as a child, the adult has

emerged from doubt rather than self-assurance. This doubt concerning adult identity raises other doubts about the ACOA's perceptions of the world.

2. Because the ACOA has not fully understood his or her childhood identity, the person may have an impaired ability to understand normal childhood identities in general. Accordingly, as parent, the ACOA will have a large blind spot when it comes to making judgments about his or her child's behavior or development.

When these two forms of impaired perceptions combine, the results can be painful for both parent and child.

If you are already a parent, you have to try to fill in this blind spot on the fly because, under otherwise normal circumstances, you can't call time-out and go back into your own childhood to reestablish your identity. If you are not yet a parent, or are about to become one, your job is a bit easier. But because you want to get on with the rest of your life, you should not dwell overmuch on what has already taken place. Rather, you should focus on understanding your past instead of mourning what you feel you did not have.

Parents and parents-to-be who are children of alcoholics must remember that their daily perceptions of what was going on in the family were routinely challenged by one or the other parent. Sometimes the challenges were direct, as in the case of seven-year-old Pat, whose mother kept on telling her that her father loved her very much and "would never do anything to hurt you." These conversations almost always took place after Pat complained to her mother that her father, with the heavy smell of alcohol on his breath, took her onto the couch, rubbed her bottom, and made her touch his penis. Unfortunately, Pat never established a childhood identity because she was a surrogate wife and lover whose own mother was lying to her.

Sometimes the challenges to a child's perceptions are less direct, as in Bill's case, when his mother pulled a curtain around the truth and did not let anything penetrate it. In either a direct or indirect challenge to the child's honest view of reality, the results are the same; the seeds of self-doubt are planted in the child's mind. If doubt is accompanied by guilt and shame, as in Pat's case, the child of the alcoholic experiences the feeling of going numb.

Blind spots become dead zones where no feeling can take place. Many ACOAs with these dead zones fully established are able to paper over the seams during their college and young adult years and think that all is well. It is not. Whether there are only blind spots of perception or zones where no feelings can take place, the ACOA has no coping mechanism whatsoever to withstand the natural shocks that children routinely administer to their parents. The ACOA either falls back on an unreal set of disciplinary rules to lock the child into a proper behavior or alternates between hopeless guilt, which turns the child into a monster, or violent rage, which often turns into physical or emotional abuse. Either way, the dysfunctional pattern established in the ACOA's childhood family is carried into the ACOA's adult family.

ACOAs can prevent this damage by trying to understand what took place in their families when their childhood identities were becoming established. First, they should come to grips with their own natural confusions about what happened. The role reversals and denial that so often characterize the alcoholic family almost always lead to feelings of confusion in children who know no other way of relating to others. Many ACOAs develop deep wells of anger in reaction to the many embarrassments and unfulfilled promises that were made to them. The childhood anger, oftentimes accompanied by real visions of violent acts, is typically so frightening to the child's mind that it must be walled in. Ironically, the fear of anger is channeled into a very critical attitude toward self and others. Thus, many ACOAs bring a hypersensitive perception of responsibility into their adult years. Once they become parents, the responsibility can be too much to bear; when the anger breaks out, the children of the ACOA are the first and most visible targets.

In even the most dysfunctional families, children learn about themselves and how to relate to other people by observing and identifying with their major role models, their parents or other adults in a parental position. Children of alcoholics are no different. The dilemma is that the child identifies with either the alcoholic parent or the enabler parent (the spouse or partner who is trying to enable the alcoholic to function or allows the alcoholic to continue the dysfunctional pattern of behavior in the family). Both parents are inadequate role models. If the alcoholic parent is identified with, the child feels out of control. If the enabler is identified with, the child may feel helpless, burdened, or hopelessly unable to cope. In either event, regardless of the laurels they garner during their young adult years, ACOAs are guilt-ridden, confused individuals on the inside.

When ACOAs as parents bring this confusion into a parent/child relationship, they tend to create the child in their parent's image. This is natural because it is the only intimate parent/child relationship the ACOA has ever developed. The pattern of dysfunction not only repeats itself, in the most bizarre of circumstances it can actually cause reversed roles, with the ACOA parent becoming the child and the ACOA's child becoming a pseudo parent. Unless the child of the ACOA receives therapy at some point in the future, he or she is likely to become the person the ACOA parent created. If that person is the image of the alcoholic parent, the alcoholism itself may repeat in the child and that child's children may adopt the personality dysfunctions of the ACOA grandparent. As you can see, under the worst of circumstances the dysfunction can easily be carried into succeeding generations, like the alternating swings of a pendulum. And already given a genetic predisposition, the odds become even greater.

Chronic Mistrust

Molly's lack of self-trust was caused by a lack of rules in her family when she was growing up.

My parents were gypsies. They both drank heavily. We had no rules for anything. They ate when they were hungry and left food out for me. If they had eaten all the food I did without. We had money, but my father was an artist and it came in when it came in. They did a lot of drugs, too, so you never knew when they were going to be spaced or straight. You couldn't even guess what would happen next.

For me today, I . . . trust nothing. If it's not there now, it's not gonna be there tomorrow. I've been pregnant twice, but I got abortions. Knowing what I know about how I was raised, I couldn't bring a kid into this world. If it were up to me, the kid could be standing on its head and think it was walking on its feet.

ACOAs develop a distrust of their own perceptions and feelings and of their ability to respond appropriately to situations. It's not surprising, therefore, that one of the most significant personality characteristics of an ACOA is the difficulty he or she has in trusting other people. As parents, ACOAs routinely, but unconsciously, distrust their children. This is not to say that ACOAs think their children are lying all the time. It is to suggest, however, that ACOA parents often doubt their children's abilities to perceive the world accurately. Consequently, one of the biggest areas of parent/child conflict, ACOAs report, is over the differences between the parent's and the child's perceptions of the same thing. This conflict is entirely normal in most families; in ACOA families it can be exacerbated to the point of hostility.

Paradoxically, in the extreme cases where the ACOA believes that his or her ability to perceive accurately is impaired, the ACOA may place all of his or her trust in the child. The parent admits to blindness and the child becomes the Seeing Eye dog. This results in an emperor's-new-clothes syndrome in which the child's view of the world is correct no matter what. Even normal parental disagreements are suppressed, and the child then dictates what is and what is not true. In a family where both parents are present, this is less the case because the non-ACOA spouse can rein in the child. In single ACOA parent families, however, no such form of control exists.

Children of alcoholics are understandably prone to develop an overly cautious nature. Sometimes this leads to the development of independence and self-reliance as a way of avoiding dependence on others. ACOAs tend to cover up mistrust of others by looking and dressing extraordinarily well, by presenting themselves as articulate and confident in social settings, and by developing a competent and effective style on the job. In fact, because of their hardworking, easy-to-please nature, ACOAs often make the best employees. They are loyal to the organization because they come to see it as family. They have learned to be protective of their environment and, hence, defend company policy. And their level of contribution to the company is often disproportionately large with respect to the level of compensation. In other words, ACOAs often work cheap because they are either too embarrassed or too guilty to stand their ground when seeking raises or promotions that they rightfully deserve. When refused the raise, they harbor a subtle resentment that, unexpressed, may eventually lead them to quit.

The more they succeed in their professional environment, the more ACOAs come to believe in the image of their success. They reject the feelings of insecurity when they come to the surface, even though the distrust of others and the feelings of guilt and shame are still operative. They harbor deep longings for the caring and nurturing they did not receive as children. Inside, there still exists a child who rejects adult logic, mistrusts others, and will likely spurn the caring of another adult when it comes. Thus many adult children of alcoholics set up a cycle of self-fulfilling prophecies in relationships, justifying the distance they keep from others.

This may go on for years until they convince themselves that the feelings of love and passion they experience for others as adults do have some validity. This is a new emotional stratum for them. When the current to the automatic distrust mechanism has been turned down sufficiently so that the emotions are allowed to dictate the response, the ACOA may even agree to marriage. A new level of emotional equilibrium within the ACOA and within his or her marital relationship will develop. If left undisturbed by outside pressures, this relationship will muddle along for years even if the mate or spouse is an inadequate partner. However, when children enter the picture, the emotional equilibrium is upset and all of the pent-up distrust and anger will come right back to the surface.

If this leads to self-discovery and healthy relationships with spouse and children, the finite period of trauma may be a good thing. However, if the trauma is plowed under and the ACOA continues to "get along by going along," everybody suffers: the ACOA, the child of the ACOA, the grandchildren of the ACOA, and the spouse, who may well be trying to keep the relationship from falling apart. During the entire period of the relationship, the automatic distrust the ACOA has of other people causes a knee-jerk reaction whenever he or she feels threatened. The trigger mechanism has been so finely tuned that even the most competent and controlled individuals have difficulty suppressing it. Therefore, the ACOA will feel an additional layer of guilt, especially when the trigger mechanism has been fired and his or her children are standing directly in the path of the response.

Chronic mistrust has profound implications for child rearing. ACOAs suppress the need they feel for others, especially for their children. On a deep level, this need may seem overwhelming. Therefore it is no surprise that ACOA parents have difficulty setting appropriate limits when confronted with the needs of their children. Ever uncertain about what to do, many ACOAs swing to being either underinvolved with their children or hypervigilant and controlling. Usually, they adopt hypervigilance as their mode of response.

Early in their lives, children of alcoholics begin to feel controlled by the needs of their parents. Yet this, too, often leads to an impulse to control the feelings and behavior of their own children. There is a fear of loss of control if the ACOA relaxes his or her rigid inhibitions or if the child refuses to feel what the parent wants him or her to feel. The result is an overprotectiveness, the fear of the parent that if he or she steps back from the edge just once, the child will be lost forever. Since most children are naturally resilient, they reject the parent's overprotectiveness and fight to go in the other direction. The tension that arises between the ACOA parent and child and between the ACOA parent and his or her spouse then threatens to disrupt family dynamics.

Pat, whose father systematically abused her throughout her childhood, exemplifies this push/pull tension in her relationship with her very young son. Because Pat's mother did nothing to protect her from her father's violence, she has overreacted and protects her son from everything and everyone.

When I used to lie in bed at night, I would cry that my mother couldn't protect me. Now I've gone in the other direction with Michael. I am so afraid of what my mother didn't do that I get so overprotective of him. I would like him to have a good relationship with his father, but I just can't trust Bill's judgment. I always think

he plays too rough with Michael. I'm afraid that something will
break and that it will be my fault. If I stood up to Bill and said, "Let
him go!" that would do more damage than letting him hurt Michael.
I just know that I'm not going to let my kid go through what I went
through. I don't care what I have to do to protect him. I just wish I
could be more sure of what I see every day. I don't know what to act
on. I don't even know when it's OK.

It's very hard sometimes to maintain the clear thinking
that effective parenting requires, but it is well worth the
effort. The energy that you invest in self-discovery will almost
always help to insure that you will do a better job for your
children than your parents did for you.

Remember, the key to surviving in your parents' alcoholic
environment was through your learning to adapt. You
learned early, and you learned the hard way, not to trust too
readily. You learned not to have expectations that were too
high or to depend upon the goodwill and intentions of others.
But you also learned to be resilient, to be able to change when
the situation demanded that you change. If you grew up in a
household where violence was ever present, you learned to
camouflage yourself quickly. If your parents denied the truth
about alcoholism, you learned that your suspicions did not go
away. Whatever traumas still linger in your memory, treat
them as lessons and not as your inevitable fate.

These lessons produced a pattern of personality characteristics and behavior that if not consciously understood may
seriously affect your children. Clearly, these lessons were
skills that you needed to adapt in order to survive. Congra-
tulations! You've survived. Now you must realize that many
of your behavior patterns are no longer appropriate or even
adequate for developing healthy parent/child relationships.
You are at the point now where you are, as Freud noted,
bestowing the sins of your parents upon your children. Unless
you take the risk to understand and accept your past for what
it was and to come to grips with how if influences you today,
you take the greater risk of carrying your feelings of inadequacy and guilt into your relationships with your children.

Your responsibility now is to raise healthy children. In the
following chapters, I will show you how.

2

Deciding to Parent
What to Expect

DEBBIE

I remember waking up at about 3:30 or 4:00 and just staring at the ceiling. I didn't know why I was awake or even who I was at first. Then I felt it again—a quick shot right in the side as if Jack had jabbed me with his knuckles. I looked over at him but he was snoring away. It happened again, only this time harder. Then two or three more times like corn popping in a pot. I realized that it was coming from inside of me, not Jack. It was the baby.

I remembered the million scenes in the movies where the wife turns over and shakes the sleeping bear of a husband, demanding that he feel the baby kicking. I didn't feel like doing that. Instead I felt the cold blade of fright cut right across my throat. I couldn't breathe; I broke out into a sweat, and I began throwing up even before I reached the bathroom. If I could have aborted there in the darkness, I would have done so. I didn't want this baby.

Debbie's crises came on as quickly as the first kick from her unborn child. From that first moment, the joy she had been expecting to feel when she first learned she was pregnant was replaced by panic. Now she knew that the decision to bring the pregnancy to term was irreversible. There was no going back now. She felt fearful, angry, and terribly alone.

She would have liked to have been able to seek the guidance and support of her parents. And she could have, she told herself, but they were both in recovery from alcoholism and she did not trust them. They expressed their concern and happiness for her, of course, but it seemed false. It was as superficial as their concern had been for the twenty-two years she had known them. Nor could Debbie turn to her in-laws. As much as she wanted to unburden herself to them, they were too "normal." They always expressed themselves clearly and directly. They were a model family and had an open sense of caring about one another and their children. Yet this ideal family of in-laws was even more of a threat than her own alcoholic parents. She knew that her husband's parents would find out her deep secret. They would come to learn how empty and inadequate she was, and they would judge her accordingly. Once they realized that Debbie was flawed and that she had transmitted "bad" genes to their grandchild, they would soon regret that their son had ever married her.

What would she say to her husband, Jack? She had always known him as a sensitive and loving person. Surely she would be able to open up to him and reveal her fears. But Debbie was angry with him for not seeing her confusion on his own. She shouldn't have to throw a tantrum, she told herself, just to get his ear. "If he really loves me, why can't he see behind the mask and offer his support?" However, wish as she might, her husband was not able to read her mind. He still saw her as strong, competent, and in control. He could not see beneath the image that she projected to the world.

Debbie grew up in an alcoholic family system which was inherently unstable and inconsistent. Like many COAs, Debbie doubted herself and constantly sought to achieve control over others and her environment. She became an over-achiever. As a child, she helped to keep the family together by cooking and cleaning while maintaining superior grades throughout school. She never outwardly asked for help and acted as if she were in charge of her life. Her alcoholic parents were always amazed at her achievements and pointed to her as a miracle. She was the first member of her family to graduate from college and solidified her social elevation by marrying into Jack's well-to-do family of surgeons and lawyers.

Before that first kick from her baby, Debbie was fine. She had learned how to compensate for what she could not get from others from the time she was a child. She read, watched television, and studied how normal people behaved in family situations. Soon she would be acting out normalcy for real, she promised herself. Debbie not only learned how to fit in, but fooled everybody including her husband and his family. But when the baby kicked, it fundamentally shook her entire support mechanism. It was as if the accumulated weight of years of performing for others had come crashing down in a moment. In that moment she decided to enter therapy, much to the shock of her husband and his family.

As hard as it is for any overachiever to admit that there is something he or she can't overcome without help, it is harder for an ACOA. Because ACOAs learn that they can rely on no one, they are the last people to seek help from the outside. In normal, functional families, reliance on help and support from others is natural. It's what is expected in any relationship. In dysfunctional families, outside help and support are usually not available. Thus, the ACOA learns very early in childhood that to rely on help is only to face constant disappointment. For Debbie to enter therapy was a major statement from a woman who had never asked for help since she was a child. She knew that once she had the responsibility of a baby, there would be no safe harbors from the storm that was building up.

JOHN

For John, the pressure to have children continued to build. He avoided it at first, as he avoided most painful issues, by refusing to talk about it. In a nice way he would tell his wife that they couldn't afford to have children because they were just starting out. "Why burden the future?" he asked rhetorically. "I'm in line for promotions, transfers, branch management. If we have a child, it might compromise everything. Wait until we're settled in a community," he promised his wife. But as the years passed and John moved steadily up the corporate ladder, his wife began to worry that they would

never start a family. Her parents began to suspect that
something was wrong with John. The more pressure they put
on their daughter, the more pressure she put on her husband.

Their persistent lack of children was becoming obvious as
they neared their thirties. All of their friends had children.
The late-night conversations in their bedroom evolved into
"discussions about our relationship." Then they became
exhortations to raise a family before it was too late. Finally
they became the kinds of direct confrontational battles that
John had systematically avoided his entire life. His wife
would begin by raising the subject of children very gingerly,
often on the tail end of "Mary Johnson's daughter dropped off
the Girl Scout Cookies today. Want some?" Then she would
often segue into how long they had been in the same community. Seeing no response from Jack, either she would drop the
subject and occupy herself with a magazine or, if her courage
were in place, she would swing him around and demand to
know "right here and now" why they couldn't have children.
At some point, she would begin to cry. Then she would
threaten to pack up and leave.

John knew that it was just a matter of time before she did
leave. Nevertheless, he was adamant: no children. Even
though his superiors were beginning to look at him as vice
presidential material and a divorce would keep him on
the administrative track until he retired, he held firm. Just
the thought of children was enough to make him panic.
Parenthood was a hurdle that he knew he could never
surmount.

I knew that she wanted kids and she knew that I didn't. Eventually it
would break us up, but I didn't care. I would sooner rot in hell than
have to fight with myself to keep from hitting my own child.

He had kept his fear of little children hidden for too long.
Their spontaneous outbursts of emotion unnerved him. Their
wide-open demands for unlimited affection and their need for
comfort made him boil with anger. "What right do they have
to demand so much?" he found himself asking when in the
presence of small children. But most of all, John feared
violence. He knew that if he were alone with a small child, a

creature who behaved as if the entire world revolved around it, he was capable of extreme physical violence. Then the secret would come out. The years of anger that he had swallowed so effectively would be disgorged and the patchwork life that he had put together would come apart in a million pieces. Nothing was worth that, not a marriage, not corporate success, not anything. John might go down with his ship, but he would do it without children.

John had survived his childhood by approaching each day as if it were the only day he had. Although he did not come from a particularly abusive family, he had none of the safety nets that most children had. Because both his parents were alcoholics, they were not there emotionally for him. He was left to care for himself; as an only child, he didn't have anyone else to turn to in his family. He grew up believing that something about him was just plain wrong, that he was unlovable. Why didn't his parents treat him the way other parents treated their children?

John carried the feeling that he was unlovable just below the surface. Each day he unconsciously put his self-esteem on the line and measured his worth against everyone else's. He met all of the challenges: at school, at play, at sports, and in contests with other children. But at home it was different. No matter how well he played Little League center field or threw touchdowns, his parents were just not interested. Nothing he did eased the feelings of self-doubt.

By the time he reached his teens, other feelings began to creep in. John noticed that children got affection from their parents that he had never gotten from his. These little kids assumed that they were lovable. They reached out and someone always picked them up. What did they have, John asked himself, that he didn't? Soon he became jealous of other children. That jealousy stayed with him, growing and growing, right through his college years. Now that he was an adult, he was not going to share his life with children.

Deciding Whether to Become a Parent

In the best of circumstances, you will have the opportunity to make rational decisions about whether or not to have children. You should give yourself time to make the choice that will be healthiest not only for you but for the children you will have to raise. If parenthood has been thrust upon you, the only remaining question is how successful a parent you will be.

Most people consider the decision to parent as one of the most important choices they will make. Most people, however, have had the opportunity to grow up in functional families where the parental role models were strong and supportive. In most ACOA families, the parents were not positive role models. Consequently, ACOAs approach the decision to parent with very mixed feelings. They want to please their spouse, but they realize that they don't have the basic parenting background and experience from their childhood that mostly everyone else does.

Are You Ready?

Simply asking yourself whether you are ready is a good start. It indicates that you are moving in the right direction because you are giving the subject thought before making a decision. Most people become parents without thinking about the effect it will have on their lives. For ACOAs this can be especially dangerous because the impact of unplanned children often greatly intensifies the emotional tensions already at work in an adult child of an alcoholic. If you can face the questions raised in this book or venture into an ACOA support group for some frank give-and-take about your past, you stand a much better chance of raising a healthy family than if you just hope for the best.

The Five-Point Safety Check

When you think about whether you want to have a child or not, you will of course recognize that being a parent involves a lot of work. People from large families or families in which the mother seemingly simply and quietly raised all of the children appear to minimize the work required, but you should not. You can slough off a large part of it, as perhaps your parents did in your case, but the results are almost always painful. It is best to recognize the amount of physical labor and emotional exertion you will be required to undertake and prepare for it. It will always be more than you expected.

On the other side of the coin, you will not be starting from ground zero. First of all, the child does a lot of the work simply by growing naturally. The child's peer groups in the neighborhood and in school also do a lot of the work for you by establishing levels of conformity. In other words, they tell the child how to act socially. You do, however, have to make sure that you approve of the groups. But if you've evidenced concern for the child during his or her infancy through preschool years, the child will generally have adopted your values. Thus, you will be more likely than not to approve of the groups your child socializes with, especially if you are living in a neighborhood where you and your spouse are comfortable and happy. It is only when the child becomes an adolescent that there is any serious rebellion, but that's how it's supposed to be anyway.

You also have what I like to call a five-point safety check guarantee with almost every child. Unless there are other complications, the following rules will apply.

1. Babies are very resilient and do not need to have *everything* done right. If you make a few mistakes, they will compensate for them.
2. A preprogrammed biological clock will direct the growth development of your child. This means that even if you spend the first months of your infant's life simply feeding and changing, he or she will still grow. Your child will grow according to a predetermined schedule over which you have little direct control—it's all genetic. In other words, in many ways your kid is on automatic from the moment he or she is conceived.
3. Babies are cooperative, social, and positive by nature. Humans are a social species. We survived by learning to communicate with one another and cooperate socially in family and tribal groups. We are survival-oriented. Your baby knows instinctively that he or she must cooperate with your attempts to parent him or her. Your baby will seek to communicate with you—first by

crying, then with gurgles and cooing, and finally by a shorthand form of speech. All of this will be in motion during the first eighteen months of the child's life. Babies want to be parented, and so will yours.

4. The instinct to parent emerges naturally. This is especially good news for ACOAs. You, too, have a biological clock that starts ticking from the moment you know you will be a parent. The set of instinctive reactions that will follow will tell you what needs to be done to take care of your child. You will have to adjust your perceptions of reality according to your background as a child of an alcoholic—that's where this book will help—but the instinct will be active all of the time.

You intensify your instinctive parental feelings by physical skin contact with your newborn child. Holding, hugging, embracing, stroking, and kissing your new baby stimulate the surface of your skin. This increases the level of your nurturing reactions. Thus, just by doing what comes naturally, holding and feeding your baby, you automatically increase your instinct to parent.

It is not uncommon for new parents to feel guilt and inadequacy if they perceive that their natural parenting instincts have not emerged spontaneously. Don't panic. Nor should you give in to the feeling that you are damaged goods. You are rational and can think through what you need to do to care for your newborn. Your instincts will emerge in time.

5. ACOAs take their responsibilities seriously. Because you are an ACOA, you know that it took a great deal of work to get where you are today. You overcame many handicaps by being more responsible than the next person. There is every reason to expect that the same person who was responsible before becoming a parent will be equally, if not more, responsible after becoming a parent.

You Do Not Need to Be Perfect

This relates directly to the first of our five points. Because babies are naturally resilient, parents don't have to be perfect. At first glance, newborns look completely helpless, and in many respects they are. They are commonly considered to be soft, fragile, and breakable, but they did manage to survive nine months of jostling inside the womb and an arduous trip through the birth canal. At birth, they are much hardier than most people commonly think. And babies are padded with a cushioning layer of fat—commonly called baby fat—which they shed as they become toddlers. They are built to withstand the everyday physical bumps and bruises that they will receive from rolling over in their cribs or kicking about on the changing table. In fact, your baby will help you with your on-the-job training.

Because of their resiliency, babies are able to adapt to their physical and emotional environment very quickly. And if their environment changes, they adapt to the change as well. Your infant's resiliency also means that you don't have to be a perfect parent in order for him or her to be healthy. In fact, there is no perfect way to raise your child.

Joan, one of my ACOA clients from a therapy group, once expressed a very painful fear that she was experiencing when she was near term. "I know that babies are vulnerable and trusting," she said. "I just don't want to hurt my baby. I don't want him to feel like something is missing from his childhood the way I feel about mine." Joan's history of emotional deprivation was much like the histories of other ACOAs. She was hypersensitive about the need to do things "just right" because her parents didn't do what was right for her. She was so fearful that she tended to overcorrect. Although *all* first-time parents express the fear that they won't be perfect, ACOAs are particularly vulnerable.

The desire to do things right is a natural motivator. It gets people ready for parenthood. First-time parents-to-be realize that there are going to be a lot of responsibilities dumped on them within the first few days after birth, and they don't know how wide a latitude they have for mistakes. What they don't realize is that there is a very broad band of normalcy. As long as they follow their instincts and listen to what they think their baby is telling them, they will do the right thing.

Fortunately for all parents, there is an expert on call to tell them what to do for their newborn twenty-four hours a day.

As you might expect, this expert is the baby itself. If you listen when your baby cries or gurgles, you will usually be able to figure out what is making the infant happy or uncomfortable. Babies have an uncanny ability to express themselves because it, like the baby's developmental process, is all biologically controlled. The words may be missing but the grunts, signs, and cries will guide a first-time parent through all sorts of crises. A significant part of parenting is learning to listen to these experts and respond lovingly to their requests. And if you don't meet their needs just right the first time, don't worry. They'll help you out until you understand them completely. If you're sensitive to what your baby wants, you will be the perfect parent no matter what you do.

For ACOAs, this is particularly important advice because it will teach you to focus your attention on your infant's feelings first and on your own feelings second. If you feel that your parents didn't listen to you or weren't attentive to your needs as a child, this is your perfect opportunity to rectify the situation. Now that you have the chance, listen to what your baby is telling you. You'll be surprised that the gratification you receive from being attentive to your child will also satisfy the child in you.

Don't Worry if You're Not 100 Percent Ready

It is the rare person who feels totally prepared for parenthood. Despite what you've read, heard in class, or learned from examining your childhood, you and many other ACOAs often feel that it isn't enough. You must realize that no one is completely ready until after the child arrives. The newborn is the missing ingredient that turns the automatic switches on and transforms a parent-to-be into a parent. When you touch your own child for the first time, you will realize that even though the doubt is still there, you have the instincts to guide you. There is no road map to parenting that covers every contingency. When you look into your baby's face for the first time and see the image of your spouse, your parents or in-laws, or even yourself, all of the missing pieces of the puzzle will fall into place. After all, where did the baby come from? The baby came from you. Thus, all the answers to your questions about what you should expect and what kind of parent you have to be will be answered by the baby itself. By listening to your own feelings and becoming very aware of your child's presence, you will find yourself in communication with him or her. Your baby will respond positively to your intuitive tendencies to nurture and you will be trained by him or her to nurture the right way. There is no mystery about this. It is a natural occurrence.

The Biological Clock

For an ACOA woman, as you begin your pregnancy, it will be comforting for you to know that you will not have to "grow" your own baby. Nature will do that for you. This may seem obvious to some people, but for ACOAs who are nervous about doing just the right thing from the moment they conceive until they send the kid off to college, it's a pleasure to realize that the baby grows automatically. Provided that you follow the advice of your physician during pregnancy and the baby's pediatrician after birth, nature will do its part to keep your child healthy and growing.

What you will be able to control are the environmental factors that are critical to the baby's health. If you are pregnant, these environmental factors are already under your control. For example, if you smoke, quit. Smoking may inhibit the flow of oxygen to your child's brain, may impair its development in minute ways, and may cause him or her to be underweight at birth. Do you work in an environment where there is cigarette smoke? Try to get transferred to a smokeless area. Do you take an occasional drink? Quit that as well. Alcohol, as you already know, is a neurodepressant. You don't want to start sedating your child before he or she is even born.

Control your child's environment by reducing all risks to your health and emotional well-being as early in your pregnancy as possible. Try to eat the foods that nourish the child as well as satisfy any cravings you may have. Consult your doctor before changing your diet drastically, but you should consider high-protein foods, sharply reduced sugars and fats, and high-fiber foods because you are now living for two people instead of one. Increasing your intake of fresh fruits will reduce your chances of colds, flu, or viral infections; taking vitamin and iron supplements if necessary will keep your resistance up, and switching to whole grain breads and cereals will provide greater nutrition for yourself and your child.

Because you are already an overachiever, you do not have to prove that you are capable of handling increased pressure on the job while you carry your baby to term. You should think of yourself as your child's environmental system and protect yourself from any pressures that will act as pollutants, and this includes emotional stress from trying to carry too heavy a work load.

You should look for and expect support from your spouse during pregnancy. Make it clear at the outset that even though you are the person carrying the unborn child, you and your spouse are in this together and you expect his help.

If you are an ACOA father-to-be, you will have to provide support. This may be the first time in your life that you are required to reach well beyond your own needs and become as selfless as possible. If you have made the decision to become a parent, then now realize that parenting begins even before the child is born. It begins when you recognize that helping your spouse through pregnancy is part of the father's job. By protecting the environment of your unborn child, you are controlling the factors that are in your area of management and leaving to the child's biological time clock the factors that are under its control.

It is important to remember than even though child development will occur in a preplanned sequence, the timing is unique to your particular child. As a parent you will not have to control the child's development. Nor should you be upset if one or another developmental stage doesn't take place exactly on schedule. In some children, development takes place faster than in other children. In fact, you shouldn't be surprised if your child accomplishes particular tasks quickly and others very slowly. Your baby isn't reading the same child-care guides that you are and, thus, can't be expected to keep to an author's schedule.

The ACOA Mother-to-Be

You're pregnant and it's a new feeling. Over the course of the past few months you began to experience physical sensations that you might never have felt before. At one moment you might feel very weak. Moments later you might feel exhilarated. These swings in emotions and the knowledge that you are no longer living just for one person are probably very unsettling. You will feel yourself flooded with emotions ranging from joy to sadness, contentment to profound hopelessness. Or perhaps you are worried because you are suppressing these emotions and are not feeling very much at all. Women report that each birth is often different from the one before. And this may be the case with you if this is a second or third pregnancy.

It is only natural for you to worry about having a normal, healthy baby. But beyond the question of immediate health is the responsibility of caring for the child. You may be wondering whether you are up to the task of meeting the demands and needs of a newborn. ACOA mothers oftentimes express concern over the possibility of either playing out the role of the inadequate parent they grew up with or overcompensating by going to the other extreme. In the latter case, they are too demanding on themselves and their children.

Debbie was preoccupied with worries about her competency as a parent.

"How many mistakes will I make? How many chances will I have to recoup? What if I create a disaster that no one can undo?" These are the questions I kept asking myself over and over. . . . I wanted to go to a hospital far away, have the baby, and never see it or Jack again. That way the baby would have a better chance than if I raised it.

In Debbie's case, just asking the questions proved to be the conduit through which she achieved greater understanding. The real danger occurs when ACOA mothers-to-be suppress all of their doubts and fears so as not to disturb the status quo. They may go on for nine months, living in a private torment while their fears about the baby continue to grow. If they don't explode into tantrums and release all of their anger and fear, they stand a great risk of becoming physically sick and impairing the baby's health. If they do let go completely, they believe they risk compromising their relationships. This can be a Hobson's choice if the ACOA doesn't admit that she is having problems which require some form of medical or psychological intervention. If you are not in any type of therapy and can't talk about it with your husband, at least talk about it with your doctor.

Quick Physical Checklist

A woman's first concerns when she plans to become pregnant will involve physical health. Here is a quick checklist to help you resolve some of your immediate worries.

1. Do you have an obstetrician/gynecologist you can rely on?
2. Does your OB/GYN have your *complete* medical and family history?
3. Has the OB/GYN put you on a diet and nutritional supplement program? Are you following it?
4. Have you eliminated all substances such as alcohol, drugs, tobacco, and even caffeine from your diet?
5. Have you and your doctor set up a personal exercise program for you (if necessary)? Are you following that program?

These questions are only a start. If you can deal with these physical concerns during the first three to four months of your pregnancy, later questions relating to concerns such as natural childbirth, breast-feeding, or any special birth or delivery procedures can be answered more calmly.

Additional Emotional Pressures ACOAs Sometimes Face

Most expectant mothers find themselves concerned about how the birth of the baby will alter the important relationships in their lives. These are emotional concerns over and above worries about raising the child. For an adult child of an alcoholic, the pressure on existing family relationships often overshadows the concerns about the baby on the way. Some of the questions my clients have faced which may help you include: How will my (alcoholic/nonalcoholic) mother deal with me and the situation? How will my (alcoholic/ nonalcoholic) father deal with me and the situation? How will my relationship with my spouse change? Will the baby enhance the value of my relationship with my spouse? Will I be able to keep my job? Will I still be able to pursue my career?

These questions, and the thousand doubts that accompany them, are a natural function of preparing for motherhood. ACOAs who are expectant mothers may have a tougher time with the related doubts because they are still struggling to find identities as individuals and therefore need to quickly establish an identity as a mother. This is an ongoing process that naturally accelerates as the pregnancy nears term. Upon the birth of the baby, most of these questions will either be answered or become of less importance as the need to care for the newborn becomes paramount. They will crop up later, however, and therefore cannot simply be dismissed.

Concerns of ACOA Expectant Fathers

Unfortunately, our culture still forces men to dismiss self-doubts or worries. The worries will persist, nevertheless, and may impair your ability to be supportive of your wife and new child. If your doubts are so serious that you feel the urgency to flee, then not talking to your spouse or partner is a great disservice and will only carry on the dysfunction you suffered as a child into the next generation. Bill, for example, spent three months fighting the urge to abandon his wife and unborn child.

From my lab table, I could see the train tracks clearly through the ninth-floor window. I could see the trains coming in from New York and from Philly in the other direction. It got so that I began to plan which train I would take to Newark. From there, it was only a short bus ride to the airport and freedom. At first it was only a fantasy during a chem lecture. Then, I actually began to see myself catching the 3:40 or the 4:10. One day I just walked to the station right from chemistry lab. The 4:10 came in and I got on. I didn't realize what I'd done until I was standing on the platform at Penn Station.

By paying attention to your feelings, even if they are painful to your spouse and to the relationship, you will solve problems instead of creating them. It is usually better to confront the truth, however disturbing that truth may be, than to avoid it. For ACOAs who have been avoiding the truth for years, becoming an expectant parent will make the reality of the truth very immediate. Thus, the *decision* to avoid the truth will be as painful, sometimes, as avoiding it.

One very common pang of worry that most fathers experience is the concern about whether they can provide for their new family. Can you earn enough money? Can you afford to send your children to the right schools and set up financing plans well in advance of their college years? Will you need to buy a house and a bigger car? On the other side of the coin, fathers worry about losing their jobs. Must you stay in an unrewarding position in the company so as not to take risks? Will you become more defensive, knowing that you have a family to support, instead of an assertive worker who takes chances in order to achieve bigger goals?

For ACOA fathers, this may mean an entire shift of strategy. Men who for years have played high-risk stakes may suddenly find themselves trapped in transitional jobs they don't want because they can't afford to lose their medical and life insurance benefits. Knowing what insecurity was like in their alcoholic families when they were children, they may swing in the opposite direction by compromising their future careers for immediate job security. Fifteen years later, will you blame your wife and children for the irreparable damage to your career?

The tendency is also for ACOA fathers to become so wrapped up in their job-related and ego-related concerns that they fail to give their wives the support they need. If your wife has not grown up as an ACOA and really can't understand the struggles you are going through, now is the best time to tell her. Let her know that you want to be there for her but that you are fighting an inner battle as well.

A husband knows that his wife will need to expend a great deal of energy to meet the needs and demands of the newborn. This knowledge may lead to concern that he might further resent the child for "taking my wife away from me."

The husband will no longer be the solitary object of his wife's attention and affection. Consequently, the husband might begin to fantasize about the type of marital relationship that will evolve after the birth of the child. Will you and your wife still have the intimacy you shared before the baby? Will you still have sex with one another as regularly as before? Will it be satisfying? Will you feel the urge to turn to other sexual partners because your wife has become a "mother"? These are all normal questions. Every expectant father confronts feelings similar to these at some point during his wife's pregnancy. The ACOA father, however, might feel as if these normal feelings are indicative of his flawed personality. He might run away from what he is feeling, become angry at himself, and spin himself into an emotional cocoon. None of this is necessary. If you can't talk to your wife, at least talk to her doctor about your fears. The doctor may recommend that you seek some short-term therapy to deal with the problems and help you become more supportive. In the overwhelming majority of cases, however, just recognizing that your feelings are normal and typical of all expectant fathers will help you to confront them while you prepare yourself for fatherhood.

Allow Yourself to Feel Love

It is important for all parents to love their children and take all steps to insure their babies' safety and comfort. This may seem obvious to many people, but for ACOAs, allowing oneself to feel love is a conscious act. In other words, if you survived your years as a teenager and young adult by shutting out your feelings because you distrusted the world, now is the time to deliberately open the door and let the feelings flood in. You cannot distrust your newborn. His or her responses are not calculated; they are totally instinctive and directed at you. The baby knows you are his or her parent and can feel nothing but love and loyalty toward you. This is biological and there is nothing you can do to alter it, just as there was nothing your parents could do to compromise your loyalty and trust in the early years.

If you can feel strong enough to lower your emotional shields for a moment and allow yourself to feel honest responses toward your parents, you might be surprised. Once you get beneath the anger and frustration, once you've admitted that you're hurt, you might feel just a touch of loyalty and love for your alcoholic parent. It's painful to allow yourself that emotion. No matter how old you are and how much you've covered up, the scars are still there and they are sensitive. No doubt it will disturb you that your childhood naiveté toward your alcoholic parent will not fade away, but the love is probably still there. The same will be true for your baby. Your baby will know that you love him or her and will respond positively to the care you provide.

Babies Are Naturally Social

Children tend to gravitate toward a positive interaction with their environment. Occasional physical or external influences may affect the baby's attitude, but if otherwise unimpeded, children move toward healthy social experiences and positive dispositions. Many ACOA parents fear that they will be unable to comfort and satisfy their children. Based on their own experiences, they understand what it was like to have grown up in a home where their legitimate childhood needs were consistently unsatisfied. If you are an ACOA, you may worry that because you were not satisfied, you don't know how to provide the comfort your baby requires. You might picture a child crying incessantly, a prototypical spoiled brat, demanding much and satisfied by very little. This need not be a fear that accompanies you through pregnancy. Once you realize that a baby's crying is only a form of communication and that you will quickly learn to differentiate among the distinct types of cries your baby will make, your fears will abate.

Benjamin Spock reminds parents of newborns that "periodic irritable crying" is often symptomatic of real physical discomfort such as colic, chafing from diaper rash or other irritants, or pain from a cold or flu. Each one of these conditions is readily curable. If the situation becomes chronic or persists too long, your doctor will recommend changes in diet, in skin creams or salves, and a change in the environment to prevent the recurrence of viral infections. One of my clients complained that she must have been doing something wrong with her newborn because he always had a cold. She was so guilty about bringing a "sickly" child into the world who would only do more harm than good that she actually began to overmedicate him so he would sleep longer hours. One of the farm wives in her rural church congregation in southern New Jersey who had raised many children during her lifetime realized that chronic colds and throat irritation are symptomatic of a dry, overheated house. As it turned out, my client's husband also had a sore throat problem punctuated by severe colds that persisted throughout the winter. Once the family began leaving open trays of water near the hot air registers in the baby's nursery and installed an inexpensive humidifying system on the hot air blower, the problems seemed to clear up within weeks—as did my client's guilt.

One of the qualities of infants and children admired most by adults is their sense of wonder. This quality is automatic. Babies are naturally awed and fascinated by the simplest leaf or any shape that catches their attention. Faces are especially fascinating to babies, and you can often see them in supermarkets staring at the multitude of people and trying to catch their gazes. This open-eyed wonder helps babies make connections with their external environment and gradually recognize familiar shapes and faces. When there are no obstacles, the infant will naturally make positive steps to integrate with his or her environment.

This is an important concept for ACOA parents. It means that one of the surest and simplest ways to get positive reinforcement from their newborn child is to provide him or her with shapes, colors, and even textures that will catch his or her attention. In what seems like an overwhelming mystery to ACOA fathers, for example, who don't breast-feed and often work during the day when the child is awake, getting to know the baby can be as simple as spending time in the evening with him or her by catching the child's attention with shapes. If you are afraid of what you will do with the baby or how can you start being a good parent, just plan to show the baby a leaf or a piece of patterned cloth, or even pictures of bright colors. Tell the baby what you're showing him or her. Make believe the baby can understand you. Soon, you will be communicating with your child without any sense of self-doubt or worry. This is what "normal" parents do.

Babies and young children usually have a positive reaction

to a warm, caring adult. Again, this is an automatic function of the species. If, because you are an ACOA, you have felt the need to compete for someone's love or have shunned love because you felt that it was too expensive to earn, you can relax when it comes to your new child. Your baby will love you because he or she is biologically programmed to do so. There is nothing you have to do to earn your newborn's love. It is already there. When you know this, it should be easy for you to love the baby right back. In fact, tell yourself as you approach the term of your or your spouse's pregnancy that, perhaps for the first time in your life, you will receive love with no strings attached. That should ease your fears and make you feel better about becoming a parent.

Parenting Emerges Naturally

The question most ACOA parents-to-be ask in therapy groups is "How can I be an effective parent when I was never shown how?" As a child, you may have watched with envy the positive relationships your friends had with their parents. These might have been in stark contrast to the tensions in your own family. As an adult, you have probably observed the interactions between your friends and their babies or young children. You may have admired the way they hold their infants and seem to meet their needs so effortlessly. Many parents-to-be—not just ACOAs—wonder whether they have the ability to love and nurture an infant. They also doubt their ability to open up immediately to a newborn's needs and know what to do when the baby arrives.

Most new parents look to their own parents for answers. You probably don't have this luxury because you never learned how to parent from your parents. If you look back at your childhood to see how your parents met your needs, you will likely find more negative situations than positive ones. Yet you probably loved your parents throughout and wanted to express that love. This was the source of much frustration. What this means now is that your new child will love you regardless of what you do. It also means that despite the negative feelings you associate with your childhood now, you were always prepared to replace them with positive feelings when you were a child. In other words, you had a natural positive feeling toward your parents that was just waiting to be tapped. If it wasn't, then you must accept that, try to channel the anger into understanding, and get on with your role as a new parent. You have to find other role models for learning how to parent. But, because you now understand your past, you are also not doomed to repeat it. Consider yourself ahead of the game at this point because at least you have a basis for correcting past mistakes.

Positive Imaging: How to Create the Parent You Want to Be

You can consciously create an image of the type of parent you want to be in several ways.

First, examine the positive and negative aspects of your own childhood and cull what pleases you the most. Did you like parts of your parents' personalities? Were there any happy times at home during your childhood? Can you remember the times with your parents before their alcoholism intervened in your relationship? If there is anything positive that they gave to you, assume that you can give it to your own children with no further effort. It belongs to you and you can transmit it.

Second, emulate your friends' parents. Did your friends have parents who were kind to you? Were there aspects of their personalities or family relationships that you can understand now? If so, bring those into your image of what you think a parent should be.

Third, emulate realistic parental role models from books you have read. Obviously novels are fiction, but fiction can be based on fact. Did you think that Nancy Drew's father was particularly supportive and helpful? Can you extrapolate the personal qualities of a literary character from the plot of a book? If so, see what it would be like to inhabit that character's personality and apply it to your situation. This is an instructive imaging exercise which will help you apply solutions to the everyday problems that will crop up.

Next, apply the same emulation modeling to parents from your favorite television shows or movies. Not all people will want to act like June Cleaver, nor can they in today's two-career families, but perhaps Elyse Keaton or Cliff Huxtable has positive personality traits that you can apply to your newly evolving family situation. You don't have to be an architect or a physician, but you can see how these TV characters interact with their children and practice the same techniques with yours. You will quickly learn to inhabit these roles, integrating them with your personality, and a positive parental role model will emerge.

And finally, allow your natural parental instincts to flow. Rather than doubting everything you do, assume that your biological instincts will lead you in the right direction. In other words, if it "feels" OK then it probably is OK. Remember, a conscious decision to parent grows out of a desire to nurture another human being. It is an extension of an already fulfilling relationship with your spouse or partner and an additional way you and your partner will relate to one another. This is all positive and natural. Therefore, instead of beginning with resentment toward the child for tapping your limited personal resources, you should be aware that you have a limitless reserve of love and caring. The natural feelings of nurturing that will emerge with the first skin contact with your child will allay many of your fears.

ACOAs Are Responsible

If there is one characteristic most adult children of alcoholics share, it is that they are responsible. They will turn their world inside out so that others will see them as responsible. They work extra hours, take on additional assignments, plan their schedules months ahead, and spend as much time as necessary to assure that their peers and colleagues view them as responsible. In fact, in the most extreme cases, ACOAs are unrealistically responsible because they take on the tasks of others just to make sure they get completed. In many situations counselors will recommend therapy to relieve the burden of excessive responsibility that ACOAs shoulder. However, being extraordinarily responsible can be a plus when it comes to being a parent.

You tend not to want to let others down, especially your

children. Therefore, you will take pains to make sure that your children are well cared and provided for. You must take care, however, that your ultraresponsible nature does not lead you on an unachievable quest for perfection. This can be damaging to both the ACOA parent and the child, not to mention the ACOA's spouse. Temper your sense of responsibility with the reality that nothing is ever perfect. Strive to do the best you can while recognizing that your children will love you because you're their parent and not because you're perfect.

Issues for Expectant Parents to Share

You will soon have your baby. With the birth, life as you have known it will be forever altered. At the same time a new and more enriched way of living will begin for you. Your goal for each child in your family should be to provide enough consistent love and caring so as to insure the development of a positive self-image. This goal is not accomplished by excessive self-sacrifice or adherence to a standard of perfection, but by the day-to-day nurturing of your child, your marriage, and yourself. If you don't take care of yourself, you can't take care of your child and your family. Your alcoholic parents did not take care of themselves and, hence, they were not able to take care of you. If you can focus on the need to foster a positive self-image in your child, I can almost guarantee you that you *will* break the alcoholism/ACOA cycle in your own family.

It is particularly necessary for ACOAs to be aware of their own tendencies to drink or use other drugs as a result of great stress. Pregnancy may sometimes bring many feelings to the surface that you cannot cope with under ordinary circumstances. The mechanisms you developed as a child in an alcoholic family may become so overtaxed that you lapse into behavior patterns you saw in your parents. Don't be afraid of this or avoid confronting it. By recognizing the danger, you will prepare for it. If you feel the need to sedate yourself, seek immediate assistance from your doctor. If he or she has your family medical history, the urgency of your fears will be self-evident. If the urge to drink seems particularly strong, consider attending an Alcoholics Anonymous or an Al-Anon meeting and seek other forms of counseling. Remember, the feelings of stress and hopelessness may be transitory, but the impact of any amount of alcohol and drugs on the developing fetus may be irreversible.

Expectant ACOA parents almost always ask themselves: Can I do it differently? Can I break the cycle?

The answer to both questions is definitely "Yes!" Try to allow yourself to recognize your feelings about these legitimate concerns without becoming overwhelmed. Anxiety is one of the ways we get ourselves ready to do what comes next: parent. Your child's life will not be perfect, and you will make mistakes as a parent. But fortunately children are fundamentally resilient and as long as you provide love and acceptance on a consistent basis, you will insure your child's good health and his or her positive physical and emotional development. Prepare for childbirth and look forward to the challenges and rewards that lie ahead.

3

You and Your Baby
The First Year

CLAIRE

Claire always handled her baby during therapy sessions as if the baby were holding her instead of the other way around. The infant made her feel complete. For once in her life, she explained, she felt as if she were an essential part of a life process instead of the extraneous appendage she felt she was during her own childhood. Many women say they feel more whole, more actuated, during the initial stages of mothering than they ever have before. But for Claire, it was far more than that.

I never wanted to let my baby down in any way. I didn't want anyone else to hold her or even to touch her. I always felt envious if she smiled or cooed for my mother or her own father. I started to get scared. This was something more than loving the baby. It was bigger. There was more at stake for me. I was putting something more on her that didn't have anything to do with her.

Claire was frightened by the intensity of her feelings of jealousy. She was the youngest of eight children in a family ruled by the terror of an abusive, alcoholic father. Claire's mother, weighed down by the burden of the four oldest children, rarely attended to the needs of the younger siblings. As a result, Claire was raised primarily by her older brothers and sisters.

I had to beg for anything I ever needed. If I needed a shirt or a pair of jeans, I had to bargain with my older sister. When you talk about a trickle-down theory of economic prosperity, I lived it. What came into the family went to the oldest boys and trickled down to me when it was used up or worn out. There was never enough money to get anything new. Even food! When we were all at the table, the best I got was what my older brother couldn't eat and saved for me.

Like many ACOAs, Claire presented a competent, tough exterior to the world while protecting her vulnerability on the inside. Her dilemma now that she was a new parent was that her extraordinarily low self-esteem was preventing her from seeing her baby as a separate person. The infant was still part of Claire, owing Claire her very life, and could not be allowed to develop as an individual.

I knew that I was a good mother on a physical level. I mean, when that baby cried, I was picking her up and rocking her before she could cry again. If she even looked uncomfortable, I was checking her diapers. I talked to her, watched TV with her on my lap, read *Winnie the Pooh* to her every afternoon, and took her everywhere I went. But I knew that sooner or later she would have to go her own way. I also knew that I couldn't allow that.

As it became obvious that by the end of the baby's first year Claire would either have to encourage the baby to develop as an individual or smother the child, she sought therapy. Her goals in therapy were almost prototypical of the types of challenges that most ACOAs face during their new baby's first year. They have to learn to provide basic care and nurturing and then recognize that separation between parent and child is part of the child's natural development.

It may seem odd to think about separation as an operant force during the first year of a child's life, but most parents with low self-esteem problems simply regard their children as appendages of their own psyches. If the child is overprotected, sheltered so excessively that the primary parent experiences anxiety every time the baby is exposed to new people or new situations, the child's emerging sense of self can be smothered. This form of psychological asphyxiation during the first few years of the child's life can result in serious impairment to his or her ability to form relationships in later years. Thus, it was critical that Claire release her baby from the emotional stranglehold she had her in.

By addressing the problem of her self-esteem, Claire was able to understand that her perceptions of the world were skewed. Because she *felt* worthless, she perceived the external world in terms of her own inadequacy.

I always felt I was never good enough for anything or anybody. That it was only a matter of time before people found out and asked me to leave the party. That was how I saw everything, even my own baby. When I held her in the hospital for the first time, I promised myself that nobody would get her away from me. I may not be good enough, but this baby was mine. Now I know why I feel that way. I haven't stopped feeling not good enough, but I know that I can put that feeling in its place. It's like walking in a dark room when you know the layout. You don't have to bump into the furniture to know that it's there—you simply avoid it from memory. That's what I do now. If I feel not good enough, I know where the feeling comes from and ditch it. It's helped my baby, too.

Your Baby's First Year

In order to be an effective parent for a newborn, not only should you know what the basic baby-care skills are, but you should be aware of how the child is developing. Learning the required skills is an obvious necessity. You and your spouse must change and feed the baby, learn to understand what the different cries mean, and be able to nurture and comfort the infant. But because it's a perfectly natural process for parents to care for their newborn offspring, learning the skills is really a matter of process. It's what's behind the process that is really important.

The first year of life will be a year of rapid growth and development. Your baby will begin to emerge from a sleepy and seemingly helpless newborn to an active and curious creature. Shapes and colors will fascinate, voices and new sounds will instantly attract, and any attention you give will delight your infant more that you can imagine. Because babies are naturally positive and prone to humor, the first year with your child can be an absolute pleasure if you allow yourself to enjoy the experience of life through your baby's eyes.

Your child will be developing a sense of separateness, an understanding that there is a difference between him or her and everything external. This is one of the critical developmental stages human beings reach, and it is essential that you help your child through it with lots of nurturing. As an ACOA, you might find that providing this much attention requires more effort than you can muster. This is where you have to make one of those blind leaps and tell yourself that even though you don't feel at all worthy, your instincts are in the right place and will guide you in knowing how to love and care for your new baby.

Talking to your child and providing as much physical contact as possible will help stimulate the infant's still-developing neurological system. They will activate the newborn and help him or her develop into a curious, aware, and intelligent child. Studies have shown that the more parents talk to their new babies and hold them, the faster the children develop emotionally and intellectually and the more self-assured they become when they reach school age. Most children will attain the same developmental level by the time they are eight or nine, but children who have been stimulated very early attain it sooner and go on to greater achievements in later years.

Critical Parenting

While you can do most of what is physically necessary for a newborn while you are "on automatic," it is important for you to recognize the critical issues of parenting for the first year. These issues involve the basic developmental steps that your baby goes through from birth to eighteen months. They involve the child's most fundamental perceptions of his or her self, the child's sense of security, and the progress of the child's natural curiosity.

A parent's critical role is threefold. First, you must help

the child develop a positive, optimistic, and healthy self-perception. In other words, parents should teach their children to love themselves. Second, make the child feel as completely secure as possible. The child should not perceive the world as a threatening place. There is plenty of time to teach him or her about the dangers of the world. Children should have a "sense of bliss" about their surroundings until their own natural sense of caution emerges. And third, encourage the child's curiosity through visual, auditory, and tactile stimulation. In other words, show the child new things about the world while you explain them; hold the child and point out his or her fingers, toes, bellybutton, elbows, or knees; and read to the child to get him or her used to your voice and the voices of other adults.

All children think they are special people and entitled to love. This is a natural developmental stage that shouldn't be compromised by the parent because the parent cannot love himself or herself and hence cannot extend that love toward the child. Because ACOA parents still have a guilty child lurking within their own psyches, they often have a difficult time relating to a newborn. The birth of the child does not mean that the parent is automatically entitled to squash the "bad child" in him or her. To squash your child is to initiate a negative personality pattern which will have painful repercussions throughout his or her childhood. This is a fundamental problem for ACOAs and their newborns.

We recognize that many ACOA parents did not receive the automatic love they felt entitled to when they were newborn infants. This is how the cycle of unfulfilled expectations and loss of childhood happiness got started in your alcoholic family in the first place. Thus, when your newborn arrives, your first negative reaction might be to act as if you were still the spiteful child you always believed you were and to take it out on the baby. ACOA parents must tell themselves that they will rewrite that script. They will activate the baby within them who wants and requires love rather than the older child who spurned love. By recognizing the child within and affirming the needs of the baby, an ACOA parent who is experiencing conflict over his or her newborn will be able to overcome negative impulses and chart a positive course.

Overreacting to the Child

"I remember when we set up the nursery," Angela told the rest of the group. "My husband, Carl, absolutely demanded that we install these plug-in intercoms that let you listen in on the baby." She explained how the devices became a form of torture that awakened her deepest fears about her self-worth.

At first it was kind of neat to listen to the baby sleeping. You knew that everything was OK up there without having to run in every five minutes to check. I'm kind of compulsive anyway, so for the first few days, these devices were great. But then things began to change, especially in the mornings. I would lie there in bed, my own brain's alarm clock going off just before the baby got up. Then I would listen for the kid's first stirrings.

I didn't want to get up and take care of this baby. I just wanted to sleep, especially during the first months after I came back from the hospital. I was depressed and I hated myself. I used to lie in bed, Carl beside me, listening for any change in the baby's breathing that told me he was waking up. Eventually, I knew that shortly after I woke up, the baby would start to move about.

Then the breathing would become panting. Then I'd hear the first whimpers. I hated those whimpers. It was just like the noise an old man makes when he gets cranky and mean. Just like my father. Then the baby would start these short little cries that were more like coughs. Then Carl would wake up and he would look at me with that awful fish-eye he had. I could read his mind. "Aren't you getting up? Don't you hear him crying? Are you just going to lie there staring at the ceiling?"

Who did I hate more, I would think to myself, Carl or the baby? Then the cries would become piercing with a little rising pitch at the end of each phrase—just like a fishhook that would get under your skin. Soon the crying would become a full-scale screaming, growing in intensity and filling the speakers that began to echo their own echoes. The whole house shuddered from the wailing. And I was paralyzed. I couldn't move. I hated myself. I knew in my heart that I was capable of letting that baby cry itself to death.

Postpartum Reactions New Mothers May Experience

As you approached your delivery date, you probably experienced a euphoria. This is a biological lift that enables you to summon the physical and emotional strength for the actual birth. In the days immediately following the birth of your baby, after the feeling of euphoria has left, there is a natural physical and emotional letdown. This is often called postpartum depression or, more commonly, postnatal blues. Most women experience it to some degree. It is marked by periods of depression, lingering doubts about your ability to cope, extreme fatigue, and maybe even a sense of hopelessness about the future.

In ACOAs, postpartum depressions may be especially severe because you may have had doubts about your ability to cope even before you had the baby, and you may have an underlying fear of failure. The depression only exacerbates these feelings. If you feel yourself suddenly gripped in a depression punctuated with bouts of crying and panic, try to remember that it is a natural physiological event. These reactions stem from the body's establishment of a new equilibrium after the strenuousness of giving birth. What you need is lots of sleep and, most likely, plenty of iron to help you get back your strength. You are entirely within your rights to demand that your husband take over most of the household chores. You have to recover your strength and resiliency so you can deal with the requirements of parenting. Talk about your reactions with your husband and your doctor, but don't blame yourself for them.

Emotional Checklist to Short-Circuit Overreactions

Essential to breaking the cycle of dysfunctional family relationships is knowing when you are overreacting to your child's behavior. To feel guilty because the baby is crying or to believe that you are unworthy because your baby is sick is to react to your own unhappiness rather than to the actual situation. If you sense that you are particularly under siege or are overwhelmed by the enormity of your role as parent, you are reacting to an inappropriate set of stimuli. Often, ACOA parents of newborns have a tendency to react to their own feelings rather than to the actual needs of the child. The overreaction might be so extreme that the needs of the child become lost to the needs of the parent. This is one of the behaviors you will have to watch out for and adjust whenever you feel it is taking place.

If you find yourself reacting to the wrong thing or reacting inappropriately to your child's behavior, before doing anything else, *stop* your panic cycle. Throw your switch to "off." Now go through the following emotional checklist.

1. What is it you feel right now? Verbalize it!
2. What specific behavior in your child evoked this response? Pinpoint that behavior.
3. Has the same behavior evoked this response before? When? What was the situation?
4. Is this a familiar or "old" feeling? When have you felt it before? Pinpoint the situation.
5. Can you identify this feeling with someone or something else that has nothing to do with your baby's behavior?
6. Who are you really mad at? What are you really sad over?

Now put your reaction on hold and deal with it after you have tended to the baby. Deal with the real source of your anger or sadness in a private moment when nothing can trigger you into a false reaction.

Calling for Help

If you feel too confused or feel drawn to react impulsively either emotionally or physically, ask for help. Demand help from someone else if you feel that you might hurt yourself or your baby. Some of the feelings of panic and siege are entirely normal in new parents. This is a new stage of life for you as well as for your child, and it is natural for you to be momentarily overwhelmed by the burden of the responsibility. If this is your first child, the burden seems that much more difficult to manage. Sometimes, simply seeking support and guidance from a friend who is an experienced and trusted parent is all that is needed. Certainly a phone call to your pediatrician is also in order. But if the feelings are too strong and refuse to be allayed by a consultation with a friend, sympathetic family member, or pediatrician, short-term counseling with a mental health professional who specializes in ACOAs is worth considering.

If you are a working mother, your company or employer may have a counseling program. Does your community or religious organization provide counseling, or can they refer you to an outreach program? If you are a student or an alumna, does your school or college have any short-term counseling facilities? If you have no resources to arrange for therapeutic counseling, call your local community mental health center.

Using Crises for Positive Development

In my psychotherapy practice, I encounter people with feelings that sometimes shift almost instantly between the extremes of joy and sorrow. Their personal stability can range from a calm self-assuredness in one moment to absolute panic in the next. Almost anyone is capable of fluctuating between extremes; however, adult children of alcoholics are more vulnerable to this fluctuation than others. Despite swings of mood and shifting feelings of self-esteem, all people, ACOAs included, can develop a more stable and consistent outlook toward themselves and others. The key to moving people toward an acceptance of change is to understand which personality "face" or point along the individual's emotional continuum presents the best opportunity for change to take place.

I have found that crisis is sometimes the best lever to encourage change. Time after time, crises present people with the opportunity to see themselves in stark relief, set off from the camouflage of their daily lives. They may have turbulent feelings during a crisis—upset, anger, confusion, or extreme sadness—but these feelings have always been present just past the surface tension of their consciousness. It takes a crisis to break that tension, bring the feelings to a head, and demand that a resolution take place.

How an individual comes to this resolution determines whether the addiction cycle will be broken. For example, how an ACOA wife chooses to deal with her husband's use of cocaine either perpetuates the enabling behavior she saw in her own mother while she was growing up or allows her to break the pattern. If she refuses to confront her husband directly and thus contributes to the addiction, her personal history as an enabler will repeat itself. If she brings the addictive behavior pattern to a crisis, she will either help him kick his habit in a treatment program or cut herself loose from an unhealthy and dangerous relationship. Either way, she will break the pattern of history. In making her decision, she will encounter feelings that are at the heart of being an ACOA: trust, guilt, neediness, anger, and self-esteem.

Similar crisis situations are a model of development for the growing child, and how the ACOA parent deals with the child's natural growth crises will determine how he or she encourages or inhibits the child's positive development. Crises provide the child with opportunities and challenges to grow to the next stage of emotional and social development. What are these forms of crisis and how will you react to them?

The Trust Crisis

The initial crisis children face during the first year is the decision of whether or not to be trusting of themselves and others and the world around them. This is a natural stage of development in the newborn. You will see the decision-making process begin when the child starts to challenge you and test the limits of the immediate environment. Your child will at first accept the rules you set down; then he or she will test the limits of those rules to see whether they bend or break, trying after each test to establish a new equilibrium. The same is true for testing the rules of the environment: Does gravity work? Is pain a constant? Does water flow? Is a flame hot?

If you waver in your rule setting and management or if the child's physical environment changes dramatically, the establishment of self-trust will be inhibited. Your child will continue to push at your rules until their outermost boundaries are found. If these rules are pushed too far or don't really exist (as is the case with most rules set by ACOAs), there will never be trust because the rules will never work. Think back to your own childhood in your alcoholic family and see whether you can remember any consistent level of trust that you came to rely on.

For Carol, member of one of my ACOA group sessions, rules became a vital component of her life because there were none in her family household. She was a rigid mother who had created an entire world out of rules of behavior, and her children marched to the beat of her drum or not at all. "I knew I was having a problem in raising them," she recalled during a meeting, "when their nursery school teacher complained that my oldest was having severe problems initiating his own projects. I realized in a flash that was because I had never given him any leeway, he had become totally dependent on my direction. He never really tested his own limits."

Children normally resolve the trust crisis by the end of the first year. Thus, it is vital that your parental presence and personality vary within a consistent and predictable range of responses. The parent's job during the first year is to ensure the development of a child who is basically trusting by nature. The formulations of a validation of self, a sense of "I'm OK," go hand in hand with this process of developing trust. However, because a lack of trust is at the center of your being an adult child of an alcoholic, it is reasonable for you to be apprehensive about how well you will do in imparting trust to your child. You can impart trust. First you have to see just how trust is fostered.

The Role of the Mother

The child's experience of its mother is absolutely crucial to the development of trust. If the mother is sensitive to the needs of the infant and effective in responding to those needs, the child's feelings of security and trust increase. The infant learns that its needs will be met in a predictable and benevolent fashion. A secure sense of self is developed in the infant when the mother provides—in Erik Erikson's words—

"consistency, continuity, and sameness of experience." With the increase in the infant's security, he or she is able to more easily tolerate the frustrations of hunger and discomfort that are sometimes inevitable. This leads the infant to eventually develop a sense of both personal trust and trust in the outside world. Children trust the consistency of the feelings of their own bodies, the urges and hunger pangs that are a part of daily existence, and learn to trust in the role of the parents or other providers who assuage those pangs and discomforts with food and nurturing.

A critical test in the development of trust in the infant and in the mother-child relationship occurs during the biting stage. The pain of teething evokes feelings of anger and rage in infants because it cannot be alleviated as easily as hunger. Children also discover much to their chagrin that the mother is of little help in eliminating the pain. In fact, the mother withdraws from the biting, which is the only activity that relieves the pain. How will you, the mother, accept the child's anger and deal with the pain the child inflicts? Can a breast-feeding mother continue to provide sensitive care, breast-feed, and nurture her baby while knowing that her infant will bite her with sawlike little baby teeth that are just penetrating the gumline?

Surprisingly, it is not the magnitude of the response that is at issue here but the sameness or consistency of it. Obviously, it is inappropriate to fly into a violent rage every time the child bites. However, it is normal for you to get angry when you react to pain. If the range of your reaction is always within the bounds of consistency, the child will learn to trust in that reaction when he or she bites. If your response is inconsistent and cannot be predicted, then the child will move on to a more serious and confrontational test of trust. The child's emotional development will be impeded. Clearly, therefore, the quality of the relationship between mother and child is a crucial factor in the development of trust and a sense of security in the child. Mothers do not have to be "supermoms." You have to convey a sense of personal trust-worthiness. You have to understand how trust is fostered and how it grows. As an ACOA parent, you have to accept your own mistrust of the world but foster your child's natural trust. As you do, your own mistrust will begin to dissipate while you nurture your baby and the baby in you.

Supermoms

Parenthood is often a time when unresolved personal issues come home to roost. While this is felt universally, it is certainly of great import for parents who are adult children of alcoholics. The subtle sense of not being quite good enough that many ACOAs carry with them is sometimes manifested in emotional swings from anger and frustration to a compulsion to be a supermom or superdad. If you find yourself having to do more for your baby, remember, it is not the number of things accomplished but the quality of the relationship that counts. Do not forget to allow yourself to enjoy the rich feelings of just being with the child when he or she is asleep or cooing in your lap.

The "I must do everything to the nth degree" personality has been described as Type A, or overly compulsive. More recently, much has been written about the Type E woman: the woman who is driven to be everything for everybody. She must be the superwife, superworker, super–adult child, and, of course, the supermom. If you find yourself tending to this direction as you see to the needs of your child, don't panic. First of all, you're not alone. This way of compensating for personal doubts is a hallmark of ACOA parents.

Susan spent years as a superwoman and then a supermom before she realized that she was actually martyring herself for her father.

I used to listen to that song "I'm a woman—W-O-M-A-N" when I was a little girl and tell myself that's what I wanted to be. Then everybody would like me. It wasn't until I was actually that type of person that I realized I was a doormat. My department chairmen, the curriculum supervisor at school, my husband, Bobby, and my father, of course my father, all relied on me 150 percent. I didn't even have space to breathe, and I took it out on the one person who couldn't defend himself—my son.

Women often adopt a form of supermom behavior as a way of compensating for negative feelings toward their families.

Chief among these, especially during the first year of the infant's life, are anger, self-doubt, resentment, and dependency. You may be angry at your own unhappy childhood; full of self-doubt because you never learned to trust; resentful of the deprivations of your childhood and your parents; and dependent upon the approval and confirmation of other people. The amalgamation of these behaviors results in a personality obsessively or compulsively driven to excel and provide for others. These feelings have been just below the surface since childhood. You may find yourself in a crisis of confidence with your newborn, questioning your adequacy as a parent, and regretting you got yourself into this predicament in the first place. And, of course, you may have nothing but resentment or even hatred for your lucky "normal" husband, oblivious to your pain, who goes happily to work every morning, confident of the rightness of the world and of your place in it as the mother of his children.

You may feel a free-floating anxiety as you hold your child or even wait for the child to awaken from a nap and begin crying. You may lie awake in your bed like Angela, waiting in a profound sense of hopelessness for the first cries of the morning to begin your day. You may resent the demands of your baby for food, comfort, changing, or simply for attention. You might notice a low level of anger building in you when your infant begins teething and your attempts to comfort do not immediately solve the problem. You may feel frustrated during this period. You may feel the baby is controlling you and dictating your life. Your anger and resentment will be accompanied by a profound sense of guilt because you may recognize that your hostility toward the infant is somehow inappropriate. You may also feel guilty because none of the baby and child-care instructions you receive address your particular problems as an ACOA.

Your first reaction should be to short-circuit any feelings of panic or rage. Again, throw your emotional response switch to "off" so that you can give yourself reasonable time for self-introspection. Understand what is really happening. The mere presence of your child and your new responsibilities are pushing your ACOA buttons. The feelings you have about yourself and the world are coming to the surface. They may wash over you with such force that you are emotionally overwhelmed at first, but you won't remain so. The task at hand is to be a loving parent, and the feelings of anxiety and anger need not prevent you from being the parent you want to be. Consciously tell yourself to shut down all negative emotions when they threaten to overwhelm you and allow yourself the emotional space to consistently do two things: touch your baby; talk to your baby.

You may want to flee, hide, turn back time, or light into your husband like a stinging wasp, but just allow yourself to risk contact with your baby. The stimulation from touching will be good for you both. And talking to your baby will also soothe the both of you. You may feel awkward at first in holding and talking to your baby. This is because of your own lack of positive contact during infancy and childhood. Nevertheless, do it anyway. It will foster a bond between you and your child. Each of you will learn to enjoy the other and receive satisfaction from one another's presence. Encourage your spouse to do it as well. The same is true for talking with your child. The human voice, essential to your child's development, will also foster the bond between the two of you. It will help develop a sense of trust faster, and it will actually make your child more verbal by the time he or she reaches school age. It doesn't matter what you say; you can even read the newspaper or a magazine aloud if you want to. All that matters is that you speak in a soothing, gentle voice, with full modulations and changes of pitch. This is therapy for you as well as for your infant.

What Are the Goals of Parenting?

Be assured, this is a question you will never stop asking yourself. You ask it now; you will ask it when you're confronted by the challenge of caring for a newborn; you will ask it again when your school-age child challenges your authority for the first time, when your teenager aggressively rebels against conformity, and when your college-age young adult suggests that your social values are passé, if not meaningless. You may never be sure of what your job as a parent is, especially if you succeed at it.

As elusive as the goal may seem from time to time, parents should aim their efforts at the development of a healthy, responsible, independent individual. You are training your child to leave you, to fly from the nest and make it on his or her own. In order for this to happen, the child must develop into a socially responsible person who understands what the rules of society are and how to navigate within them. Ideally, the child should also develop a positive self-image. This can happen if the naturally positive self-image the child has at birth is allowed to evolve and is not impeded by the negative imaging that parents sometimes impose. Thus, your goals are to keep your child healthy and safe, to encourage the development of a positive self-image, and to develop an independent, responsible, and social individual.

Most parents eventually find that *when* the first words are uttered, *when* toilet training is completed, *where* he or she attends preschool, or *whether* he or she is elected class president and ultimately becomes a lawyer or a doctor does not matter in the end. What matters is that you have done your job to create a responsible person. What that person chooses to become or how that individual lives his or her life becomes less of a parenting issue the more successful the parents have been as parents. During the first year of the infant's life, the groundwork can be laid for the healthy development of self-esteem and a positive view of the world. Once this foundations is set, all the rest will fall into place surprisingly easily. You can help your baby along by giving him or her a feeling of being loved and cared for and, through your consistency and even discipline, showing the child that he or she can trust the world and predict outcomes of behavior. Once that takes place, the child will feel safe and secure when interacting with the outside world. You will notice it by the beginning of the baby's second year, when a sense of responsibility begins to develop. Address the fundamental goals of parenting from the start, and you will establish a pattern of successful development that may surprise even you. Your ACOA background need not be an impediment to this, as long as you are able to switch off your negative feelings, realign yourself to reality, and get in contact with your baby's immediate needs. During this first year, your consistent caring attention to those needs will foster the development of trust and well-being in his or her emerging personality.

The Father and the Newborn During the First Weeks After Birth

In the first few weeks after your child's birth, both mother and child will be tired. This provides an opportunity for the father to establish himself in the expanded relationship with his wife and to begin the bonding process with the baby through his nurturance. The birthing process and getting adjusted to life outside of the mother are particularly tiring for the baby. Thus, in the first weeks, the child will be drifting in and out of sleep. This is normal. Slowly, your infant will make his or her constant presence felt more and more.

The newborn baby is the most helpless and dependent of all earth's creatures for a long period of time. This creates its own opportunities, however. While the dependency may be frightening to the parent as well as to the child, it is also somewhat comforting to know that you will have plenty of time to relate to the baby. You don't have to be there twenty-four hours a day to establish yourself as parent. While your wife is getting her energy back, you should assume as much responsibility as you can while getting to know your baby's moods, learning to identify its different cries, and responding to the needs that come up when you are at home.

Confronting Inadequacy

Many new fathers become aware of feelings of inadequacy. This is normal and is to be expected. However, in male adult children of alcoholics, this feeling is especially exaggerated when it comes to assuming leadership. If you were the child of an especially strong enabling mother, you might have a weak male image for which you have been overcompensating throughout your life. You might have relied on your spouse for strength, but now she's just had a baby and must rely on you. You may find yourself terribly alone for the first time since childhood.

"The biggest problem I had after the baby was born," Andy expressed in a therapy session, "was that I couldn't differentiate myself from my father. I guess he was actually pretty strong, but to a kid he looked weak and helpless. Mom did everything. When she said jump, he jumped—and I did, too. Then when my wife, Jane, had Cindy and then came down with a virus during postpartum, I found myself doing the laundry, shopping, cleaning, cooking, and having to serve everybody. That was the event—if you can point to any one in particular—that precipitated the divorce, even though it took place years later."

If you had an alcoholic mother, your father may have had to assume many of the household duties. Thus, your situation now as a provider for a new baby and a spouse who must have bed rest during the next few weeks may be painfully reminiscent of your own childhood. You may even experience the nightmarish desperation that haunted you throughout your early years. All of these feelings, whether from a strong or weak father, will be accompanied by a strong dose of guilt as you try to fight them down and cope with the first few weeks of a new baby.

Stop the panic by realizing that nature has now taken over and will set the course. Your infant is already preprogrammed to develop. Most of what needs to get done will take place as part of the normal processes of growth. Assume for the moment that all your fears have been anticipated by a grand scheme. That scheme has provided for your anxieties, guilt, and human shortcomings by setting both infant and mother on automatic pilot. Everything will be all right. All you have to do is give your new baby and your wife love, attention, and care and they will thrive. It's nice to clean a dish once in a while, but that's what you should be doing even if there were no baby. You should provide as much physical care as you can. Spend as much time with your baby and your wife as you can. You will find that within a few months, you will have integrated yourself into the family system and assumed a role of leadership that may have frightened you throughout your life. The mutual satisfaction will be reinforcing for all parties in the family, and a healthy bonding among the three of you will result.

Responding to the Child's Needs Versus Spoiling the Child

Much has been written about whether one risks spoiling the child by consistently responding to his or her distress or whether letting the baby "cry it out" helps develop a more resilient and healthy individual in the long run. We can lay this debate to rest very easily. In the first few weeks after birth, there is no such thing as spoiling a child by responding quickly to the newborn's cries. In fact, by not responding, you actually teach the child to become frustrated and angry in order to get a response. Ultimately, the child will learn that displays of anger and frustration get your attention, and you will have created the very personality you were trying to avoid.

Responding quickly to a newborn's stress in the early weeks will teach the child to be secure, reinforce the infant's trust in his or her parents, and teach the child that the outside world can be depended on, and that he or she is not alone and isolated in the universe. Children who are abandoned or who are given only minute amounts of attention never develop these feelings. The result is a lot of unnecessary sadness during childhood, and it probably explains some of the sadness you felt growing up. Don't repeat the pattern. Your child is a needy creature. How he or she relates to you in addressing discomfort greatly influences the child's future relations with others.

Try to let yourself respond naturally to the upset of the child. Remember, you do not have to do everything just right. But if your baby's distress is allowed to elicit a constant and positive response from you, he or she will quickly confirm his or her natural sense that the world is a safe, caring place. On the other hand, the child who is forced to "cry it out" also develops a set of expectations of the world. This child will come to see the world as an isolated environment, full of danger and unhappiness, and will not learn to trust and will not give trust in return. Studies have borne out the positive effects of routinely responding to the cries of a baby. Indeed, a healthier and more mutually satisfying attachment tends to develop between responsive parents and their trusting child.

Establish a Routine

If you have dutifully read your baby- and child-care book, you already know the importance of establishing a routine—this is for the sake of the child as well as the parents. Your baby will learn to find comfort in fitting into a routine, and it will help your parenting later on down the line when you want to set more complex rules and limits on your child's behavior. Moreover, you need the comfort of getting into a daily routine and rhythm with your child. Let children know that their ·expectations can be timed according to your responses and that there is a quid pro quo to your existence. It will enable you to pace yourself and help you to make it through particularly trying days and nights.

Routines work best when they are established early. This is simply because both the parents and infant will quickly get used to them and fall into the habit of, for example, mealtimes according to a specific schedule during the day. You must remember, however, that the purpose of the schedule is the baby's best interest. Therefore, use consistency and not rigidity in applying the routine. If you listen to your baby, you will know when it is time to vary the routine. Also, you will attune yourself to your baby's biological clock and reinforce it with the schedule. Why swim upstream, as many first-time parents do, when you can go with the flow and let your baby do a lot of the work? In other words, let your baby establish some of the scheduling at first. Listen to the messages your baby gives you in the form of cries or sniffles when he or she wants to sleep more or eat more. Keep track of how long the baby can go between meals and the length of naps. See if responding to some "demand feedings" makes the routine easier or more difficult.

What is most important is to aim toward the same times each day for feeding, napping, nightly bedtime, playtime, separate times with mother and father, reading, and bathing. The more you can perform these activities in the same location, the better. The baby will become more familiar with the surroundings and will learn to associate the setting with the event. This will aid in his or her sense of comfort and security and enable the child to make rudimentary predictions about what will happen next. All of this works toward positive reinforcement with respect to the environment. But remember, each baby is an infant unto himself or herself. Some will tend to be more difficult or easier than others in establishing schedules at different stages of their first year. Comparing, while it cannot be helped, should not be valued as a yardstick. This child is different from other children and from older siblings. Your child is unique and will develop according to his or her own internal clock. You must recognize the differences between children and refrain from berating yourself or your parenting abilities because your child's schedule is different from that of the baby's next door.

When the Child Is a Burden

It is naive to believe that after successfully negotiating your way through your childhood years in an alcoholic family, or becoming an overachiever despite insurmountable odds, or managing to establish yourself in an upscale life-style after having suffered in a dysfunctional family, you are living just to bear and raise children. Obviously, parenting is important or else you wouldn't have opted for it. But parenting is only one aspect of your identity, albeit a critically important one.

Accordingly, as central as the child is to your sense of self, you might also have a job and a life as an independent human being. Thus, it is no crime to admit that at times the baby will be a burden to you. At times you might wish that you had never had children. This is no more damning than to say that at times you wish you had never got married. No one will find you and throw you in jail for these thoughts.

The truth of the matter is that all parents in all circumstances have entertained the thought that perhaps their children are less than joyful bundles. And there are times when even the best of parents simply want to be alone—no kids allowed! You don't have to feel guilty, therefore, when your responsibilities become so overwhelming that you wish you didn't have them. Remember, the family situations in modern society are unique in human history. Even a hundred years ago, if a parent in a rural environment wanted to be freed from child-care responsibilities for a while, another family member would take over. And in aristocratic or plantation households in the previous century (or even today in very wealthy families), children would often be raised by nannies, au pairs, mother's helpers, or nurses. The parents only saw their children after they were fed, rested, cleaned, and dressed. When the child misbehaved or became too troublesome, the nanny would whisk the child away to the nursery.

In middle-class working families, no such luxury exists. You must raise your own children, often with no respite, until they are ready for school. It is no wonder that even the best of parents need to take a break. The danger is not in wanting to take a break, but in forcing yourself to not recognize you need a break and in making the child pay for it by sending mixed signals.

Babies are very smart creatures and very perceptive, too. They can pick up your feeling of apprehension about touching them and handling them even if you are not consciously aware of it yourself. For instance, if you are hurried and feel burdened about having to pick up and comfort your baby, he or she will sense that fact. If this happens occasionally, it's no real problem because babies are resilient enough to compensate. Besides, the vast majority of interactions with you are more than enough to comfort the child. However, problems arise when apprehension occurs habitually. Then you are consistently sending the signal "You are a burden to me" or "I don't have enough time for you."

If you sense this is happening on a regular basis, then you should seek some form of counseling or at least relate it to your spouse. If you're the mother, you are more likely the principal caregiver, and so when you feel you're giving mixed signals, the sooner you call for help the better. If you're the father, you may have more room in which to navigate, if you are not your child's principal source of care and comfort, but that room is not without limits. The problem is not that the baby is a burden but that you are not *admitting* the baby is a burden. If you can admit it to yourself and to the baby, you will be a more consistent parent, and consistency is the issue, not unlimited selflessness.

Therefore, the key is to understand what your limits and

needs are and to address them with the baby's interests in mind. If you find that you are not a bottomless well of parental feeling, that's OK as long as you admit it and give your child some "quality time." If you make the child the brunt of your mixed feelings, you do both the child and yourself a disservice. In other words, it's OK to reach your limit and get tired. Just don't pretend that you can relate to your child without conflicting emotions when you're in as much conflict as you can be. Admit it. Say that you're upset. Recognize that tonight won't be one of the nights when you point out the stars in the summer sky to your new baby. If not tonight, then tomorrow. If not tomorrow, then the next night. But at least you won't be transmitting negative feelings to the baby. If you let yourself deal with the issues and responsibilities of parenthood honestly, you won't create an emotionally impossible situation for the child.

When Counseling Is Necessary

In the unhappy situation when you're not too busy to hold or touch your baby but simply too resentful, you have to examine the situation carefully. If you turn your resentment or anger off and go on automatic, you can, in effect, jump start your natural parenting instincts. If, however, no matter how hard you try, you're having serious emotional reactions to the baby, then you should seek counseling as quickly as possible. Because intimate contact between parent and child—especially mother and child—is critical, not being able to establish that contact can cause long-term emotional damage. You can be helped through this if you obtain professional psychological counseling to address the issues. Through counseling, it will be possible to sort out the conflicting feelings that are getting between you and your automatic parental instincts. You will confront feelings, many of which are old and familiar, so they won't get in the way of caring for and loving your child.

Basic Housekeeping Rules

Although you can't completely child-proof a home, you can remove obviously dangerous objects and make routine checks for safety on a weekly basis. Remember, your child will find a way into places where you don't know you have places.

- Make sure all electrical wall outlets have protective plastic inserts.
- Doubleknot electrical cords to keep them off the floor and out of the baby's reach.
- Cover or remove all sharp objects in the baby's crawling range.
- Remove all breakables—china, glass, picture frames, mirrors, ceramics, etc.—from the tables where your child will be crawling.
- Make sure all tables and chairs are stable and cannot collapse on the baby, who will surely try to pull them over. (If you don't want the baby to use your rolling lamp tables as walkers, remove the casters and replace them with rubber cups.)
- Keep pet foods away from the baby and control the dog and cat. If you are worried about how the dog will react to the baby, keep them separated or get rid of the dog.
- Lock all doors to rooms you do not want the baby to enter.
- Put up barriers on all stairways that the baby can crawl to.
- Remove all forms of poison and skin or eye irritants— cleansers, perfumes, household chemicals, and paints and varnishes—from where the baby can get at them.
- Keep all aerosol and spray cans out of the baby's reach.
- Keep silverware, especially knives and forks, away from the edges of tables, where the baby can knock them off.
- Every cabinet and drawer that your baby can reach should be locked.
- All medicine containers should have child-proof caps and be kept well away from the baby.

Disciplining the Baby

As a general rule, discipline should be gentle but consistent and firm. In the case of biting, show your displeasure and pain by removing the child from whatever it is she or he is biting and saying no. If you have a teething toy, hand it to the baby and encourage him or her to bite *it*. The chewing is not the negative behavior; biting another person is. Thus, you want to focus the infant's attention away from what is negative and on what is positive.

As children begin to navigate along the floor during the first year, they unavoidably get into places where you don't want them to be. There is really no such thing as a child-proof house, even though you've tried your best to create one. The active orientation of children to the outside world, which is a result of natural curiosity, will manifest itself in self-confidence, self-assertiveness, and a trust that they can do no wrong. This is all very healthy behavior at first. However, children will ultimately cross forbidden boundaries. They will put themselves in jeopardy by touching dangerous objects. They will create messes in places where you don't want them to be.

Your first reaction as an ACOA parent might be to feel guilty about your child's misbehavior. You might brook what you take to be naughtiness to a point beyond normal endurance and then explode in anger. This is not a healthy reaction. You should set well-defined limits on children's behavior and rein them in gently when they go over the line. Children will challenge you and will test those limits—they have to test in order to establish a sense of trust. It is your *job* to make sure that your discipline is unwavering, albeit loving and benevolent. If you can't develop a consistency in your response, a child can't learn to trust in consistency and predictability. Therefore, discipline is a necessary and vital component of parenting. Physical discipline—striking the child—is not.

Positive discipline means that when you say no to one form of behavior you get the child's attention with another form. If you remove your finger from between the child's sharp gums, you should offer something else. If your child is playing with a dangerous object, don't just whip it out of sight and say no. Show the baby there are other things to play with. In other words, always try to be positive, even though you may have an ACOA voice ringing inside you, punishing you for the behavior of your child. Your answer to that voice should be that the child is doing what comes naturally. You, by providing a positive direction, are encouraging that natural curiosity and assertiveness by channeling them in a new, safe, and acceptable direction. You are developing high self-esteem in your child and inculcating leadership qualities. Be proud of what you are doing and take pleasure in your attempts at success.

Stay Alert to Your Baby

Keep attuned to all signs of your baby's real physical discomfort. If you notice a different type of cry, it might be a sign of pain or illness. Monitor the baby regularly to make sure that everything is all right. You will get used to his or her schedule, so if something is amiss, you will notice it immediately.

Finally, remember that there will be times when you will find it difficult to comfort your baby and to figure out what may be causing his or her discomfort. The challenge to the ACOA parent is to not put your self-esteem on the line in these circumstances but rather to solve the problem with the baby. Remember that the child's body is growing, and learning to adjust to the world outside the womb is a difficult task all by itself. If the baby is sick, it is all the more difficult. Holding and rocking the baby will work well no matter what the source of the upset. And when nothing you do works, call the pediatrician or consult with an experienced parent.

Remember also that the one central psychosocial task during the first year of life is your baby's establishment of a sense of trust. Most new parents who are also adult children of alcoholics are concerned about imparting a sense of trust to their children when it still remains a difficult issue for the parents themselves. As a result, there is a tendency to under- or overcompensate. You should not worry about this. It is a normal part of everyone's struggle to parent effectively. Remember that the most important factor is the development of trust, not the quantity of what you provide for your child. The quality of the relationship is based on the way you instill a sense of individuality and independence in the child. But if you find yourself feeling particularly angry or confused about caring for the baby, perhaps your own trust issues and worry about competence are getting in the way. ACOA support groups or individual counseling can help you sort out your feelings on a short-term basis and may help you to a feeling of self-assuredness. However, your natural parental instincts will soon take over and you will be a successful parent for your newborn.

4

Toddlers
18 Months to 3 Years

LYNN

It was as if my arm had a mind of its own. I had never hit him before. It was something I had made up my mind never to do. I didn't want my baby to grow up under the reign of terror I had known, and now I was just as bad as my father. How I hated to think I would now be like him. I feared that more of his traits would soon start popping up in my personality.

Lynn had never hit anyone in her life before—she had always been terrified of violence of any kind. This time, when she slappped her son, Tommy, it was as if the violence had come out of nowhere. In an instant, she had wound up and slapped her son across the face with the full force of her might. His defiance and disapproval, his refusal to do what she wanted, seemed to trip a wire that Lynn didn't even know was there. She could only stand in shock as Tommy, his eyes wide, his screams full of hurt and indignation, wailed like a siren.

Lynn was fifteen years old when her father finally began his recovery from alcoholism. Now a mother of a twenty-six-month-old son, she continued to feel distant from her father, having not yet come to terms with her anger and the vague longing of wanting something from him, albeit undefined. She had an easier time coping with the anger, but the longing left her queasy and just on the edge of a migraine whenever she thought about it.

During his drinking days, her father had behaved like an irrational monster, and Lynn learned it was best to stay out of his path. Consequently, she spent most of her time and energy trying to avoid any encounters with him. He was not usually physically abusive, however, and she could remember being hit by him only a few times in her life. But the emotional assault was just as bad. He was a very angry man, and there was little she or anyone could do to please him. "He was just as rotten whether or not he was drinking. Only when he was drinking, he smelled bad."

Lynn solemnly promised herself that she would never subject her children to the angry moods and incipient violence she had had to face as a child.

Yet, in an instant, there it was all over again. The quiet fear that she was really like him reached across the years, and she was shamed and worried over the impact this would have on her son and their relationship. It was only through discussions with a friend and participation in a therapy group that Lynn was able to examine her anger and her desperate need to take control of each and every situation. She learned not only that her reactions to her son's demands and his refusal to cooperate were natural, given her background, but that she was not forever condemned to approach her past with fear and misunderstanding. She learned that because she was an ACOA who needed to exert control in all situations, she was bound to be on a collision course with a toddler, who between the ages of eighteen months and three years needs to wrest some control from his parents as a means to assert his own identity.

In the Eye of the Hurricane

You will find that the period of the child's life between approximately twelve and eighteen months is markedly pleasant. You have a year's worth of parenting experience behind you, and it's much easier to feel relaxed around the child. Your baby has also adjusted to life in the outside world by now and has developed into a responsive, happy little person who is often contented. One-year-olds tend to be receptive and take direction easily. They listen to their parents and obey simple instructions without obstinancy or discussion.

Shortly, however, this period of contentment will end with the thunderclap of No! Just as an airplane passes through the eye of a hurricane back into the tumult of the storm, you are about to enter one of the most turbulent periods of your child's life. The stress and pressure of the next year and a half will test your resiliency and will likely force you to confront some of your deepest misgivings about your own abilities and background.

Your child is talking more now, actually developing more and more into a little individual with a mind of his or her own. The child will soon distance him- or herself from you, and begin to show independence by refusing to obey your instructions. You will hear the word *no* again and again as an assertion of your child's independence. *No* will be a long and drawn-out sound on the cutting edge of a whine; it will be shouted at you from behind the closed door of your child's room; it will punctuate your child's refusal to move from the front of the checkout counter in the supermarket; and it will be repeated in staccato bursts as you try to wrench the latest breakfast cereal, grabbed off the shelf, out of your child's hand. *No* will be expressed in all types of circumstances. It is a mark of the child's emerging personality as he or she sheds the shell of "baby" for "toddler."

You should expect resistance from your child shortly after he or she reaches fourteen months. This resistance will grow in intensity as the child reaches twenty-four months and encounters the world more and more on his or her own terms. In the child's own way, this resistance in the form of refusing to go along with your instructions is an infantile way of taking charge of his or her life. This is normal and healthy. It's what has to happen for the baby to become an older child. However, understanding that it is normal will not stop you from feeling, just for a moment, that you have given birth to a monster. It will happen again when your daughter reaches age twelve and your son age fifteen. But by then you will have thicker skin.

No matter who you are, the toddler years are a stressful time for a parent. Ideally, you have had a reasonably good year and a half in which your nurturance and bonding with your baby produced a mutually loving relationship. You are going to need to look back on the best of those days now as you ask yourself, "What did I do to deserve this?" You might even feel that your child's mood swings and temper tantrums are nutritionally related, and you might be right. Switching to whole-grain breads, drastically cutting back on sugar and fats, and adding more complex proteins to your child's diet will indeed help. But what you and your baby are going through is inevitable. The tantrums, the fussiness, the noes are a necessary part of your child's separating from you as a totally dependent baby. It will be important for you, as an ACOA, not to take all of this personally because it will only make a difficult period even worse.

The Terrible Twos: Autonomy Versus Shame and Doubt

Just as your baby has had to develop trust as part of evoluting as a person, so he or she will now have to resolve the conflict between having a sense of autonomy and having one of self-doubt and shame. Like the trust crisis, this crisis is an important milepost on the way to a healthy personality. Child psychologists have identified this crisis as taking place between the ages of eighteen and forty-two months, but these ages are only approximations and may vary widely from child to child. Don't be chagrined if your friend's child goes through the terrible twos at twenty months while your child waits until thirty months: respect your child's uniqueness. Because you are an ACOA, you will sometimes tend to think in black or white or two-valued terms and evaluate your child as: ahead of schedule, good; behind schedule, bad. Avoid this kind of thinking when it comes to your child because it is completely meaningless and will only end up frustrating you.

The autonomy-versus-shame-and-doubt stage develops at the same time the child's muscular system allows independent walking and the toddler gains a greater control over the use of fingers and thumbs. Thus, the child can navigate independently to a greater degree and can hold and manipulate objects with a greater degree of dexterity. At this time your child is also gaining mastery over language and is forming more complex phrases. He or she may begin to feel anxiety over toilet training and is experiencing all of the tensions and stresses that accompany bladder and anal retention. In other words, between eighteen and thirty-six months, your child is coping with many of the same tensions that adults have to cope with, only your child does not have any coping mechanisms. Toddlers must learn and adapt to their own personalities while they learn to exert control over themselves.

This stage of development holds both positive and negative aspects for you and your child. First of all, your baby is growing up. He or she has begun to reach out to explore the world. A personality is emerging—awkwardly, to be sure—and traits that will stay with the child for the rest of his or her life will now start appearing for the first time. Your child's ability to hold on to objects and manipulate them is his or her first demonstration of caring and concern. If, however, it is turned into a negative force, your child will use this ability to grasp or restrain. It is up to you to guide the child through this period so that caring and concern are manifest rather than holding back and grasping. Similarly, your child's fascination with letting objects go can be representative of a personality that lets things pass in a relaxed way or one that destructively hurls or drops things. Again, the way you react to your child will have a great deal to do with which aspects come to the surface and are encouraged, either consciously or unconsciously. If you understand that your role is crucial to the positive resolution of your child's development crisis, you can approach the terrible twos as a challenge instead of regarding them as a nightmare only to be endured.

Your child has a job during this period as well. It is at this time children learn to regulate their own behavior so that they fit in socially with other people. Children who do not resolve this crisis positively—and the parents who sabotage their attempts to learn to be adults—find when they get older that they have become antisocial or asocial and have to relearn all the rules. If you are an ACOA and your parents didn't help you through this crisis, you probably had to relearn the rules the hard way when you were older. You may still not have learned the rules and have to consciously watch your behavior in difficult social situations.

During this learning process children will demonstrate the tendency to demand that they be in charge. It is of course a difficult task for you to blend permission for the decisions two-year-olds can handle with prohibitions against actions they cannot adequately manage. It will not require a great deal of tact and patience for you to enable a child to choose between pancakes and a hamburger for lunch, but it will to refuse to allow your child to throw the puppy down the stairs to see whether it can fly. However, you can walk the fine line by consciously adopting a positive tone whenever possible, even when it means saying, "Why don't you roll the ball for Spot so he can chase it?" or "I think Spot would rather play with his bone," instead of "No! Puppies can't fly." In other words, you *can* train your child out of negative behavior by setting a positive example, as difficult as that may seem at certain times.

Granted that the excessive use of the word *no* and the apparent glee two-year-olds take in defying their parents may drive you up the wall at times, you should never lose sight of what is really happening to your child and the charming qualities that underlie this behavior. Despite their persistence in making unreasonable demands, children during this period are engaging in an incredible flurry of activity. They are often so curious that they charge headlong into one adventure after another. Although it is often difficult to understand their speech, they are prone to rattle off string after string of seemingly endless questions, all of which make sense to them and relate to their explorations of the world. As illogical as he or she may sound sometimes, your child is asking you to help shape the world so that he or she can understand it. And the impossible demands your child makes are simply ways to test the outer boundaries of reality. Of course you can't take everything your child says seriously, but you must realize that it is serious to your child and reinforces the trust mechanism that the child developed during the first year after birth.

Between two and three years of age, your child is a blend of dependent baby and autonomous toddler. The mixture of increased development of motor, social, cognitive, and language skills has opened up a whole new world for your child. These little people are quite imaginative and are apt to play at adult roles, usually the roles they see their parents playing for real. However, they are often easily frightened by the thoughts they have that accompany the roles they play. Because they have not developed the ability to adequately distinguish between fantasy and reality, they often mistake their imagination and dreams for actual experiences. For example, a child of a friend of mine, in acting out his mother's morning schedule of packing her briefcase and going off to the office, actually got caught up in the task, packed his backpack, and walked out the front door. He was halfway down the street—violating his parents' rule never to leave the house on his own—before he realized that he had only been acting out a fantasy. By the time he realized that he wasn't his mother going off to the office, he was lost and frightened. Luckily, a neighbor saw an unescorted child on the sidewalk and swooped out of her door before he reached the curb. My friend quickly installed an eyehook on the storm door that the child could not reach. But as this example illustrates, your two-year-old is both fascinated by the world and frightened by it. And like the curious kitten, he or she may make decisions which involve consequences far more serious than anyone can imagine.

The ACOA's Challenge

The challenge that the ACOA parent faces in raising the two-year-old is most formidable: to provide an appropriate amount of growing room so the child may discover what the world contains, while at the same time serving as a "spotter" who catches the tumbler if he or she falls from the trampoline. As a parent, you must moderate between providing too much and too little protection. Also, because the two-year-old is typically unable to distinguish among the decisions he or she wants to make, your child may struggle for a sense of autonomy and self-regulation. How you accept your child in this struggle will have a great effect in determining whether he or she will become self-reliant and autonomous in the world or suspicious, full of self-doubt, and dependent upon the decisions of others. Your role is clear:

1. Help your child by supporting efforts to make choices and accepting the consequences of those choices.
2. Support your child in exploring the world without blame or shame.
3. Guide your child positively, not negatively.
4. Help your child understand that it's OK to make mistakes but not OK to hurt friends or other creatures.
5. Constantly reinforce the message that your child is a good person and worthy of a happy life.

Remember that it is likely your alcoholic parent did *not* do this for you. Thus, you are working without role models or examples—you may be flying blind. As one of my clients expressed over and over again in group, "The hardest thing about raising my kids during their terrible twos was that I never *knew* what was right or what was wrong. I had a big blind spot. I only hope that what I *thought* was the right thing to do was, in fact, right. I went entirely on instinct and what I was able to cull from people I respected in the outside world." Good advice. If you don't know what's right—ask your friends. If you can help your child experience the world not with shame or doubt but with a sense of self-reliance, autonomy, and confidence, he or she will be more likely to develop self-control, willpower, and respect for others.

Children at this age are apt to develop a sense of mastery and free choice to retain or reject. The trust that the infant developed is repeatedly tested as a toddler in his or her stubborn attempts to choose what he or she wants, make demands, reject your suggestions summarily, and inappropriately eliminate all possibilities. Your child will test, again and again, his or her trust of self against your control. In other words, you and your kid will butt heads over the most seemingly mundane of issues: milk versus lemonade, candy versus an oatmeal cookie, and a hot dog versus that last piece of spinach. You will say to yourself, "Never, never, never give in." Your child will simply say No! As parents demand more mature social behavior, all children resist and assert their rights to self-control. It is a battle of wills for a year and a half, but ultimately the child will emerge with a more mature personality. Your job is to make sure that you don't damage that personality by making your child feel guilty and ashamed. To do this you have to overcome some of your deepest fears as an ACOA who was emotionally abused during this period in his or her own childhood.

It is likely that when you were a child, you were taught not to master the world but to become critical of yourself and demanding of others. This self-judgment resulted in a strong sense of shame and self-doubt. Thus, when your two-year-old confronts the same issues, you may feel particularly threatened by it because it reminds you of your own perceived shortcomings. The job for you is not to lay the same guilt on your child that your parents laid on you. Consider this: The sense of shame that you might have felt resulted from a feeling of being exposed and of having your deficiencies known to others. We all know what it feels like to be "caught with your pants down." The exposure of your shortcomings is painful and embarrassing. As a parent, you have to understand that your child will make mistakes in public and will be ashamed sometimes. You don't have to like these situations, but you should accept them without making the child feel guilty or more ashamed. Guide the child and change the behavior without condemning the person. Be comforting and supportive when your child becomes frightened, and diplomatic when deciding matters for the child that are beyond his or her awareness. Above all, don't deliberately squash your little child's personality. You don't have to give in to every demand, but you should provide choices and support even when you can't go along with what he or she wants.

Tantrums

Children between the ages of eighteen and thirty-six months will try out their assertiveness by using tantrums as a means of behavioral control. Tantrums are simply something that most children have to go through on the way to growing up to be responsible and self-assured. You don't have to like them—no one does—but you should be prepared to handle them as a natural process. It is not unlike a scale that on the way to becoming balanced will first swing wildly to both extremes. So, too, your child will swing from being very reasonable, sensitive, and acquiescent to being a loud, screaming bully who is angry and demanding. It is important for all parents, especially ACOAs, to see and understand their children's tantrums in the context of their development. The child is growing through this period of tantrums toward a more mature personality. This sense of standing back and observing your child's behavior from a developmental perspective may not prevent you from overreacting in response, but it may keep you from blaming yourself for the child's behavior.

Simply stated, tantrums are a childish attempt to get what the toddler wants and to get your attention. Children at this age are cognitively, socially, and *morally* immature in a world that they see almost entirely in terms of their own wants. This egocentrism will be revisited in about ten years when, as teenagers, they renew their quest for satisfaction in terms of demands that must be met. At age two, however, the immaturity of the demands are much more apparent. These children literally cannot see the world separately from their own wants. Thus, they take it out on their parents. You should not take it personally. Your child is not blaming you for anything, even though the demands may make you cower behind your own perceived weaknesses. The child is doing what is expected. You must do the same.

The best advice for dealing with tantrums, again, especially for ACOAs, is not to overreact so as to encourage the child's behavior and reinforce the child's need to throw a tantrum. No parent who enjoys sanity will want to knowingly encourage a child to throw more tantrums, but it is easy for ACOAs to do so inadvertently. If, because of your childhood experiences, you feel it necessary to get right down on your child's level and wrangle with him or her in the midst of a tantrum, you will only encourage another tantrum because the child knows he or she can get your attention. You might even give in to what your child wants just to stop the tantrum. Ultimately, your child will learn to use your weakness to his or her advantage.

Jean, for example, grew up in a large family in which there was little parental nurturance due, in part, to the sheer number of children and the dysfunction brought about by her father's drinking. She and her sisters were treated like second-class citizens and were held accountable for fulfilling domestic responsibilities. The boys, on the other hand, were rulers annointed by the father and had no real chores. They got into trouble (boys will be boys), enjoyed special privileges, and had veto power over anything their sisters wanted. Jean became an angry little girl. But, over the course of growing up, she directed her righteous anger inward, at herself.

I felt like something must be wrong with me. I mean, people would not treat you bad unless there was a reason. I never realized it then, but I must not have liked myself very much. I still don't like myself. I just don't feel good enough, not smart enough or anything. I worry that I am not a good parent for my daughters. I do not want them to feel like I feel—angry all the time.

However, Jean's insecurity and unresolved anger have caused her to overreact to her own daughters' tantrums. In her attempt to impart a good feeling about themselves to her daughters, Jean has inadvertently taught them to use tantrums to get what they want. Because her own childhood needs and frustrations were suppressed, Jean began to express them as explosive tantrums and ultimately passed this behavior on to her children. But, like Don Quixote seeing his image in the mirror for the first time, Jean was immobilized by her daughters' tantrums, which only pointed up her weakness. She couldn't react righteously to her daughters' tantrums because, like many ACOAs, Jean was unable to express her legitimate demands in intimate relationships. She feared that the anger she felt might get out of control, so she kept it in rather than display it.

The twins are almost three, and they know the rules about picking up their toys before we go out or before bed. Yet most times it seems I end up doing their job myself. It seems it would be much easier if I did it. I don't want to yell at them because I do love them so, and, anyway, they don't listen to what I say in the first place.

By continuing to pick up their toys in the face of the girls' tantrums and their refusal to cooperate, Jean reinforced their immature behavior. They became bullies, pushing their mother around because Jean didn't have the means to control her own anger, recognize her own childhood feelings of rage and inadequacy, and behave like an adult in the face of childhood frustrations. There was nothing wrong with Jean's daughters because *all* children—yours included—will continue to display tantrumlike behavior as long as it works. Your children, like Jean's girls, will demonstrate great persistence in making their demands. They will throw tantrums in front of other people or in public. They will discover who ultimately gives in to tantrums and who does not. Once they understand that, they can effectively control whoever it is they want to control simply by threatening to throw a tantrum in public.

The inadvertent reinforcement of a child's manipulative behavior can also take place without the parent's giving in to tantrums. Oftentimes a child demanding a piece of chocolate or an ice-cream bar is more concerned with receiving attention than with the item being sought. Remember that even if you scold the child in public, you are giving the attention he or she is seeking and reinforcing the manipulative cycle of behavior. Thus, your child is encouraged to continue these excessive public demands. You are training your child to display negative behavior and might as well give him or her a set of instructions entitled: How to Control Your Parent. You should develop more appropriate and successful ways to direct your child's behavior.

How to Control Your Child's Tantrums

Your basic strategy should be to reinforce positive and cooperative behavior in your child by giving that your attention and praise. If, for example, Jean were to notice one of her twins whining or throwing a tantrum, the first course of action would be to see whether there is any real or legitimate danger. Having ruled out a genuine cause for concern, Jean should learn to display a nonreactive expression, as if nothing were going on. This is difficult to do, especially in a crowded store, but practice will make it possible. I've seen parents consciously turn a deaf ear to a child's obnoxious behavior, even when other shoppers or patrons gritted their teeth at the screams. It's not the other patrons the child is trying to control, it's the parent.

If your child sees that you are not reacting to the first wave of temper, he or she will turn up the volume in a pitched attempt to get your attention. Your task will be not unlike riding a bronco. You only need to hold on until the storm passes. This is usually the most difficult part, but if you are persistent and can hold your own temper, it is guaranteed to pay off. After a while the tantrum, like any storm, will blow itself out. Now, it is obvious that you can't bring your child to a crowded restaurant and expect his or her cries to go unheeded while all the paying customers nod their approval to you. You have to pick and choose your battlefields. If you notice that your child is beginning to use tantrums to get your attention, then you can't take that child to public places where the tantrums will affect other people until you've managed to control them.

Ignoring a child's screaming fits is best done in the privacy of the home. When the fit has passed, and the child seems lucid again, you can tell your child that you won't take him or her anywhere as long as the misbehavior continues. If your son or daughter throws a tantrum in a public place, after the tantrum has passed, tell him or her that that place is off limits until you are convinced there will be no more public displays of bad manners. Once you've made your decision, stick to it. Don't say, "OK, just one more chance. Now be cooperative." Your child will interpret that as a sign that you can be manipulated by an empty promise. You have to make your word good by saying, "I told you that until you behave properly in public, I'm not taking you back to that restaurant again. Let's wait a week. If you show me that you can behave, then we'll go back. I know you can do it."

When you see your child playing calmly or fighting for his or her opinion in a positive way, praise the child's behavior. It is important not to bring up the tantrum, but rather to focus on how much you enjoy your son's or daughter's company when you share an activity. Engage your child in a conversation about his or her activity. Ultimately—and this may take three or four months—your child will learn not only that tantrum throwing does not get the results he or she wants but that it does not even get your attention.

Calling Time-Out

Where deliberate distraction used as a limit-setting technique worked during the first six or so months of your child's life, it will be increasingly less effective after a year and a half. Time-out is the tactic most useful during the next two years. Remember, the purpose of a time-out is to control your child's behavior in a positive way without throwing a temper tantrum of your own. It is a method of setting limits on your child's behavior. Before you begin, remember to stand your ground and within reason make sure that your child understands that when you set a limit, you intend to enforce it. You must persist in consistently following through with your instructions. The challenge, as always, is to balance appropriate limit setting with excessive control. Unless you back up your prohibitions on forbidden activities, your child will learn to be difficult to manage and may also come to feel out of control.

Time-out is a disciplinary procedure wherein the child is literally removed from involvement in activities for a brief period of time. It works quite simply. You must first explain to your child that it isn't helpful to either party for you to yell or spank him or her, so you plan to use time-out. He or she must be quiet during the time-out period. Use a timer to insure fairness. Having given the child fair warning—usually a repetition of two or three times to make sure that he or she understands—the child will be prepared for what ensues. If the child breaks the rule again, you must follow through in order for the method to be successful.

Generally, time-out may be used from about the age of eighteen months to ten years, depending upon the maturity of the child. The procedure is to remove the child for a brief period of time to an unstimulating and boring place so "you can think about how you have behaved." For a time-out to be effective, you must invoke it immediately after the inappropriate behavior and after you have given your child a fair warning. For instance, if your twenty-month-old son becomes aggressive and starts hitting his sister—younger or older—remove him right away to the established time-out area for two minutes of quiet. If he screams or throws a tantrum, inform him that the time-out begins when the tantrum has passed. Your child may continue to test your commitment to the time-out procedure by continuing to whine during the time-out period. If this happens, determine what constitutes the behavior level you want to set, and reset the timer. Try to remind yourself that his behavior is under his control.

Remember that you are not punishing your child for crying or whining. These, under many circumstances, are legitimate attempts to communicate, and if your child cries silently during the time-out period, you might choose to ignore it. It is the violent tantrum you want to control; you don't want to tell the child that feeling remorse or sadness or that "feeling" at all is bad. If the child attempts to shout at you during the time-out period, you must ignore that. Let your child know that there are always appropriate ways to engage in conversation, but shouting across a room or from room to room isn't one of them. Be firm and consistent, but not angry. Let your child know exactly where the boundaries of acceptable behavior are and how you will enforce them. If he or she is having a "sad day," be understanding and comforting. However, if the"sad day" turns into bullying and fighting, let the child know that you will be supportive but not pushed around.

If your child is throwing tantrums and becoming nasty because he or she is ill, then you should respond to that as well. Many times, a low-grade fever, headache, or pains from stuffed-up sinuses or clogged ear passages will sap children's resiliency and make them prone to crying and temper tantrums. Ask your child if anything is wrong. If so, treat the cause, not the behavior.

If your child regularly throws tantrums during certain periods of the day or when certain people are around, make careful note. Does he or she become especially cranky or violent after eating certain foods? Note that as well. Many children have reactions to excessive amounts of sugar or experience a cranky lethargy if they don't get enough iron. If your spouse or you have any food reactions, look for them in your children as well. If it is food or a vitamin deficiency that is causing behavior problems, talk to your child's pediatrician. If your child has an occasional reaction to sugar or chocolate, remove the food from his or her diet. If your child's behavior seems to unravel at a certain time in the afternoon or early evening, perhaps he or she is tired and needs a nap. Determine the regularity and causality of your child's tantrums before you get worried and impose punishments. Many times, you are punishing behavior that is simply a reaction to a food or an event.

When you do invoke time-out, it is important not to be excessive about the length of time. The general rule of thumb is one minute for an eighteen-month-old, two minutes for a two-year-old, three minutes for a three-year-old, and so on up to five minutes. After age six you can increase the length of time measurably so that an eight-year-old can spend up to fifteen minutes in a time-out if the transgression warrants severe punishment. Remember, however, that the effectiveness of the length of time varies from child to child, and five minutes may carry the same weight as twenty minutes if spent in silent contemplation. In no event should you punish a child for more than thirty minutes. You want to improve behavior, not break your child's will or spirit.

In selecting the time-out area remember to choose a neutral and unstimulating setting. Most likely, sending a child to his or her room if it is filled with favorite toys, pictures, or a TV set will not do. On the other hand, do not send your child to a basement, bathroom, closet, or garage. This is not prison, and you don't want your child in a dark or unfriendly place. These places are also dangerous, and inflicting emotional trauma on a child is tantamount to abuse. It is unhealthy and unnecessary, even if your parents imposed the same punishment on you.

Spanking

Simply put, spanking is an unhealthy and abusive form of punishment. There are volumes of legitimate research that all come to the same conclusion: Spanking causes physical and emotional damage and creates people who will in turn abuse other people. Renowned experts such as Frank and Theresa Caplan of the Princeton Center for Infancy and Early Childhood, as well as pediatricians and child psychologists, speak to the point that spanking is in reality the assault of a bigger person on a smaller person. It is intergenerational violence. Contrary to its supposed intent—which is to teach discipline—spanking teaches fear, endurance of pain, low self-esteem, and violent aggression.

It is now generally believed that children can be taught to be both cooperative and well behaved without ever having to be physically or emotionally punished. They respond remarkably well to praise. But some parents may still find the need to slap a child's bottom under certain extraordinary circumstances—such as a youngster's hell-bent intention to run out into the street. In this case, you are jolted into action by your immediate concern for the safety and physical well-being of your child. If it is literally a life-and-death issue, such as playing in traffic or putting fingers into a live electrical outlet, your concern may become paramount and overstep the bounds you would normally adhere to. In that case, don't punish yourself for it. But usually, given use of clear limit setting, time-out, and physical restraint (holding the child from hitting another child) when necessary, you will probably be able to handle the impulsive child without ever having to resort to spanking.

Given the history of many parents who are also adult children of alcoholics, the issues of discipline, control, and spanking are often a source of critical concern. We know that many ACOAs have been subjected to combinations of physical, sexual, and emotional abuse or general neglect during their childhoods. Over the course of my career in counseling, I have often heard both the conviction of parents wanting to provide a different childhood from the one they had and the worry that they may repeat the same pattern. My clients have reported:

She is not going to have to put up with what I did.

I know what it's like and I am not going to let my husband lay a hand on my son.

I am going to be real different. I am going to do it right this time.

I just get so angry sometimes. I feel like I could kill him, I get so mad.

Sometimes I feel out of control, just like my father.

I let my kids walk all over me and then I overreact over nothing at all.

It's the task of adulthood to take what we can use from how our parents raised us and leave the rest behind. This is something everyone must face. It becomes more complicated when you become a parent and more complicated still if you are an ACOA. If you should find that you are losing both your patience and temper all too frequently, and/or you are resorting more and more to spanking, it is well worth your while to seek professional guidance from a mental health professional who has been trained in ACOA issues. This person can help you to sort out and separate your emotional baggage from your behavior as parent. It is hard work, but it is oftentimes quite helpful.

Toilet Training

Your child's single biggest accomplishment during the period from eighteen to thirty months is toilet training. It is this feat that heralds the child's feeling that he or she is grown-up. Toilet training has become an almost mystical event in families, causing parents undue amounts of pride or shame, but it is simply the gradual readiness of the child to learn sphincter muscle control. It has become, however, much, much more. It is the opportunity for a major advance toward autonomy and self-reliance. It is also a stage where a struggle for control may be played out between child and parents. On the other hand, it may also serve as an opportunity for the child to continue to develop positive self-esteem within a loving and trusting parent-child relationship. It does *not* mean that the parents are good or bad people, failures or successes, winners or losers. However, the attitude you feel as parents and express either directly or indirectly to your child is a crucial determinant as to how smoothly the toilet training will go. If you take it slow and easy, your child will follow suit. If you get crazy and use it to predict whether your child will be a success or failure in life, you will create a great deal of unnecessary tension.

First of all, you should recognize this as an axiom: Human beings use toilets, therefore your child will toilet train him- or herself at some point. Although the majority of children show clear indications of a readiness to begin toilet training between eighteen and twenty-four months old, a wide variation in age is entirely normal. What is not acceptable is to try to rush the child before he or she is physically ready. That will only result in frustration and a sense of failure for your child. On this point almost all experts in pediatrics and child psychology agree: Do not push or rush your child into toilet training.

Children vary greatly in both the age at which they will begin to be toilet trained and in the length of time it takes to complete the training. Some children are reasonably successful in only a few days, while others take many weeks or months. Almost all children will have good days and bad days. Most children will have accidents when they are supposed to be toilet trained, but "forgot." The arrival of a new sibling or family tensions will also affect the child's schedule and result in accidents. Children whose parents are in the process of getting divorced will very likely experience accidents and might even forget they are toilet trained as an unconscious means of bringing their parents back together. The child hopes that by becoming a helpless baby again, the parents will unite to care for him or her. Children might also think—as you did—that the parents' problems are their fault and blame themselves. It is your job to keep that from happening by constant support and positive reinforcement.

It is important not to impose your own sense of readiness on your child. In toilet training, as in other tasks that children must master, a parent's regulating and pushing do little to help develop a sense of self-reliance. In fact, toilet training that is either rushed too early or pushed too rigidly may contribute to developing a compulsive, fearful, or aggressive nature in the child.

There are many clear indicators that your child may be ready to begin toilet training. They are:

1. The child understands what is said—a recognition that the child knows what you are telling him or her to do.
2. The child has the ability to express wants or needs.
3. The child can *without help* raise and lower his or her own pants.
4. The child displays increased attention to the act of elimination.

5. Upon your invitation or inquiry, the child notifies you when a bowel movement has passed.

6. The child expresses a desire to act "more grown-up."

Once your child has indicated a readiness to begin toilet training, it will be important to discuss with him or her your intention to ask about every five minutes whether he or she needs to go to the bathroom. You should also ask your child to tell you if he or she wants to go. When your son or daughter begins to ask you, then increase your time between checks from every five minutes to twenty-minute intervals. Often children initially tend to forget and they feel bad if they miss the opportunity to succeed. Therefore, you need to remind them if they fail to remind you. When your child begins to consistently ask to go to the bathroom, you can extend the period between checks to an hour or two hours. Throughout this process it is very important for you to reinforce your children's behavior with consistent and meaningful praise. Praise them for telling you when they want to go to the bathroom and also when you check and find them dry. But, while it is important to praise, don't make a grand production out of it.

Try to be as relaxed as possible about toilet training. If, for example, you find your son's pants are wet, just acknowledge this fact and ask him to change. Your attitude to successes and failures in toilet training is a significant aspect of the child's learning to be trained and to feel good about himself or herself. If you are too rigid and too hyper about how and when the toilet training is completed, the issue will expand into a struggle for control. And by all means, do *not* show disapproval because of failure. Again, remember, your child will be toilet trained. The only person who can make an issue out of a perfectly normal process is the parent, not the child. Your child naturally wants to succeed. Help him or her do that.

If there is too much resistance from your child to toilet training, it may simply be too early, so try again in a month or so, even though the child expresses a desire to wear pants instead of diapers. Don't allow the child to move out of diapers until he or she really is toilet trained, but don't make the diapers into a badge of shame.

It may be hard for you as an ACOA to take as relaxed a position toward this as you might like. This is often due to both a felt need to be in control and the feeling that your self-esteem and worth as a parent are on the line. As one of my clients once explained:

I was feeling like such a success because Jennifer was toilet training herself, I wanted to call my father and tell him how good I was doing. Then when Chris was born, Jennifer seemed to fall apart. She wanted to wear diapers again, began wetting her pants in nursery school, and forced the teachers to tell me that I had pushed her into nursery school too soon. It had nothing to do with me. As soon as Jennifer became acclimated to having a new baby in the house and felt that we loved her just as much as before—more even, because she was our special daughter and he was our special son—she retrained herself in a few days.

If you find yourself feeling overstressed about toilet training, just consider that these issues are yours and have nothing to do with your child. Unless you can genuinely remain patient throughout this proces, it is best for you to seek some help. Toilet training usually works best when the parents allow themselves to trust the child's capacity to grow and mature without coercion. Generally, if parents wait until the child is ready to train himself or herself, the toilet training will go smoothly and not take on any additional or undue issues.

Guilt

When looked at in the context of your child's resolution of the issue of autonomy versus shame and doubt, toilet training is a major milestone. There are also many other events that occur throughout each day which are fueled by your child's curiosity, thus imparting to him or her a sense of autonomy and mastery. Or your child's legitimate attempts to explore the world and create his or her own sense of identity can be rejected as a transgression of the rules, consequently imparting to the child a sense of shame and a feeling of guilt. Any examination of rule-oriented societies will quickly reveal how the qualities of autonomy and shame or guilt are balanced against one another. In our society, we regard autonomy as a virtue. Strict obedience to rules is considered a vice. Consider this as you evaluate which rules to enforce and how rigidly you want to enforce them.

Even after your child has been successfully toilet trained, the issue of guilt may continue to worry your child. It might be manifested in a demonstration of dependency. For example, he or she might repeatedly ask to be taken to the bathroom to urinate, only to find that nothing much happens. In addition to successfully seeking your attention, this might also be your child's way of struggling with the guilt he or she may feel when an accident happens in bed or in his or her pants. A client of mine once had a moment of insight about this in therapy.

It wasn't until I saw my three-year-old son peeing every five or ten minutes that I learned something about how I was raised. My mother always told me that it was shameful to wet my pants. I believed that, and would go to the bathroom the moment I felt that I might have a drop or so of urine to pass. As I got older, I didn't go quite so often, but, I tell you, even today, every time I'm under stress it's off to the bathroom. Drives my wife crazy, but I could never explain it. Then, when I saw my son doing the same thing—bang—it hit me.

It is no doubt clear to children by the latter part of their toilet training that their parents are not entirely pleased when slips occur in their mastery of it. Continual visits to the bathroom, therefore, are attempts to avoid the shame of an accident. Thus, a child may pester you with what may seem to be an unreasonable number of requests for help. Be prepared for this behavior and try to allow yourself to be patient with this dependency.

Dependency

Although children are much more mobile now than they were at one year old, remember that they still feel the need to be, and are still, quite dependent. The dependency may be manifested in many ways, such as hanging on to skirts, being underfoot, and hiding behind you. Your child may also feel shy when addressed by other adults. You may see a separation fear manifested as crying, upset, or a frenzied holding on to your hand when the child feels you will leave him or her with a baby-sitter or another adult.

For many parents, but epecially ACOAs, the period in their child's life between eighteen months and three years may awaken uneasy remembrances of what it feels like to need love from another person. Your child's dependence can awaken the long-suppressed feelings of isolation and anxiety that you experienced at this age. It may become further complicated by having to address your child's neediness at the same time that you're aware of your own feelings of dependency. One of my clients poignantly remembered the first time he left his two-year-old at a YMCA day camp:

Jeff had been anxious all morning. He knew something was up. Mommy had gone to work, as usual, but I hadn't settled in with my newspaper and coffee. I packed him into the car along with a change of clothes and a diaper. Now he knew something was wrong. We drove the ten minutes into Hightstown and stopped at the camp meeting site. I walked him over to his group counselor—wearing a happy-face badge with a number three on it—and said goodbye. "Make this quick," the counselor told me. I couldn't believe I was taking orders from a sixteen-year-old snot who probably still chewed bubble gum. Anyway, I tried to make it quick by saying, in my most casual voice, "See ya later, Jeff," and sauntering off to the car. Didn't work. He began trumpeting like a wounded elephant and I was back in a flash.

Next I tried the direct approach. "Jeff," I said, "you're going to have day camp today. Todd here is your counselor. And you and he are going to have lots of fun. So, I'll see you later on." And I sauntered off to the car again, only to turn around to see a tearful Jeff standing by the door, looking at me as if I were abandoning him forever. Now other parents were staring at me. I was failing!

Finally, I just walked Jeff over to his group, told him to wait there for his counselor, and ran back to the car. By the time Jeff discovered I was gone, I was pulling out of the driveway. I can still remember seeing him standing there in the middle of his group crying away in misery. He was alone, abandoned, and I had done the abandoning. In that moment, I was crushed. I was angry at him for pointing out my failure and shortcomings. But, basically, I was the child, standing there abandoned as I had been throughout my whole life. I went home and didn't stop crying for the rest of the day.

Many ACOAs ask themselves how they can take care of their children when they were never adequately cared for themselves. Anger is often a typical response. Sometimes you may resent your child for being so needy. You will ultimately, however, direct the anger at yourself. I have found that the child is usually the mirror bearer, reflecting the parent's own need and dependency from the past into the present and allowing him or her to see what silently remains after all the years. If you can allow yourself to accept the feelings that are truly yours, the resentment toward your child will probably dissipate quickly. Of course, if you have difficulty sorting these feelings out and you can't quite get a handle on them, you should consider entering short-term counseling.

Tempted to Be Offended

As self-worth is an issue with most ACOAs, it is bound to come to the surface during the terrible twos. Try not to be personally offended by your children's behavior and try not to punish yourself for their actions and your difficulty in coping with them. Admittedly, this will be a difficult time for you. These suggestions might help you get through it with less friction and worry.

1. At the first sign of a tantrum, check whether there is a real cause for alarm: danger, illness, fear, genuine sadness or concern.
2. It is your child's behavior that you do not like, not your child. Make sure you convey this when setting limits.
3. Never ignore a child who is aggressive to you or to his or her siblings.
4. Use of a time-out can be helpful to your child and you because it gives both of you a chance to step down from confrontation.
5. React to your child, not to your own feelings for the child in you.

Remember that your child's toddler years are a vital and creative period of development. During this period of your child's life, you must strive to create an atmosphere that will enable him or her to grow into an autonomous and self-assured person. Central to a smooth transition is the genuine conveyance of trust and love for your child. While, as with all stages, it is often easier said than done, the more clear you are about *your* issues, separate from *your child's* issues, the more confidence you will have in your capacity to parent and the more you will trust your child's capacity to mature.

5

Taking the Initiative to Separate
Ages 3 to 6

PAT

The first time I took Susie to nursery school, she was a little tearful, but she really handled it quite well. I wish I had. Having been sexually abused by my alcoholic father since I was very young, I am really concerned about her. Back then, I kind of felt like something wasn't right, but I did not know it was so wrong. And when I did learn that it did not happen in other families, I felt like it was I who was to blame. I just felt so dirty. My fear is that Susie would not necessarily know what was wrong if some teacher or somebody tried something with her. So, when I left her off, it all came right back to me. I was worried. For all of her four years, I have made sure she has been protected. I have been in control. Now she is out of my hands, and I do not know what to do. I feel so upset, so out of control. Everything I have done might be blown. I know it is not right, but I did not want to let her go.

As children enter this period of their lives, they begin to separate from their parents and encounter the world outside the immediate family. One of the tasks parents are charged with is to encourage this initiative and create, as best they can, an environment that is safe for exploration. That was not easy for Pat. She faced the panic that flooded her thoughts as she realized she could no longer maintain absolute control and protection over her daughter. As a result of projecting her own need to have been protected from her father onto her daughter, Pat found herself caught between doing what she knew she had to do—help Susie in her transition to nursery school—and feelings that implored her to never let her daughter out of her sight.

ROBERTA

Roberta's situation is more common, but no less unsettling for parents. It is typical of those many times when a physical separation from the child is in order. It could involve putting the child to bed for the night, dropping him or her off at day care on the way to work, or leaving him or her with a baby-sitter on the way out for an evening with your spouse. Your child cries and expresses the absolute horror of being abandoned to strangers. This experience evokes painful feelings in all parents who don't want to see their children unhappy, but for ACOAs like Roberta, the experience can be too painful to bear.

We let Jerry's mother take care of Janie when we went out the other night. And she wailed. My God, she wailed with such sadness. She likes Jerry's mother, but that didn't matter. We weren't going to be there, and she wanted us. She was crying, screaming, grabbing at us as we went to leave. We talked with Janie and assured her we loved her and we would be back later, but she did not want to hear it. She said, "You don't love me." It took Jerry's mother to hold her so we could even get out the door. I hated it. I just felt so bad for her. I felt as if I were abandoning her, and I know what that feels like from my own life. But what were we to do?

Initiative Versus Guilt

After your child has resolved the crisis between autonomy and shame by age three, he or she will confront a new crisis centering around the resolution of initiative versus guilt. Children who are rewarded for showing initiative and risk taking will develop a sense of purpose and direction. Children taught by their experiences that trying new things and showing initiative will result only in failure and criticism will develop a sense of inhibition and guilt. This is a major developmental stage for your child because it can have life-altering results. Often the children who succeed in school and exude a sense of self-confidence are those who were rewarded for displaying initiative and taking risks in their preschool years.

The hallmark of this stage of development is the child's ability to get around independently. Children tend to be quite curious and inquisitive and by age three have the motor skills that allow them almost free access to their immediate world. The usual style children adopt when engaging this world is a headlong charge. They have a great sense of mastery—actually a greater sense than in reality—and they risk exceeding their own limits of competency and skill. Accordingly, they face the inevitable consequences of risking injury from accidents and criticism from their parents when they go too far.

Your child will probably not have adequate judgment for distinguishing what he or she should or should not get into. A child's tendency is to get into everything in his or her path. Of course, this can be maddening for a parent as well as exciting as you see your offspring display navigational and cognitive skills for the first time. You have to be constantly on your toes, however, because at any moment the bookcase may come tumbling down. As charming and as genuine as your child's reckless-abandonment approach to the world may seem, there is also the legitimate concern that he or she may get hurt. The challenge for you during this stage, therefore, is to support the child's initiative in taking on the world while being at the ready to intervene should he or she get into real danger.

There is a need to balance your guidance and restrictions with trust and respect for your child's personal autonomy. Children whose attempts at initiative taking are thwarted by anxious, hovering parents are as much subject to feelings of guilt and inhibition as those children who are given so much space to operate in that they repeatedly suffer from failure and frustration because they have exceeded their capacities. In the first case, the parent's overidentification with and difficulty separating from the child restrict the child's normal development toward independence. While there was a need for zealous protection during your child's infancy, the continuation of this protection past age three makes adequate resolution of your child's initiative-versus-guilt crisis difficult. As Tim, a thirty-three-year-old ACOA currently in psychotherapy, explained:

I know my mother loved me, but I think if it's possible she loved me too much. I feel like I grew up in a plastic bag. There were restrictions for everything. When my friends wanted soda, I had to have juice; when my cousins wanted ice water, I had to have straight tap water; and when I wanted to do anything, I felt as if I had to hold myself back. It was as if I was going to break, or that I would screw something up if I tried. My mother was happy when I behaved in this reserved way and very nervous and worried when I didn't. So I became a "good" boy. Good, that is, until I discovered drugs and sex as a teenager. I am recovering and I now realize that it was she who was afraid of breaking. I wish I could have seen it then. It has taken me a lot of work to feel that I can actually be in charge of my life.

Tim's mother was overprotective and kept him from taking risks in the real world. She inhibited his natural urge to explore, and as a result, kept him inhibited until he reached his teens. Then, he sowed his wild oats in an uncontrolled way. However, being underprotective and neglectful can also restrict the healthy resolution the child needs at this stage. The negative influence is twofold. First, the underprotected child develops a sense of unworthiness and of being unloved. "Why else," he might ask himself, "would my parents not be there for me if there weren't something wrong with me?" The child is given so little parental involvement and protection that he or she feels guilty when impulsiveness leads him or her to exceed social or physical boundaries, perhaps resulting in the inflicting or receiving of pain. As Jonathan, another one of my ACOA clients, explained:

My father left when I was real young. I didn't know him. I know now that he was an addict. My mother, on the other hand, was always butting into my business when I did not need her to be and was never there when I wanted her help. It's still like that with her now. I can't wait to move out. Anyway, I feel like I can't do anything right. I want to try, but I don't let myself go and really do it. School, sports, making friends, I am always afraid I will screw it up. I feel like it will never change.

Because it is so important that children emerge from this stage with a sense of initiative which will serve as a solid foundation for their feelings of ambition and purpose, you should understand how the process works. The emotional struggle between developing a sense of initiative versus developing a sense of guilt and trepidation may be compared to the balance between the child's mastery over the environment and responsibility for his or her actions. Your child is more mobile and full of energy than at any point in his or her young life. Children at this age tend to be inquisitive and are eager to learn and perform tasks well. The progressive increase in their cognitive development has led to their further acquisition of language and given them just enough adequacy in verbal communication to let their vivid imaginations embellish what they thought you were saying to them. Increased cognitive development also allows children to engage in more thoughtful planning ahead. In this way, the child can develop strategies and in turn acquire a sense of direction and purpose. Your child at this point is beginning to understand consequences—that if he or she does *A*, then *B* might result. You can see that if allowed to carry out this development to its highest levels of attainment, your child will nurture skills that will last a lifetime. Unfortunately, not every child gets this chance. The real world crashes down in the form of parents or consequences, and the child learns to develop guilt, frustration, and a sense of failure. How does this happen?

Balancing out a newly developing sense of mastery are the child's feelings of guilt and responsibility. Now, more than ever, your child is aware of his or her freedom and ability to take action in this world. But with this awareness comes a feeling of anxiety. The feeling is not unlike what Western civilization has experienced in the age of the bomb. We are the most powerful civilization in history because of the tremendous power we have harnessed. But what are we to do with something that has the potential for destroying all life on the planet? We are at the same time all powerful but capable of wiping ourselves out. Your child at ages three to six is in a roughly analogous, albeit a far less dramatic, situation.

As part of a natural tendency to keep this assertion of personal power in check, children at this stage begin to develop a conscience and a capacity for self-observation. Children are now equipped to balance out the drive toward initiative and mastery by internalizing their parents' rules and regulations. They are more able to observe, guide, and punish themselves for their actions. The challenge for your child is to effectively regulate his or her exuberant growth potential with a now-internalized parental mind-set. The danger is that the child may learn to be self-indulgent and impulsive on the one extreme, or on the other extreme may overmanipulate and control him or herself with guilt.

The reality is that at this stage of development, children can do more than they ever could before. In order to insure a significant self-regulation, they must learn to set their own limits. It is your responsibility as parent to help your child through this process. It is not your job to overregulate and overcontrol, but to help your child learn to discover the balance between, for example, being too impulsive and being too inhibited or being too trusting and being too shy. What are the issues pertinent to this critical stage of your child's development?

Separation: For the Parent

Perhaps the hallmark of this stage is your child's separation from you. Not that separation and the quest for independence weren't taking place before age three, but now the quest has become more significant. Those first wobbly steps your child took as a toddler have become giant strides toward independent adulthood. Children during this period are expanding their world beyond being in the home with their parents. They may be entering nursery school, preschool, Bible school, or kindergarten, and are entering into expanded family relationships and relationships with peers and authority figures outside the family. How your child relates to you will never be quite the same after his or her first social experience outside the family. As the child's parent, you are no longer solely at the center of his or her world. Children want to share their life and experiences with others now, an indication of normal and healthy development. However, there may be a feeling of loss because of the major change your relationship is undergoing.

The loss of the way things used to be is actually a shared experience. You and your child will at various points probably be feeling some ambivalence about his or her growing up and moving into the world outside the family. This apprehension, however, will be experienced quite differently by each of you. Parent and child are at different life stages, but beyond that, they are now clearly separate people. Despite your child's wish to be just like daddy or mommy and his or her fantasy to always be with you, your child is becoming his or her own person even as early as age three and a half. Each member of the family may attempt to resist this process— and in ACOA families the resistance might be strenuous and painful—but the separation is inevitable. Therefore, it will be helpful to understand why there may be an increased difficulty in letting your child go and in what ways this may be manifested.

Alcoholic families tend to be out of balance in terms of the amount of personal space allowed and the nurturance given to a child. There tends to be either too much space provided, so that the child risks feeling unloved and uncared for, or so little space that the parent emotionally or physically intrudes on the child, often resulting in difficulty in establishing a healthy separate identity. Children who were never made to be accountable for their actions become adults who are asocial or even sociopathic at worst or at best have great difficulty establishing relationships with other adults. Children who are allowed no personal space whatsoever to grow by parents of the opposite sex are—at the most extreme— victims of incest in the family. Father/daughter incest in otherwise normal-looking families is an example of this form of family dysfunction. At best, children who are not permitted to separate from the family at this stage may tend to grow up very shy, afraid to leave the nest, or afraid to have experiences normal growing children relish having. Regardless of the set of circumstances displayed in these dysfunctional families, the child often grows up having developed an effective personal style for both making connections with other people and disengaging from them.

Pat is an example of this scenario. The victim of incest with her alcoholic father and neglect on the part of her mother, who allowed it go on, Pat came to know all too well the confusion of both intrusion and abandonment. She grew to feel quite out of control and very dependent in her relationships. Consequently, it was no surprise that when she brought her young daughter to kindergarten, Pat felt an almost gut-wrenching urgency.

I don't know exactly what was wrong. I just did not feel right. Here I was asked to trust strangers with my daughter. It was so hard. I had to force myself. It was like a piece of me was cut out and left at the school. And when she started to cry, oh boy, it was just too much. Eventually the teacher had to ask me to leave. I left, but I wanted to just keep holding on. I did not realize it so much then, but I felt as if I were being abandoned.

Actually, considering Pat's history, her reactions at school were quite mild. Other parents in similar situations might never even consider sending their children to preschool at all. These parents tend to be very clinging and create in their own children mirror social images of themselves. They, in turn, pass this developmental dysfunction on to their children's generation.

Remember, allowing a child to separate is hard for most every parent. It gets more complicated when you are an ACOA for the simple reason that your parents did not do an effective job during this crisis when you were young.

Bob, whom we introduced in an earlier chapter, was nine when his alcoholic father died and he was expected to take his place as the man of the house. He learned to hold both his childhood needs and his tears inside. To this day, he carries with him a rugged self-reliance that blocks him from asking for help from his concerned wife or even his therapist for fear of being seen as weak. But unresolved feelings, like carrier pigeons, eventually come home to roost and always bring their message with them. As with Pat, Bob's medium was his daughter's enrollment in nursery school.

I had done a thorough job researching all the programs available and knew rationally that this was a good choice, nice setting, impressive preschool curriculum and credentials of staff, good child-teacher ratio. I even contacted parents who either used or were still using the school for their own children. And it still wasn't enough for me. I could see a reasonable amount of concern, given the news reports about child abuse, but I was totally irrational. I wasn't behaving out of control, but on the inside, I had lost it. I was really afraid for her. For at least the first month, from the moment I brought her there in the morning, I could hardly wait to come and get her.

There is no question that Bob and Pat are loving parents who want to do the right thing and provide the best care for their children. In both cases, however, there is clearly an edge of something more than their caring that is being played out in the drama. It is as if they catch a fleeting reflection of themselves as children in the teary separations that occur when they bring their children to school. In that brief but powerful glimpse, the despair which they knew once before as needy young children is felt once again. Separation is an awkward experience for all parents to deal with, but even more so when as children, they weren't helped through this process by their own parents. If you are in this situation, there is little you can do but try to understand that what you went through shouldn't be allowed to make your child into the victim that you became.

Let your spouse handle the moments of separation, if possible, or try to deal with your own feelings by talking them out with a friend. You can even try to talk them out with your child as long as you don't make him or her feel responsible for your unhappiness. Your child is not a shoulder to cry on at this time; he or she has his or own feelings of separation to deal with. But if you can make it clear that you miss your child because you love him or her and not because you are afraid, it will take the mystery out of your behavior.

Separation: For the Child

Growing up is both an exciting and a scary experience. As much as going to school offers the lure of no longer being a baby but of being a big boy or big girl, it is only natural that a child might feel somewhat in awe of the prospect. Children have come to rely on the safety of home and their relationships with their parents and siblings. They pretty much know by now what to expect at home, but for the huge new world that awaits them, they have only wonder. Children at this age rely on the tales brought home by their older siblings, conversations with their parents, expectations based on television, and their own vivid imaginations. Simply put, because there is only a limited amount of hard data available, it is only reasonable that a child might have some trepidation about leaving home.

The question you should ask is "How can I minimize my child's anxiety about leaving home to go to school?" The answer will be based in part on the atmosphere you provided for him or her in growing up. How children do at any given stage is related to how they came to know themselves previously. Your parenting has a cumulative effect on your child in that if you have imparted a sense of trust and love early in his or her life, it will be easier for the child to feel autonomous when the time comes to separate. The more your child feels as if you have been pushing him or her away during the years from two to three, the harder it might be for the child to actually leave the nest to go to school. The issue of trust will take on a renewed significance as the child becomes a teenager.

Both forms of trust are based on the foundation of trust developed in infancy. Thus, your child's development is like a set of building blocks. If one block is missing, you might still be able to erect the structure, but the stresses and strains will have to be borne by other blocks. It's like building a house without completing the foundation. When there is a weak foundation the best you can do is find the weakest spot and fix it if possible. This is the case most ACOAs find themselves in. Because your own foundation is weak in critical areas, you might not feel right about much of what you must do to provide a basis of trust, confidence, and self-worth for your child. Yet, as a survivor, you have learned to go forward. This has guided you since childhood. Now that you are a parent, you have to identify the weak spots in your own foundation so they don't haunt your child as they haunted you.

In order to help your child deal effectively with the task of separation, it is imperative that you have a clear understanding of the ownership of personal issues touched off by your child. The more aware you are of unresolved feelings about your own problems with separation and taking the initiative, the easier it will be to see and respect your child as an individual working on his or her own issues.

Identification: Under- and Overinvolvement

Children at this age really admire their parents. They tend to be fascinated with their parents and like everything they do. The fact that they wish to be just like daddy or mommy is reflected in their drawings and play activities. They will want to build things with tools the way daddy does or take care of babies by pretending to feed them as they've seen their parents care for their younger siblings. This process of identification is how the child develops a sense of identity. It is through this process that a unique character is developed. While it may be very flattering indeed to be so greatly admired by your personal fan club, the process of identification is sometimes frightening for parents who are ACOAs.

For Roberta, it was other family members who pointed out the similarities between her and her baby.

When she was between two and four years old, Janie used to have the most horrible tantrums. It was like she was possessed or something. Once when my family was over, she threw another fit, screaming and yelling, crying uncontrollably on the floor in the middle of the room. She could not be calmed at all. That's bad enough, but everybody pointed and laughed and said, "Look, it's a little Roberta." My mother, my aunt, my older sister all said that's exactly what I was like when I was that age. And then the fear shot through me like a cold chill. If Janie is like me in this way, maybe she will pick up the other hangups I have been working so hard to come to terms with. I am so indecisive and demanding. I hate feeling dependent on Jerry, but I do and in many ways I'm still impulsive, indecisive, and demanding. The last thing in the world I want for her is to have my flaws, especially the self-doubt.

If you are unhappy with yourself, as many ACOAs are, having your child want to be just like you can be a real source of concern. It is all the more reason to work on your feelings of devaluation because, like it or not, your children will look to you as a model of how they will be as adults. They will also learn from you how people act in relationships: parent and child, husband and wife, and how males and females differ and also relate to one another. Daughters will learn about being a female by watching their mother. What you say and do and how you demonstrate dealing with men and other women convey a clear message about how you value yourself as a person and as a woman. The daughter who sees her mother quietly accept repeated emotional disappointment without making reasonable demands on a husband who is unfaithful and having affairs with other women is learning not to expect fair or equal treatment from a mate and that disappointment goes with the territory when one is a female. Children learn about adult roles not only from your behavior, but also from your attitudes and beliefs. They may be more subtle, but no less powerful, messages.

For fathers dealing with their sons, the issues are equally critical. Even if you as an ACOA father sense your own weakness, you should try to be decisive as an example to your son. If you can't make a decision, don't berate yourself in front of him and certainly don't blame him for your shortcomings. Act with deliberation, but don't act hastily so as to make a mistake that you later have to correct. In other words, try to imagine what your role is and play to it. Don't, however, confuse abuse or bullying with strength. Being firm in your resolve is strength; admitting your mistakes is strength; shouldering a responsibility is strength; and facing down a tough issue is strength. Deliberately making someone else unhappy is weakness.

Connecting

The period after the terrible twos is often a pleasant time for both parents and children. The storm has mostly passed and children are very involved with their own lives. They will play by themselves or alongside other children now and are enjoyable for parents to watch. There is a lot of hugging and caring expressed and received by parents and child. It is often a time when children begin to feel an especially strong connection with the opposite-sex parent.

When we remember that this is a period when children identify with being a boy (maleness) and being a girl (femaleness) and also begin to learn about relationships, we can then realize that a mechanism for this learning is their relationship with the parent of the opposite sex. This shows up in the many proclamations made by boys that they are "going to live together with mommy forever" and by girls that "daddy is the most wonderful person in the world. He loves me and he is going to marry me when I grow up." The notions of being a mamma's boy or daddy's little girl have their roots in these early events.

It is crucial that the tendency for boys to be drawn to their mothers and girls to their fathers be recognized as a normal part of healthy development. Don't be overly alarmed if, for example, your son displays affection, possessiveness, and even jealousy for your wife and seems less interested in you. Take note of what feelings emerge inside you. You may feel left out, annoyed, or resentful. Try to sort out your feelings before you react to your son. When you respond, try to give a message that is appropriate to the situation by filtering out the old feelings of loss or possessiveness that may emerge in you. In a similar fashion it is important for the mother to be aware of her feelings, which may range from a balanced appreciation of his affection and admiration to deep satisfaction and possessiveness to repulsion that he wants to be that close.

Children at this age don't really know about sex, and they also don't understand marriage, so don't respond as if they were adults. They are beginning to learn how to make connections with the opposite sex and the appropriate boundaries of behavior. You are the teacher, and the lesson learned is in your response. It is here that many ACOAs run into difficulty.

Most COAs are raised in homes where the emotional boundaries between parents and children are unhealthy. In many instances the boundaries are so rigid that the emotions necessary for healthy nurturance are not present. In an even greater number of alcoholic families, boundaries of behavior are so vague and ambiguous that, for example, a mother who is upset automatically becomes the child, as if the cord was not yet cut. The confusion is worse still in incestuous families, where the boundary violation goes beyond the emotional and into the realm of the physical. It is only reasonable that when these children become parents themselves, they will experience conflicting feelings and be somewhat confused.

There may sometimes be a tendency to be drawn too much to the aggrandizement of the child. If you feel inadequate and before you is a little person who thinks that the sun rises and sets around you, you might want to soak it up like a dry sponge. Certainly, if you've had an especially bad day, having your child look up to you because you're important in his or her life is just the kind of lift that most normal parents want. If somebody in the world thinks you're special, that can be the impetus you need to go out and do a good job, be strong, bring home the bacon, or set the world on its ear. These are good things. However, if your relationship turns into a form of hero worship that you actively encourage, it may damage your child's personality and perspective over the long haul. You may be expecting too much from your child. You may try to make yourself larger than life for a child who must eventually come to appreciate you as a human being with all the shortcomings real flesh and blood people have. What a shock it will be to him or her, just like Biff in *Death of a Salesman*, to find out that father is a human being after all.

If you indulge in being worshipped, you might inadvertently foster a restrictive and exclusionary relationship with your child. The danger is that this could lead to a symbiotic attachment wherein parent and child feed emotionally off one another while excluding all others. This is unhealthy. If this were to happen the child would never develop the initiative to encounter the world of boys and girls his or her own age. If you find that love you are receiving from your child has awakened a deep and old longing, seek professional help sooner rather than later before you do too much damage. Only when you sort out your own needs and feelings can you begin to trust that your response to your child is healthy and good for both of you.

By the end of this period, children move beyond their attempt for exclusive involvement with the opposite-sex parent. In doing so, they will have incorporated some important discoveries about themselves in relationships. They also need the opposite-sex parent to respond favorably to their affection without becoming overinvolved. Boys and girls need to feel valued and loved while learning that their parents are in love and are a team.

Comparison

Children in this age group are entering a very social world. Whether the setting is preschool or kindergarten, they can see how other children and their parents behave toward one another. They are observed by the outside world as well and evaluated by teachers and other parents. This is a particularly anxious time for the ACOA parent who has low self-esteem and is afraid of being judged by others as an inadequate parent. You may find yourself trying to live your life through your child. You may also notice a panicky feeling that your child is a reflection of you. Your child might be short for his or her age, or seem to have a more limited vocabulary, or be too immature in contrast to his or her peers, or have one of a hundred imagined or perceived shortcomings that all point like a blinking red beacon to your own particular perceived failure as a member of the human race.

There is a natural tendency in all parents to compare their child's progress to that of the other children in his or her peer group or class. The problem comes only when this interferes with your seeing your child as an individual separate from you. This tends to occur for ACOAs when questions about self-worth are aroused. If you feel flawed because you came from a dysfunctional family, you may be concerned that you will be found out through your children. This is a natural way for you to feel. Most ACOAs complain about just this fear when they send their children into the world each day. But remember, your child is not you. He or she will not carry your private fears out into the world unless you force them on your child. Your child needs you to be aware that he or she is a separate individual with his or her own set of needs. You should not inadvertently ask your child to carry your emotional baggage for you or even to share the load.

Type A Personalities and Comparison Child Raising

It is no surprise that most ACOAs who survive dysfunctional childhoods become Type A adults in order to compensate for their feelings of inadequacy or perceived lack of control. The psychological basis for this is straightforward: "If I really demonstrate to the world that I am self-reliant and extremely responsible and perform my duties as parent or employee beyond reproach, then *they* won't see how fragile and insecure I really feel." The cycle perpetuates itself if you ask your children to do the same. If you expect your child to carry the burden of your self-esteem issues by excessive comparisons with how he or she is doing in relation to his or her peers, you may set the stage for two unfortunate consequences. Your child may come to feel that the only way to keep your esteem and love is if he or she is perfect and does everything well. The other possibility is that your child may feel there is no way to live up to your standards and rebel by becoming antisocial or an underachiever. In the first case, the Type A personality is perpetuated by the child's attempting to become the parent's angel, while in the second the child chooses out of frustration to become a sinner. In either case, the decision is indirectly forced upon the child and he or she gets a raw deal in the end.

Remember that your child will naturally try to emulate you or your spouse or separate from one or both of you. All of these forces will occur in sequence from time to time. Just as you should have learned, but did not, from your parents about how to be an adult, your child will attempt to learn from you. Inadvertently you will show combinations of strength and weakness, the positive and negative. It can't be helped. If you make the mistake of forcing roles upon your child, burdening him or her with your own need to excel, then you are distorting the natural forces that comprise your relationship. Let nature take its course. Your child will need to separate from you and return to the nest to take examples of your behavior into the world. By understanding this, you will set the best example for your child.

Try not to judge your parenting. If you are reading child-care guides to help you be a better parent, try to focus on being successful, not on identifying where you've failed. Just as you should not compare your child with other children, you should not compare your parenting with that of non-ACOA parents or other parents in your community. Don't compete as a parent—you don't have to and it's unhealthy for your child. As an ACOA, you have the tendency to set up competitions in all arenas and to take the tiniest issues and blow them out of all proportion. Remember:

1. The issue is raising healthy children, not children better than those next door.
2. You and your neighbors or siblings are not in a race to see whose child reads first, is toilet trained first, rides a bike first, or establishes the first financially successful lemonade stand on the corner.
3. All children develop at different rates throughout their lives. There is a wide variation in what is considered normal.
4. Your child is first and foremost a separate person from you. If you find yourself spilling your feelings and personal issues onto your relationship with your child, stop. Do not beat yourself up over it. Do not impose your emotional burdens on your child. Seek the help of friends or counselors.

Your child from ages three to six is entering an exciting period in which the world becomes an alternately engaging and threatening landscape. Whether your child becomes fearful of the outside world or embraces it with a healthy curiosity and drive to explore will, in large measure, depend upon how you encourage your child to test his or her initiative. Knowing that you were probably severely impeded at this age should help you to not stand in your child's way. On the other hand, if you overreact and push an unready child into the conflicts of the world, you are causing potential damage as well. If you read how your child is behaving and what he or she seems to need, you will have an easier time than if you dictate your child's needs and provide for them automatically.

6

Middle Childhood to Preadolescence

Ages 6 to 12

LAWRENCE

When Jeremy was about six and a half he asked for a set of little tools like his other friends had gotten. He was eager, and being reasonably educated I know it was important for him to have this hands-on experience. I found myself fearing that it would only be a matter of time before he realized that his dad, whom he admired so much, couldn't do anything with his hands. My own father was an adequate person. I think he was pretty smart, but he never applied himself. He wasn't around all that much, but when he was he wasn't much of a role model. He never really showed me how to do anything, and he told me early on that I would never be any good with my hands. He was right, I guess, although I wonder if I just lived down to his expectations. Despite the fact that I'm completing my Ph.D. from Princeton, I know I'm making it harder on myself than I have to, and I'm reasonably certain it is related to my father's age-old difficulties with following through. Anyway, I don't want Jeremy to think of his dad as a pinhead. And I don't want to hold him from developing his confidence and competence in both the physical and intellectual realms. I felt awfully separate from other kids when I grew up. Jeremy's doing well now, and I don't want to mess things up for him.

Industry Versus Inferiority

Between the ages of six and twelve, your child will go through the crisis of industry versus inferiority. This is an especially unique time of life in that each ending is really a new beginning. At the start of this period, the child goes through the rite of passage of beginning first grade and more deeply entering into life outside the immediate world of the family. At the end of this period, at about age twelve, the child marks the passage from childhood into early adolescence.

This is the time when children are eager and ready to learn how to do things. This readiness is recognized in every culture by the beginning of some form of systematic instruction. Children look to parents, to teachers, older siblings, and elders of all kinds to teach them how to perform various tasks. Children develop a sense of industry in that they seek to be productive by using the tools and utensils of adults. As children progress through this stage, they not only want to do things, but they want to do them well. It is this potential to develop a sense of mastery that is at the heart of this stage.

Developmental psychologist Erik Erikson says it best when he refers to this period as a time when the child's "exuberant imagination is tamed and harnessed" in the performance of tasks that are essential for entering adult life. School is the focus of much of this learning. It is there that your child will further develop verbal, writing, and reasoning skills in a context where he or she simultaneously addresses the need for social skills.

During this period, children also experience fascination with the work people do and sometimes even explore vocational skills. They are intrigued by work and often talk about what they want to do. Children at age six or seven convince themselves they want to be police officers, firefighters, soldiers, sailors, plumbers, teachers, ballplayers, doctors, or dancers. They become fascinated with performing the tasks of almost anyone they come into contact with or see on television. But while they are apt to follow parents around the house and want to participate in the cooking, vacuuming, fixing-up, and yard work, they also seek to perform tasks on their own or with friends.

Their vocational self-concept first begins to develop

through identification with parents, teachers, and other significant adults by way of their imagination. Children role-play by pretending they are mothers, teachers, or doctors. As children progress through this stage, what they choose to do and how well they do it become increasingly important. At an earlier age, the child will play at activities with no real attention given to the quality of the results. In this stage, however, the notion of play takes on a worklike quality. Mere play is not enough for your child. He or she needs to perform well. This success is necessary to developing the sense of satisfaction one gets from completing a job well done.

In order for your children to develop a sense of competence, they need to feel that their efforts at being productive and creative are rewarded. It is important for them to know that they planned something out, followed through, and performed well. Unless children have enough of these positive experiences, they will develop a sense of inadequacy and inferiority.

A child who feels inadequate may tend to withdraw from activities and interactions with peers who are perceived as more competent. It is, therefore, important that as a parent you don't inadvertently encourage dependent involvement with you. Fortunately, there are a great many opportunities for children to explore and test their abilities through the tasks that are available at school and at home. Your child will be looking to you to provide guidance and sometimes to structure activities. But your child needs to know that he or she has completed a task successfully and that you recognize this accomplishment. Throughout this process, it is imperative that you both reward your child's successes and address mistakes as opportunities for new learning, not as evidence of failure. Because of the critical parent they harbor inside, this is sometimes a challenge for parents who are ACOAs. This question of "How can I give to my child what I wasn't given and continue to find hard to give to myself?" will be addressed throughout this chapter. However, suffice it to say now that ACOAs must make the separation between the needs of the child they are raising and the needs of the child within them. Once these are differentiated, an ACOA will able to satisfy one or both sets of needs in such a way that the child the parent is raising will receive what he or she requires.

A Caution to ACOA Parents

Your child is now formally encountering the world outside the home on an almost full-time basis. Just as you may be going out to work, your child is getting more and more accustomed to using outside activities as a source of much new information. He or she is encountering children of different socioeconomic groups, races, and values and, consequently, sees himself or herself in contrast to them. Your child is also increasingly exposed to the influence of other adults and authority figures. Much of his or her daily activity will be focused on teachers, but he or she will also interact with other parents in joining the scouts, community sports, and church or related activities. It is only a matter of time before your child will in some way begin to compare you to these other seemingly wonderful adults. If you harbor a certain emptiness or self-doubt inside, as most ACOAs do, it is quite likely that it will be touched off by the comparisons and complaints made by your now more worldly child. Be prepared for this to happen and try not to beat yourself up when you hear these tales of wonder about the accomplishments and feats of other adults.

There are many scenarios in which this potential crisis is played out. Bill's story is just one of many that frequently come up in group. Bill is an ACOA who is married and has two boys, aged six and eight. He grew up in an upper-middle-class family in which his dad, although a successful professional, was also an alcoholic. As a means of compensating for his feelings of inadequacy, known only to him, Bill completed law school, was selected for *Law Review*, and put in six days a week at his firm when he was hired. Bill's workaholic tendencies also became a function of his genuine concern and desire to provide for his family. The larger the caseload he took, the more money he made and the more valuable he was to his growing firm.

When I got home, my son was in a whining mood. I asked how he did at soccer and although he did OK, he starts crying. And as we were talking about the game, I asked John what was wrong and he says nothing. Then he says he doesn't know and then it leaked out. "Everybody else's dad was at the game but you." It hit me like a brick in my face.

Despite all his years of achievement and professional success, Bill still felt like a failure before his son. Comparisons with the other fathers immediately flashed through his mind: they were bigger, stronger, smarter, better able to take on the responsibilities of raising a boy, and most of them were better looking than he was. He was never much of an athlete, as his sloping shoulders revealed, and felt he couldn't even fit in on the sidelines. It was as if all his efforts at being a super-achiever in his own chosen field accounted for nothing. Before him now was the revelation that his young son had compared his father to the other fathers of the neighborhood and found him wanting. He, too, perceived his father to be a failure.

Similarly, Jill was confronted by the disappointment of her eleven-year-old daughter, who had returned home after attending a birthday party at a classmate's house. Although Debbie had seemed happy when she first came home, her mood soured considerably toward evening. As Jill reported the conversation for the group:

JILL: Debbie, what's going on? You seemed so happy before.

DEBBIE: Nothing.

JILL: You don't seem like *nothing* is going on.

DEBBIE: I hate this house! (Runs to her room. Jill follows her.)

JILL: Honey, what's wrong?

DEBBIE: (Now crying.) Oh, the Beckermans have everything so nice. Their house is so pretty, and they are always giving Mary nice clothes. Her father went out and bought pizza and sodas for us. Dad keeps that old clunker in the driveway. We don't have anything here.

Jill lives in a small university town in a very affluent part of New Jersey where the lower middle class and upper middle class share the same schools and grocery stores. Their children become friends and the many differences in upbringing that divergent incomes bring are often quickly discovered. As Jill subsequently revealed to the group, she knew all along what must have been troubling Debbie, and that it really— logically—had nothing to do with her. All the children of graduate students and university junior faculty encountered many of the same feelings. Yet like many ACOA parents, Jill felt that she must be at the core responsible for Debbie's upset, and this overshadowed what she rationally knew.

I felt like I had failed her. It was beyond the money and beyond the divorce. I knew we gave her what we could . . . and I got angry. She seemed so ungrateful. It was as if she were telling me that I wasn't good enough. I knew she wasn't saying that. I know it's really me. It gets very confusing.

It is also important to remember that as children progress through this stage of their lives they will be making comparisons between what they know (themselves and their immediate family) and the outside world. This is a part of the separation process that will continue in a different form into their teenage years. A commonplace occurrence in this process is children blaming their parents for what they perceive as shortcomings in their own lives. A need that isn't met, a friend with better toys, a family with a bigger television set and more channels on cable, a friend's house with a pool: all these are forms of comparison for which children will routinely blame their parents because they cannot see beyond the immediacy of the different life-styles.

When this happens to you, you need to focus the spotlight back on your children and ask what is really bothering them. The tendency among parents who are ACOAs is to focus on themselves and feel as if they've failed. When you hear the first complaints from your seven- or eight-year-old, don't panic. First, recognize that these feelings of self-doubt and failure are what the overwhelming majority of ACOA parents would typically feel in this situation. Remember, too, that these feelings are not unique to you. We would expect, given your personal history, for them to show up at some time in your life because they were an integral part of your childhood. Although the feelings are powerful, remember that they are only feelings, and they most likely aren't at all a true measure of your performance as a parent. So, without denying to yourself the existence of these doubts, act as a healthy parent would.

Quick Healthy Parent Response

1. Listen between the lines to what your child is saying about him- or herself.
2. Reassure your child of his or her abilities and self-worth. Don't pour on the praise or overdo it, which will sound hopelessly corny. Just tell the truth, but stress the positive.
3. Remember that your child is a separate person from you and will have to face some struggles by him- or herself. Give the child the space to do that without emotionally abandoning him or her.
4. Sort out your feelings of failure away from your child. Work out your feelings with a friend, spouse, or professional counselor. Don't bring your fear of failure into your child's life or make him or her carry it as emotional baggage.

Try to keep in mind that your child values you highly just as you valued your parents. Even though they had let you down, you would have bent over backward for words of praise from them and a recognition that you were surviving just fine in that environment. Your child, in the same way, will really value words of praise from you.

However, your child is still a child who needs to complain and compare the greener grass on the other side of the fence with the grass you have painstakingly raised. These comparisons are sometimes used by children as clubs to extract concessions or outright goodies from parents. If your son or daughter wants something from you, he or she knows how to play to your weakness to get it. Jill's daughter, for example, wanted desperately to belong to the horsey set at her school. Never mind that she had been afraid of horses since a pony stepped on her toe when she was four—now she wanted to belong to the riding club at school because that's where her friends were. Her strategy was to make Jill feel like a failed parent for not providing a healthy physical and emotional outlet for her daughter. She learned how to do this from her older friends.

Jill let Debbie play to her weakness until a friend reminded her that in that community all the children played off parent against parent as a kind of game. Jill realized that she was taking seriously what was a not-so-serious attempt by her daughter to impress older children at her school. She eventually realized that despite her daughter's complaints and her old scripts that told her she was not a good person, she was believing an illusion, not reality. You will find yourself in similar situations as your children grow. They will try to convince you that you are failing because you haven't provided them with what they really want at that moment. Almost any of the other parents in the community, they will tell you, are better than you. Remember, this is not real. It is a game. Your children value you highly, but want all the goodies they can get. You can be firm with them even while keeping your own head above water.

Lying and Other Transgressions

One of the great moral dilemmas faced by all parents occurs when they are confronted by dishonesty in their children. The situation is often much more awkward for parents who are ACOAs because dishonesty is a strategy that the active alcoholic uses on a daily basis. In many alcoholic families there are few parental guidelines. What is taught about right and wrong, truth and lies, is often negated by the actions of the alocholic parent. Because of the disease, the addicted parent often makes promises that are never kept; this fosters distrust in the child, who views these broken promises as blatant lies. Fortunately for most children of alcoholics, there is an adult, usually the nonalcoholic parent, who, although an enabler, nevertheless upholds a value system and usually follows through on commitments. In families where both parents are alcoholic or equally dysfunctional, children have no role models at home for clearly and consistently defining the boundaries of right and wrong. If you were a child in an alcoholic home, you knew that your drinking parent was routinely lying to you, even though you wanted desperately to believe that what he or she was saying was true. Thus, you have a deep weak spot when it comes to dealing with deliberate and consistent untruths. Be assured, if you find that your child is lying, and that weak spot is irritated, you are almost sure to overreact. Here is what you have to remember before you fly off the handle.

Where there is a dearth of guidance at home, children develop their sense of morality from their peers. Consequently, the acquisition of a healthy conscience in the absence of parental guidance may be a function of whether the environment provides a positive or negative influence. Accordingly, there may not be internalized checks and balances when it comes time to parent. However, many ACOAs compensate for their lack of adequate parental guidance as children by developing a rigid code of right and wrong. The rigidity is key. For many ACOA parents, this is an inflexible schema that defines every aspect of the parents' and child's lives. If you are in this situation, you have to be aware that your child is not an ACOA and did not grow up with the same lack of parental guidelines you did. Your code of right and wrong was helpful earlier, of course, because it provided a much-needed structure, but chances are it will interfere with effective parenting as your own child grows.

When confronted by a child who is misbehaving in some way, ACOA parents like yourself are prone to se only black or white, good or bad. There is no gray area. In a similar fashion, when you as an ACOA discover that your child has lied, you may too quickly and incorrectly assume that the child is like the alcoholic parent; you, the ACOA parent, are a fundamentally bad seed no matter how hard you try to succeed; you are a basic failure; or the child has to be disciplined to within an inch of his or her life so as not to show up your flaws ever again. None of these assumptions are likely to be true, and many of them are downright harmful.

There is a tendency to come down very harshly on the child and make a much bigger deal of the situation than is warranted. For example, I remember the story of eight-year-old David and his older sister's baby-sitting money. Both children lived near the Rutgers University campus in New Brunswick, N.J., with their recently divorced ACOA mother, Joan, a client who had returned to graduate school after ten years of marriage. Joan was already under a great deal of stress from the dissolution of her marriage and the demands of the children and school, but it had gotten worse since she had invited her boyfriend of six months to pool his resources with hers and move in with her family. Now, she felt, the whole world would condemn her: her own mother, who had been the enabling parent; her ex-parents-in-law, who chastised her every night over the phone for inviting her boyfriend, Alan, in to share a house with "Karl's adolescent daughter"; her ex-husband, Karl, who immediately stopped paying child support in protest; and even her friends from the housing development where she and her family had lived. "It's too soon," they whispered over the phone. "You're only going to regret it."

The first screams from Joan's adolescent daughter— "Where's my money?"—were the opening salvo. Thirty dollars in baby-sitting money from over two weeks' worth of work was now missing from the daughter's table. Suspicion immediately fell on Alan, whose spending habits had changed with his acceptance of a new research assistantship. Joan was beside herself. Had she invited a criminal to live with them? Strangely silent in the tumult on the third floor of their apartment building was David, who sat on his bunk and watched his sister and mother turn over cushions and look under chairs. Then Alan returned from the laboratory building, and he was immediately questioned by Joan and her daughter. Pleading ignorance and finally getting mad, he left the house, promising to pick up his clothing by the weekend. In her mind Joan was now truly alone.

The next day, David was playing with a new Hot Wheels car he said he had borrowed from a friend at school. The following day, two more cars turned up. Joan's suspicions were aroused, and for the first time ever she searched under her son's bedding. There she found two ten-dollar bills. She confronted him when he came home from school, but his imperious attitude thwarted her attempts to shame him into telling what she now knew was the truth. Her daughter joined in when she came home from school, but David would not relent. He had found the money. His father had given him the money. He had borrowed it from a friend. He had been carrying grocery bags for Mrs. Mitchell next door. Finally in desperation, Joan grabbed David and shoved him through the partially closed bathroom door. He began screaming and vowing to call his father.

I felt as if I didn't stop him here—right there and then in that bathroom—he'd get out of control. It was the lying that got to me, not the stealing. All kids go through a stealing phase; I remembered that from basic child psych when I was an undergrad. But the lying, and then the brazen denial of it, changing the truth each time I asked. That was my panic button, and I went absolutely nuts. I slammed him against the wall, while Karen squealed with delight, and jammed a bar of soap into his mouth. "I'll teach you not to lie," I said to him. "When I get through, you'll never lie to me again. Never, because I'm gonna wash every lie out of your head!" He was gasping for air, but I kept right on washing out his mouth with soap. I was becoming emotionally drained at this point and felt as if my entire life had crashed around me. I didn't want to go back to school, to deal with either kid anymore, to see Alan, or even to go on living.

She had held his squirming head down into the sink and scraped the bar of soap along the inside of his front teeth so that the bitter shavings would fall into his mouth. She still loved him, she told herself, but had to save him from what she believed would happen to him if the pattern of lies became his entire life.

Unfortunately, she had acted on her feelings of panic. As an ACOA, you will find yourself confronted with such feelings on occasions when your children commit varous serious transgressions. There is a definite need to respond and respond quickly and decisively. But your response has to be measured nonetheless. Usually no one incident will cause irreparable damage to your child's personality. However harshly David was judged, the incident was soon resolved. Joan realized that all children go through some form of a lying and stealing phase. It is how the parents react to that phase that determines how the child will emerge.

Some children will shoplift just as an experiment. It doesn't mean that it's right. If it's handled in perspective, and if the child is held accountable, he or she will understand that stealing is wrong. Lying and cheating are similar phases. Your child will undoubtedly tell you many small lies. Either out of fear of retribution or out of a misconceived sense of convenience, your child will either tell you what he or she thinks you want to hear or what will deflect blame from him or her and place it elsewhere. If you think that your son or daughter will stand up straight-shouldered, look you straight in the eye, and confess to chopping down the cherry tree, think again. That will never happen. It is likely that when your child has lied, you will have to ferret out the truth by oblique conversation and much emotional support. You don't have to say that it's OK to lie, but you might have to admit that sometimes a lie helps a person confront the truth on the second or third pass. Eventually, you must stress, the truth must come out and you will never punish your child for telling the truth.

On the other hand, when some ACOA parents feel panic over their child's transgressions, they don't spring into action. They do nothing at all. It isn't a matter of not caring. Rather, they care so much that they are afraid their rage may get out of control.

Backing off may prevent you from overreacting, but it also sends a message to your children that might prevent them from developing healthy social relationships and a healthy sense of responsibility. The message basically says that you can manipulate others to get what you want by being selfish and uncooperative. This type of parenting actually is another form of enabling. As long as Susan picks up her son's toys, she is teaching him that he does not have to be responsible. As in Joan's case, there is a need for a response that is appropriate to the event.

Childhood is in many ways a series of experiments. As the child grows older, the arena may change, but the event is basically the same: to explore strange new worlds, outside and inside. During this period of life, children desire to be less dependent on their parents and more connected with their peers. This will continue in different forms throughout the teenage years. The reality is that between the ages of six and twelve years your child will at some point lie, steal, or in some way be dishonest. Do not try to send the child back to the factory for a recall. You haven't failed as a parent. This behavior, however disturbing to you, is a manifestation of the process of experimentation that occurs in normal development.

By the time children are six years old, they basically understand the difference between right and wrong, although there are some gray areas that might still be confusing to them. However, if your child has taken something that does not belong to him or her, chances are the child knows he or she shouldn't have. If you directly confront your child about it, he or she may also lie by either denying having done it or blaming someone else. There are several reasons why a child may act in this way.

Avoidance.   Your child may have taken something not out of need or a feeling of deprivation, but out of curiosity—just to see what it would be like to take something. He or she knows the difference between right and wrong and may simply be experimenting with "the dark side." The child may feel confused by both having taken something that didn't belong to him or her and being confronted about it by you. In this case, lying may be an attempt to avoid punishment.

Lonesomeness.   No matter how well adjusted a child may seem, he or she may not yet feel at home with peers. Your child is clear in the desire to be less dependent on you and may feel as if he or she is in the middle. Your child may be feeling lonesome and unhappy. As a young client of mine once revealed about her need to feel accepted as a fourth grader, "I wanted to fit in with the other girls but Darlene, the most popular girl, did not like me for some reason. She would get the other girls to make fun of me. So I stole a whole box of candy bars from my father's store and passed them out to get them to like me."

The Need to Fit In.   Children sometimes steal things so that they will be accepted by their peers. This is an offshoot of feeling lonesome. Usually, the child pulls a prank of some sort in an effort to fit in with a select peer group. What it amounts to is a test wherein the child proves him- or herself worthy to be in with the crowd. My client's fourth-grade behavior exemplifies this need, as does most of the preadolescent gang activity in middle-class neighborhoods and the hazing rituals surrounding neighborhood clubs. Or, like David, the child may steal to acquire toys that will help him make new friends.

Powerlessness.   In some children, an act of lying or stealing may be connected to a pervasive sense of powerlessness. If your child's environment has impaired his or her development of a sense of trust in him- or herself or in others, the child may reason that cheating is the only way to get what he or she wants or needs. These children usually have poor self-esteem and a family life in which they feel devalued and ineffectual. Alcoholism is often present at home, and the lack of love and security produces children who are damaged and often need love as well as professional counseling. In an ACOA family this can manifest itself when the parent, who is so crippled by the responsibilities associated with parenting, feels completely overwhelmed. His or her own self-esteem is so damaged that the parent actually makes the child the victim of his or her own weakness. Thus the child feels unvalued and has low self-esteem as a result. Accordingly, the child is at high risk for committing juvenile crimes and entering the juvenile justice system as a youthful offender.

How to Confront Your Child

When faced with dishonesty on the part of your child, be prepared to respond in a way commensurate with the crime. While it is imperative that your child know that you do not in any way condone lying or stealing, it is crucial that you do not imply that your love for him or her is conditional on good behavior. You may disapprove of the child's actions, may be disappointed and angry, but your child must know that you still love him or her. By demonstrating that you love and value your child in the face of the negative behavior, you are teaching him or her about trust and self-respect. You are teaching your child that you value him or her as an individual and the behavior disappoints you, but doesn't lessen the child's value in your eyes.

It has already been established that it is not helpful to act on the automatic impulses that many ACOA parents have by either coming down too hard on your child or ignoring the dishonest behavior altogether. Both extremes do a disservice to you and your child. One way to find out what an appropriate response would be is to ask yourself what you would have wanted your parents to do if you were the child. You'll probably realize that you would want to be confronted, treated fairly, given guidance, told to make some sort of restitution to set things right, and made to feel loved and nurtured. It is your job as parent to do the same thing.

Confront Your Child. Directly confront the child with what you think he or she has done. Don't try to trick a confession out or force it out with threats. Let your child know that you know that he or she has lied to you or taken something that did not belong to him or her. Confront your child with the evidence and let the child explain it, if he or she can. If you sense only lies, push on them until your child gives them up. Show your child that lies cannot stand up to the truth. However, remember that this is not a form of ancient torture. You are not actually trying to wring out a confession and in so doing reducing the child to jelly. All you want is for your child to understand that you know what he or she has done and that you want him or her to assume responsibility for the act and the truth.

Treat Your Child Fairly. During the entire process you must be fair. If your child has an explanation, listen to it. If he or she claims there are mitigating circumstances, consider them. If your child absolutely maintains that he or she is not guilty, keep the book open until you have definitive proof. In other words, just because this is your child, don't summarily throw away the Sixth Amendment. However, you don't have to make a federal case out of it either. Strike a balance. Let your child know that you are aware that he or she may have misbehaved even though you value him or her no less because of this behavior. He has disappointed you *because* you respect and value him as a person. Thus, stress that you love him, show him that you value him, and explain that nothing can make you stop loving him.

Your child does not need you to be taken in by lies or to ignore the problem. Rather, you are needed to set limits and, like a referee, call a foul when you see it. Be direct with your child by stating your concern. "I know you took the candy from the store and I want you to bring it back." Or, "You hit your sister, now go to your room." Don't ask if the child did something if you already know he or she did it. You might just be setting the child up to lie, which solves nothing. But if your child wants to explain, hear him or her out. Regardless of what your child says, however, trust your own judgment and act appropriately.

Be aware of passing the issue off on the other parent. If you are concerned about the child's leaving crumbs on the floor, own up to that concern. Don't say, "Wait till your father gets home." Or, "Don't you know how hard your mother works to keep the house clean?" Be direct by taking personal responsibility for what concerns you. Your children will get the message and will be less apt to be confused or feel they can get away with something.

Remember you want to teach children about the meaning of responsibility. You do not want to break your child's will. Be fair and judicial in your response. You may choose among a variety of responses: ten minutes in a time-out, forfeiture of a favorite TV show, paying for damage out of a weekly allowance, returning a stolen item (under your supervision) to the store and apologizing to the storekeeper, and so on. Implement the consequence as close in time to the negative behavior as possible and make the punishment fit the crime. Always insist that your child make reasonable restitution whenever something is broken (if it wasn't an accident) or stolen. There is no need for arguments or recriminations; your child needs you to be firm, just, and fair.

Comparisons

You already know that your children will have a tendency at this age to make comparisons between you and their teachers or the other adults they encounter. As this is part of the process of seeking independence and discovering the world outside the family, it is considered a function of normal, albeit annoying, psychological and social development. In other words, you don't have to like it, just accept it as a phase. It is equally important, however, to consider the tendency of ACOA parents to make comparisons between their children and others. And this is as annoying to your children as their comparisons are to you.

Adult children of alcoholics are prone to derive a sense of self-validation from others. Years of inconsistency, double messages, and disappointments have led many ACOAs to develop an external orientation to life. It is only reasonable to expect that when they become parents, adult children of alcoholics might continue this external orientation by perceiving their children as public indicators of their worth as people and validity as parents. The notion is that if my child is doing well in school, if he or she is popular, respected, a good student, and a good athlete, then I as parent am OK. On the other hand, I do not feel as if I have any worth at all if my child does poorly. In either event, this constitutes an attempt to live life through another, and that is a problem because it blurs the distinction between parent and child as separate individuals and hampers your effectiveness in being there to parent your child.

Our culture is competitive by nature, and, as such, it fosters comparisons. From comparing your baby's eight-and-a-half-pound birth weight—"He's a big boy all right, the biggest they've seen in over a year!"—to your daughter's completing MIT in only three years—"The girl's a genius, I tell ya, she's smart as a whip"—parents use their kids to compete with other parents. Throughout their school years, children are measured against each other by their physical appearance, popularity, athletic ability, and academic success. However, in ACOA families, the problem of comparisons can not only be commonplace but became a form of dysfunction. Listen to Daniel's story:

Only in looking back on it do I realize that I have been a dancing bear seeking my mother's approval all my life. Scholar-athlete in high school, Ph.D. from Princeton, you'd think that it'd be enough. Nothing ever was enough for her, and I am afraid that even though she's dead five years now, I still never feel pleased with what I do. So when my girls do so well in school and I so get excited, I sometimes confuse who I am happy for. Me or them? Donna just won the junior's state swimming championship, and I was very mindful of my wanting to share with her the thrill that I felt, and how proud I am of her. But I also made sure to convey that I would love and feel proud of her no matter where she placed as long as she tried her hardest. I've really got to watch myself.

Part of the unfortunate residue from growing up in an alcoholic family is the feeling of being inadequate. A great many ACOAs who have felt this way have dealt with these self-doubts by overcompensating and trying to be the perfect student, father, wife, or employee. The act of reading a book on child care might be a manifestation of the tendency. The problem is that too often the inner voice spurring you on and telling you that what you've done is not good enough continues to raise self-doubts. It continues to taunt you into thinking that no matter how hard you try, you will never please the voice that holds the carrot of approval just beyond your reach. You begin to believe the voice and doubt your own abilities. Despite all of your attempts to bribe the voice into silence by achieving what it wants, the voice is never satisfied.

Remember that your self-worth issues preceded your children and are not connected with them. Try to make clear that your loving and valuing your children are not conditional upon their success or bringing home the first-place trophy. Of course, you will be happy for them if they do win what they set out to, but you'll care for them regardless. Your children will be looking to you for cues as to whether you approve of them. If you say the right words, but your attitude conveys another message, your child will feel confused and not good enough. This, in turn, could inadvertently set off the cycle of your child's overachieving in order to gain your love and approval.

Sometimes the grades children get and the number of goals scored in soccer are subtly used by ACOAs as an offering or message to their alcoholic parent, especially if he or she is still actively drinking. In this case, the child would unknowingly be fulfilling a mission in the parent's life. It is as if the child's parent might be saying, "I gave birth to a healthy baby who did well in toilet training, is well adjusted and sociable, and now is really bringing home the laurels. Didn't I do a great job? Isn't it amazing how well I've done considering how little you've given me?" Maybe what you're really saying is, "Please stop drinking and love me and my child." In this scenario the success of the child is used both as a weapon of anger against the alcoholic grandparent and as another demonstration of the ACOA's achievement combined with a plea for validation from the alcoholic parent. In the face of enormous evidence that the alcoholic parent is unable to give, many ACOAs still feel compelled to secure their parent's love and approval. Try to be as clear as you can about these feelings. Be aware of your own use of denial, because unless you understand what you are doing, your child can easily get caught doing your bidding. This is your struggle with your own past, and your putting it to rest can come only from within you—not your child. If you are concerned that your tendency to feel unsatisfied is spilling over into your relationship with your child, get some help and talk it out. Consider joining an ACOA support group or therapy group or entering individual counseling. You owe it to yourself and your child.

Broaching the Subject of Alcohol and Other Drugs

One of the major tasks of every parent who was raised by an alcoholic parent is to prevent as best as possible the cycle of addiction from beginning all over again. You have been expending a goodly amount of energy working on yourself so that the open wounds you've carried since childhood would heal. It is now time to focus your concerns about this "family disease" directly on your children.

The experts on addiction are in complete agreement that the most effective method of prevention is education. The best place for the education to take place is in the family, and the best time to begin is around the age of five. The age doesn't really matter; rather, your decision to begin to talk generally about alcohol and other drugs should be based on your child's emotional maturity. If he or she is able to understand the concept that someone's offering a drink, a cigarette, or a pill is unsafe, then your child is ready for a discussion with you provided that you keep it on the child's level.

The first place to begin is by examining your own attitudes about alcohol, including how you use it and other drugs. This is especially important because your child will learn by casually observing the habits and patterns of use of alcohol by you and your spouse. Most children first taste alcohol in the home as part of a family ritual, usually on holidays. In some families, alcohol—wine—is an integral part of a religious ceremony. This is all the more reason to be sensitive to how alcohol is presented in the home and to what you say about it to your child.

Try to sort out whatever conflicting feelings you might have about alcohol so you can allow yourself to enter freely into discussions with your children about substances. Don't think of this as a one-shot deal. What you are really doing is giving your children permission to ask questions about alcohol and other drugs when they arise. If you inadvertently send them a message about how uncomfortable and tense you feel about the subject, you risk their learning that this is a family secret that we don't talk about openly.

Your children eventually need to know about how your parent's alcoholism may predispose them to addiction, but a discussion of this kind with a child who is too young may cause him or her to feel frightened. Scared is *not* what you want. What will help children to "just say no" when offered alcohol or other drugs is a strong sense of themselves as capable and valued individuals who know the dangers of such substances. You have an opportunity to help build your child's self-esteem in your daily interactions, and can educate him or her about alcohol and other drugs in special planned talks, but more frequently the subject will come up in normal conversation about the world or the fact that grandpa is coming to visit.

In your discussion with your child, listen closely to what he or she is asking you. Answer questions as best you can (you don't need to know all the answers at the time) and provide answers for questions your child didn't ask but which you think him or her capable of understanding. Your goal in these discussions is to establish a general awareness of alcohol and other drugs and how their use can turn into an illness like the one grandpa has. Be prepared to cover the following questions:

• What is alcohol?
• What are drugs?
• Why do people use them?
• How does it make you feel when you use them?

- Is it wrong to use them?
- Why do some people keep drinking or keep taking drugs?
- Why does my grandparent have to drink so much?
- What is alcoholism?
- Can I catch it?
- Did you ever get drunk?

Be sure to remember to let your children know that you are willing and interested to talk with them anytime about anything they might be wondering about. If you mean it, they'll be asking you about all sorts of topics in addition to alcohol and other drugs. Especially as they approach age twelve, your children will have questions about their changing bodies and doubts about their feelings. By opening the channels of communication with them early, you can help them navigate through to adolescence.

7

Adolescence
Ages 12 to 19 Plus

DON

We really want to be there for our kids. We do not want them to feel that they can't talk to us. As a matter of fact, Joan and I both encourage them to talk about anything. Alcohol was one of the subjects we discussed with Bob. He's seventeen and our eldest. We all agreed it is both dangerous and foolish to drink and drive, so we made an arrangement that if he ever had too much to drink he would call us for a ride. We told him no questions asked. We wouldn't hassle him and we'd be glad to come and get him. Bob's a pretty popular guy in school and one of the top athletes in baseball and football. We know there's drinking going on out there with kids his age, and we just don't want him to get hurt. For a while, when he was a sophomore, things worked out pretty well. A couple of times he had too much to drink, and we came and got him. By the end of his junior year, it got to be a regular Saturday night thing. After a football game, he and his teammates would go out and get smashed. He would call us up and . . . we'd come and get him. I don't mind getting him, but we started to get pretty concerned. It was as if by our actions we were saying that it was OK to get drunk all the time. Then his cousin got busted for possession of cocaine, and although Bob said he never did drugs other than trying marijuana once, we started to really worry. Joan's father was an alcoholic and who knows if that's a factor. We'd hate to think he could have a problem, but this is scaring the hell out of us. That's why we came in for counseling.

BILL

My father was an alcoholic and we didn't have much of a family life. And it kills me that I've worked my tail off for my kids only to feel like I've been shit on. They storm to their rooms and hide. They say, "Leave me alone." They don't want to do the stuff we used to do as a family. And when I ask what's wrong, I'm told, "Nothing." I really feel angry. Moreover, I feel hurt that they're treating me this way. I don't feel valued, loved, or respected.

RUTH

I feel like I can't control her anymore and that frightens me. I don't want her to get into the rebelling that I did. I hated my parents. They treated me like the black sheep. They were all so righteous about how I should behave while ignoring the fact that my father drank too much and my parents had a terrible relationship. I rebelled all right. Dated lots of men who were much older than I. I also drank and used drugs, too. I didn't like myself much then. Once when my boyfriend wanted one of his buddies to join us in bed, I went along with it. Got married after I got pregnant. He used to beat me when he was in one of his drunken rampages before he died. Oh, the life I led. I only date gentlemen now and expect my children to behave properly. I get absolutely furious with Meagan when I see the way she dresses. She is fourteen going on twenty-five and has a figure that gets noticed. She is starting to slip in school, and I am afraid for her. I can see the pattern starting all over again.

These crises are but three examples of the many situations you may face as an ACOA parent of an adolescent. Your child is in the throes of a struggle which, no doubt, is the most demanding his or her conscious mind can recall.

Identity Versus Role Confusion

"Who am I?" your adolescent son asks himself. "What am I going to be?" your fourteen-year-old daughter wonders. "How can I get them to like me?" These are among the wave of almost constant questions your child will now be asking. He or she began seeking a personal identity at around age thirteen and will continue in this search until just after age nineteen. In this psychological stage, adolescents are confused about their roles and try to find their identities amidst many conflicting challenges and opportunities. As in the story about the lady and the tiger, they have many doors to open, but the challenge is knowing which one is the right one. Moreover, although child psychologists have said that this crisis occurs after thirteen and ends at around nineteen, it varies more widely than any other stage. Your child may enter this stage as early as ten and at twenty-two still be struggling for an answer to the same issues. Some perpetual adolescents never leave this stage.

As many of your friends who are parents of older children have no doubt already told you, this is indeed a time of excitement and plenty of confusion. This should come as no surprise, because you remember that adolescence represented a divide or watershed between the two worlds of childhood and adulthood. If you can think back to your own teenage years, the sun had not quite set on your childhood and yet there were still only glimmers of the coming dawn of your adulthood. You were full of hope and nostalgia while you picked your way through the many choices that seemed there for you.

Now you are a parent and will see this from the other side. Like all parents, you will occasionally feel confused at the moments of adult behavior that creep up between bouts of childlike demands and childhood needs. You, of course, only see the surface of what your adolescent is going through. The confusion, frustration, occasional anger, and tantrums only give you a hint of the chaos that your son or daughter is experiencing. Try not to judge your child too quickly or harshly, for there are greater forces at work than even you can remember.

This stage begins with your adolescent's attempting to integrate experiences from childhood into a new understanding of self. Throughout adolescence, your child will be shopping for a new identity—going from one store to the next just trying on different roles in a frenzied effort to find something that fits exactly right. This becomes a very difficult task when the child's size keeps changing. The growth process of this stage is second only to the rapid changes that occurred almost ten years earlier. It is little wonder how hard it is to find a role for oneself when we consider the dramatic emotional, cognitive, social, and physical changes that are taking place. And so the child continues to run from place to place, role model to role model, in a desperate attempt to find something about himself or herself that can be taken into the future. At the same time, the adolescent's body is changing, hormones are flowing, and desires are welling up for the first time that frighten your child while they hold out the promise of great pleasure. At the end of this stage, the adolescent who has successfully resolved the crisis of identity versus role confusion ostensibly now knows who he or she is. Now your child can move on to the next major task of making interpersonal commitments. Luckily, when that next crisis occurs, your child will be an adult, and will probably no longer be living under your roof. Therefore, brace yourself at this stage. It may be the last one you will witness from a ringside seat, but it'll be one you won't forget.

Your child is in the process of developing a new sense of self. He or she will be struggling to integrate the self he or she came to know in childhood with the emerging self of the present. All of this will take place within the context of your child's social milieu and how he or she perceives fitting in. Adolescents are self-conscious almost to the point of a paranoid sense of hypervigilance. In an effort to resolve their psychological crises, adolescents must be able to distinguish between their own personal identities and those of others. It is inevitable that they will suffer from some role confusion. As a result, they may question their intelligence, competence, physical attractiveness—especially in terms of the opposite sex—and even their sexual identities. Explorations of the worlds of homosexual as well as heterosexual behavior are not uncommon around age thirteen to fourteen or even later. Adolescents also wonder about how they fit into the world of adults and the workplace.

Unless your adolescent children can develop a sense of identification with one or more role models, they will experience doubts and insecurity. This identification, whether it be with an individual or cultural role model, will give a sense of direction and purpose to your children's lives. It is also this need to identify that can lead your children into associations with the wrong crowd. The more adolescents feel isolated, confused, or empty, the more prone they are to lose themselves in groups that provide them with a sense of belonging and a structure of values they can commit to in the absence of any internalized values. Thus, adolescents are particularly vulnerable to the appeals made by religious groups or cults, the requirements and advantages of membership in gangs, or, at the very least, the values personified or emblemized by cliques and social groups at school. Adolescents may also feel unable to make, or resistant to making, any important life decisions as they pertain to personal, educational, or vocational goals.

Adolescence seems to recapture earlier stages in your child's development in that prior psychological crises are relived. Children will again address the issue of trust in the search for a person with whom they can identify. They will experience renewed desire to assert their will autonomously in the world. They will also seek to take the initiative by acting out dreams. Finally, they will seek to feel productive by seeking the occupations that seem unique to their wants and goals. The risk throughout this stage is role confusion. There will be periods of real emotional chaos. These mood swings and changes in behavior may even resemble those of a child who is abusing alcohol or other drugs. Nevertheless, all of this is quite normal. I hope that by understanding the adolescent process you may be able to minimize your impulse to overreact. Instead, you should serve as a loving and patient reference point in the stormy night of adolescence.

Who Am I?

You can define adolescence as a time when the question "Who am I?" is answered much less frequently than it is asked. Your son or daughter has developed a heightened sensitivity to outside approval. There is a very strong need to have self-esteem affirmed by others, especially friends and peers. Through interaction with other members of the group, a sense of identity is reinforced. Sometimes, because of the exclusive and sometimes secretive nature of these friendships, parents feel rejected and no longer important in their children's lives. For ACOAs, this may be especially critical because it once again provides an opportunity for you to feel betrayed, rejected, abandoned, shut out, frustrated, and devalued. If you see your adolescent shutting you out and you begin to experience the familiar feelings of rejection and frustration, stop for a moment and catch your breath. Remember, a temporary rejection of parental values and expectations is a normal function of the process of identity formation. This is not a personal indictment of you. Your adolescent child might be rejecting your values or your immediate supervisory presence in the home for the moment; he or she is not rejecting you.

The reality is that you are still important to your child, even if he or she won't admit it. While feeling accepted by a peer group is something to be cherished and while rejection by peers is upsetting, your child is still most interested in how you feel about him or her. Considering how fragile the adolescent's self-esteem may be at this time, it is important that you carefully measure your words to him or her. You may inadvertently contribute to self-doubts if you are excessively critical or judge the external features of the child too harshly. If you get stuck in not accepting your child's hairstyle, clothes, or music, you may be building barriers. At this time of life your child needs bridges, not barriers.

You don't have to fall on your face over your child's latest favorite musical performer or screen idol and you don't have to like the way he or she is dressing (provided it meets with your moral standards), but it is important that your teenager feel accepted by you. Certainly, it is wise for you to reinforce and focus emphasis on behaviors and characteristics of your child which you consider positive. But don't overdo it or you might be orchestrating the next area of rebellion. Just mentioning how much you agree with an adolescent's choice of rock group XYZ might be the kiss of death for it. At the same time, haranguing your son or daughter about how awful his or her choice of a friend is can be enough to give that friend the imprimatur of your disapproval. This was the case with Ruth.

It was so important to me that Meagan know right from wrong and develop high moral standards, especially as far as men are concerned. And I know I pressured her too much then. I got so that I would get hysterical if her room wasn't cleaned. I would lose it over just about everything. I told her she was hanging around with the wrong crowd, but all we would do was fight. Then she got pregnant and my dream that she could have had a better life was shattered.

Teenagers tend to serve as emotional barometers for their families. They do this in two ways. The first is in their well-known propensity for rebelling. You say white and they say black. You tell your son no and he argues yes. This is a natural part of adolescents' attempts to find themselves. In this case, although the atmosphere seems stormy, the barometer is reading normal. Some ACOA parents tend to take their children's argumentativeness personally. Some feel they have probably failed as parents. If this is the case with you, try to let yourself see your child's actions as the natural events they are. Your child is in the process of trying on new roles and ways of seeing him- or herself, and will sometimes contrast him- or herself with you. Without conscious awareness teenagers know that the only way they can really see themselves is to see themselves as separate from their parents.

The second way teenagers serve as emotional barometers is by pointing out areas of imbalance in the family. Although they may not mean them to, their actions may also serve the function of red herrings. It's as if they were to say to you and the community, "Something is wrong in my family and nobody wants to admit it." This may take the form of provocative dressing or sexual acting-out in response to parents' prudish "Victorian" expectations; inexplicable failing grades in high school subjects despite high aptitude test scores, in the face of a father's exclusive focus on good grades as opposed to getting to know the child; or repeated transgressions of home or school rules of conduct in response to poor communication and marital conflicts. In each case, you as parent must put aside your feelings of having failed and instead address the problem. If you find situations like these occurring in your family, seek the help of a family therapist or a mental health professional skilled in family therapy. Oftentimes when the family as a system is helped to change, the problems of the teenager will take care of themselves.

Alcohol, Drugs, and Adolescents

It is a sobering fact that many teenagers are exposed to and use mood-altering chemicals on a regular basis. You may be surprised to learn that alcohol is the primary drug of choice. Health professionals classify alcohol as a drug because it is a powerful central nervous system depressant and its use, along with that of marijuana and cocaine and its derivative crack, represents a major danger for young people. This is not to say that PCP, barbiturates, amphetamines, and even LSD don't pose a problem. They do, but they aren't as frequently used and they aren't generally as available as alcohol, marijuana, and cocaine. Surveys have repeatedly demonstrated that the vast majority of high school students have tried alcohol or other drugs at least once and that well over half use alcohol on a regular basis. If that isn't bad enough, about a third of all teenagers questioned report having been a passenger in a car with a peer who was drunk while at the wheel. Alcohol is the most popular of all drugs, and, like it or not, you must address the use of it and other substances with your child.

Teenagers take drugs and consume alcohol for a variety of reasons. Alcohol is legal and very available. In some states it can be purchased in the local convenience store by anyone who shows proper identification. Alcohol—particularly beer—is seen by many as one of the rites of passage into adulthood. Many a teen has paid the dizzying price for having been "drinking like a man." The modeling of adult activities like drinking may also be an attempt to win acceptance by a teenager's peer group. Considering how desperate teens often feel in wanting to fit in with the most popular cliques, we can well understand how alluring the use of alcohol and drugs may be. But consider also that the teenagers who are the most susceptible to using and abusing mood-altering chemicals are those who do not like themselves.

Alcohol and Self-Esteem

All adolescents confront the issue of self-esteem. The dramatic increase in the time spent in front of the mirror is an indication of concern about how your adolescent will be seen by others. Some young people with particularly low self-esteem discover the use of alcohol and drugs as a means to cover up these feelings of self-doubt, loneliness, and inadequacy. This inevitably proves to be an ineffective coping mechanism because when the high wears off, the feelings of personal dissatisfaction return with a vengeance. Worse, there is a "rebound," a more intense feeling of personal dissatisfaction because the adolescent has so severely medicated his or her nervous system with a depressant that the low overcompensates for the drug-induced high. In addition, the child may feel guilty for having used the drug in the first place, thus leading to further upset and self-hatred. If the alcohol or drugs are generally or easily available, a depressed state of mind may then justify repeated use of the chemical substances. Because of the possible development of a physical and/or psychological dependency, this can progress into a serious problem within a relatively short period of time.

Is your child prone to this type of depression? Have you discovered that your adolescent has been drinking regularly or using drugs? Have you thought about taking preventive measures? Do you even know what to look for? If you're an ACOA, are you even able to face the problem of alcohol or drugs in your own family? Have you come to terms with the fact that you may be predisposed to alcoholism? These might be some of the most important questions you will ever face with your adolescent children.

Prevention

If only you could prevent the cycle of drug and alcohol abuse from resurfacing in the next generation. By now, I am sure, you are aware of the increased risk of your children's becoming substance abusers because of the presence of alcoholism in your family. Perhaps you abstain or are a controlled drinker, but because you are an ACOA your children may possess a genetic predisposition to manifest the disease. The reality is that you can't absolutely prevent this from happening. Your child has a mind and a body and will make his or her own choices, but you can set the stage so that he or she may make appropriate and informed decisions. The first thing for you to do is to examine your own behavior and attitudes in regard to the use of alcohol and drugs. Your child by now has learned from both you and your spouse what you have to say about alcohol and how the two of you have used it. If you can clearly see your values and pattern of alcohol use, you are in a good position to discuss the subject honestly and openly with your child. Some ACOAs are so rigidly opposed to alcohol use that they inadvertently set up a power struggle whenever the child uses alcohol and drugs as a means of rebellion.

You may discuss alcohol and drug use with your child within the context of a planned meeting or family discussion, or as an impromptu series of questions, answers, and opinion sharing as a result of what your child saw some friends do at a party. The ad hoc discussion may also arise as a result of a news broadcast of drug-related stories in your community or in the neighboring high school. No matter what form your exchange takes, it is important that you encourage this kind of frank and honest, no-recriminations discussion. Note, however, that it won't work unless the honesty is mutual. Teenagers have minds of their own and seek your opinions and input, not a lecture. They want to know about you. Chances are if you share your feelings, they will also. This kind of self-disclosure is reciprocal.

It is important that in your discussions you convey your interest in how your child sees him- or herself and the world. Alcohol and drugs are just one of a cluster of issues he or she is facing. Remember, adolescents are working hard to establish their own identities and so are struggling to find meaning to their lives, to feel accepted and a part of a valued group of peers, and to come to know and like who they are. Without intruding, discuss these problems which characterize adolescence. Be sure to let your child know that longing and self-doubts are quite normal and that you value him or her. Affirm the specific attributes and talents that are unique to your child. However, don't patronize your child because, like any adolescent, he or she will recognize being manipulated. If your child senses that you are honest, his or her barriers will drop very quickly.

One of the first things you must discuss with your children is your family's history of alcohol abuse. You owe it to yourself and to your child to be honest in detailing the history. Now, unlike when you were dealing with your eight- or nine-year-old child, you can be frank about difficulties you experienced in your alcoholic family. Don't deliberately scare your child, but don't gloss over the pain you felt, because your child will understand much better where your fears are originating from. Adolescents need to understand the potential dangers they face, and it is imperative that any secrets not previously shared be told now. Your child needs to appreciate the possible genetic predisposition to abuse alcohol so that he or she can look out for it. Your child will ultimately appreciate your honesty and your decision to entrust him or her with this information.

Be fully prepared to answer your child's questions and also to offer information for the questions not asked. You don't need to be an expert on alcohol and drugs, but it would be helpful to have some basic knowledge. Remember, it is likely that your child knows only what he or she has picked up from friends, and most of that information will be incorrect. Take the initiative to obtain the correct information from your local Council on Alcoholism, community mental health center, library, or bookstore. If you don't know an answer to a question, tell your child you don't know and try to find out the answer together. It can also be a starting point for future discussions, insuring an ongoing process of communication. One or two *lectures* will not adequately address the issue. Be aware that you are sharing information with your child about a common *medical* problem that the two of you may have. You carry the genetic predisposition and so may your child. Each of you should help the other understand this problem and live with it.

These are some of the questions you should explore with your child. If he or she doesn't ask them, you should raise them in your discussion.

- What will I do if all my friends drink or take drugs?
- How can I fit in if I don't drink?
- What if everyone I go to a party with gets high?
- What if my girl- or boyfriend wants me to drink or gives me a joint or asks me to snort a line of cocaine?
- What if I am curious about what it feels like?

• How come my grandparent drank so much when you were young?
• Did you drink a lot? Did you take drugs? What kept you from becoming an alcoholic, too?
• Can you still become an alcoholic?
• Will you be like my alcoholic grandparent?
• Will I be like my alcoholic grandparent?

Try not to fall into the role of expert. You will be most effective if you foster an atmosphere of mutual discussion and sharing of feelings. If you push what's right or wrong your child may feel you're trying to control him or her and will consequently stop sharing with you.

In addition to the use of discussions and written materials, some parents act out real-life scenarios with their children in which the child is faced with a decision whether or not to use alcohol or drugs. This helps the teenager to anticipate difficult situations and practice coming up with effective and safe solutions. Some parents and teenagers also come to an agreement on how certain situations will be handled. The well-known use of the contract not to drive after drinking is one example. In this case the teen knows that it is OK to call parents without fear of reprisal. If you and other parents get together, you can rotate shifts on weekends so that no one family has the burden of chauffering the whole group of adolescents. This also allows you to share information passively so as not to make your kids paranoid. Unlike the way Joan and Don were handling their son's drinking—they avoided the obvious—the contract can be used as a way to insure the child's safety and identify a budding alcohol problem that is calling out to be addressed. Remember, your child may not intend to drink or use drugs at a party, but the terrible weight of peer pressure and the exposure to embarrassment and social censure if he or she does "just say no" might be enough to overpower any normal person's resolve.

Limit Setting

As much as adolescence is a time when children will challenge many rules and regulations, it is also a time for artful application of rules. They are so busy questioning why things are the way they are that the world often seems topsy-turvy and out of control. The last thing adolescents need from you is inconsistency. They need to count on your love, acceptance, and enforcement of limits. This is called limit setting. Of course, they won't admit that they need it; they don't have to. When teenagers were younger they found comfort and security in your gentle and consistent enforcement of boundaries. As they get older, they push against those boundaries in order to test them, themselves, and you. And although it is their job as teenagers to find their identities by pushing against parental boundaries, they will again experience a sense of security when they find the guidelines as firmly in place as they were once before.

Your child, however, is no longer merely a child. As an adolescent, he or she will fluctuate between acting like a child and an adult, with a gradual and often subtle increase in adultlike behavior. Therefore, you must be prepared to enforce the rules while remaining flexible enough to consider reworking the boundaries. It is imperative, however, that you enforce the rules until they are changed.

There is a need for limit setting and rule enforcement for all sorts of activities: bedtimes, curfews, age at which the child is allowed to date, study times, performance of chores around the house, acceptable clothes to wear to school or church, drunk-driving contracts, and the following through on all sorts of activities. There is no set system of rules that fits every family's needs and values, but whatever your rules are, they must be clearly understood by the child as a set of expectations. Ideally, this will be achieved before the rules are initially enforced. This way, there will be no surprises for the child, and he or she can anticipate the consequences of decisions to behave in certain ways. Thus, make your rules clear and explain them fully to cover all possible contingencies. Make sure your child knows them in advance. Thus, because your child knows what is acceptable and unacceptable behavior, any tendency for the child to be unfairly singled out and persecuted by you is to a large degree minimized. As a result of your consistent application of the rules, the adolescent is able to develop a sense of responsibility and mastery over his or her own fate.

Some parents find it helpful to develop along with their child a set of consequences. This mutual negotiation will help create a sense of fair play. Consequences might range from loss of phone or TV privileges to being grounded for certain lengths of time. As before, the consequences should be appropriate to the infraction. If too great a penalty is imposed, you may inadvertently foster a pattern of rebellion that will spring from your child's sense of powerlessness. Be fair, but be consistent.

As we know, parents who are ACOAs often swing from a tendency to either come down too hard or avoid the issue by looking the other way. In Bill's situation, he looked the other way until it was too late.

The night she came home drunk from a party and got sick in the kitchen was when I finally woke up. My wife and I both had to own up to the fact that we had been ignoring the possibility that she was drinking. I think we wanted to avoid considering the possibility that my father's alcoholism had been reborn in this generation. The levels of scotch and whiskey in the bottles we kept only for special party occasions had been consistently down. The bottle of special 101 proof bourbon that we had in the cabinet was almost empty. My wife and I looked at the bottles, looked at one another, and made an unspoken decision to deny what it might mean.

Although you might feel that you are a failure as a parent for having perpetuated a bad seed, you needn't ignore a potential problem that calls for your attention. Only by being as clear as you can about your own self-esteem and issues relating to the family you grew up in can you find that balance point between being hypervigilant and overreacting to your teenage child and letting things pass without enforcing limits. It's not easy, but that is your job as parent. You may consider joining a parents' support group. Many have found this to be helpful.

Sex: Physical Maturity and Social Responsibility

Perhaps the most important and difficult area to enforce limits in is the area of sexuality. Teenagers are now on their own a good deal of the time, and you cannot rely on your constant presence as a deterrent to behavior that you disapprove of. Your sons and daughters are sexual creatures just like you and will have as many opportunities to make decisions about sex as they will about the use of alcohol or drugs. As with the latter, you need to encourage open communication, trust your instincts and observations, and realize that ultimately it is your child who will, through his or her behavior, make the final decision.

The line of demarcation between childhood and adolescence is the rapid psychological development and glandular changes that take place. These changes will begin at about age ten in girls and twelve in boys. It is wise to provide information about physical maturation to your children in the form of written materials and in conversations with you well before the onset of puberty. As to the exact level of maturity and readiness to discuss such matters with each child, you must use your own judgment. Chances are they are more ready than you think, so don't wait too long.

It is quite normal at this time for children to be infatuated with movie stars, rock stars, celebrities, even their teachers, and in general very curious about the opposite sex. It is also possible for some healthy and well-adjusted children to be drawn to same-sex peers. The advent of homosexuality is beyond the scope of this discussion; however, it is important to recognize its possibility as a function of some children's healthy development. Most children, however, will be fascinated and almost obsessed with the opposite sex. What will begin in early adolescence as shy interest will normally progress to active risk taking later on.

If you feel awkward about the idea of talking to your children about sex, you are not alone. This is not a function of being an ACOA. However, how you talk to them or approach them on the issues of sex may be directly related to your ACOA background. For example, an ACOA's mother who experienced poor impulse control as a teenager as a reaction to her dysfunctional family might be inclined to frighten her daughter with tales of the "woman's curse" and that "boys only want one thing." Certainly, a girl needs to be informed about menstruation before her first period and about romance and pregnancy, but she needs to be told in a way that will minimize her apprehension and reinforce her positive self-image. She isn't cursed any more than you were as a child, and she isn't about to rush out to get pregnant if she understands what her body processes are. It is your job as her mother to explain these things. It is usually best if fathers talk with their sons and mothers with their daughters in matters of sex and bodily maturation. But in both cases you should leave room for the other parent to talk with the child as well and to answer questions your child may have.

Young teenagers want to know about sex, but in addition they want to feel that their own physiological development is normal and that they seem attractive to the opposite sex. It is important that you discuss how pregnancies happen as well as the potential dangers of promiscuity. Undue emphasis should not be placed on these matters. It is usually most helpful if they are merely included along with other issues such as dating, romance, relationships, safe sex, and love.

All parents tend to be worried during these years, so reassure yourself that you are experiencing the normal protective and caring instincts of parenthood. Excessive worrying might be an indication that some of your own issues about trust, intimacy, and loss of control are coming to the surface. As an ACOA, you must take note of these feelings and come to terms with them in some of the ways I have indicated previously. Remember, if your child has been relatively well adjusted before the onset of adolescence, he or she will probably carry a sense of morality and values with him or her. When your teenagers begin to date, you can then let them know you trust their common sense.

The responsibilities that accompany this aspect of adolescence should be handled as an extension of general limit setting. Relevant issues and parental expectations may include adherence to a time to be home from dates and some form of itinerary: "Who are you going out with? Where are you going? Who else is going with you? How are you getting there and who's driving?" Is this the third degree? You might have thought so when you were a teenager, but now the shoe is on the other foot. You recognize now that you have a legitimate need to know. You should also recognize that the answers to these questions are not confessions to be extracted by a Grand Inquisitor if you and your child have already established a rapport of trust and respect. It is also entirely appropriate for you to make sure a parent is present at teen parties whether your child is hosting it or is a guest. You should make clear the consequences for not adhering to these expectations. However, try not to come down like the gestapo, because you are almost sure to incite a sense of rebellion.

Looking at Adolescence in Perspective

Adolescence is a period of storm and tempest whose severity depends more on the child than upon how you react to it. Of course, you can make things easier or more difficult for your child and the rest of the family, but the actual severity of your adolescent's emotional swings will find its own level. This is a time of tremendous emotional and physical growth, which takes place at the same time the adolescent's horizons are rapidly expanding. For at least three to five years during his or her teens, your child will behave as if in a pressure cooker. These years are full of excitement and strife, but they are temporary, and you should look ahead to the clearing after the storm.

It is easy for the adolescent to get lost in a world of conflicting emotions, perceived responsibilities, and very real demands. This is where you come in. You can be the reference point, the voice in the darkness that helps your child work out the mysteries that surround him or her. You've been there before and know some of the territory. If you can remember how you felt and the problems you experienced—especially as an adolescent child of an alcoholic in a dysfunctional family—you can be a great resource for your child, helping him or her to find a safe passage through.

In your children's searches for self-identity, they may experiment with roles, sex, alcohol, chemical substances, and narcotics. They will undoubtedly make mistakes, even if it is only the smoking of an occasional marijuana joint. Your job is to attempt to foster an atmosphere in which any potential harm will be minimized. This does not mean never letting your kids out of the house; rather, it means doing your best to keep the lines of communication open. There are several ways this is best done.

1. Convey to your children an accepting interest in their opinions, feelings, and ideas, even if those ideas seem strange to you or downright off the wall.

2. Patiently and with great understanding accept your children's need to rebel and to be different from you in their searches for identity. Remember what you went through when you called your parents "fossils" and taunted them by playing the latest rock and roll groups at top volume on your stereo. Your kids will do the same now with "MTV" or the late night video show. You wore long hair; they may wear blue-tipped and spiked hair.

3. Respond to your teenagers' direct and sometimes subtle requests for information and your attention with an honest and nonjudgmental sharing of your feelings. This can be serious because when you rebelled as a teenager, experimented with drugs or alcohol, and engaged in premarital sex, there wasn't AIDS. Your love-ins or be-ins might have put you at risk for an arrest for trespass, lewd behavior in public, or disturbing the peace, but they didn't put you at risk for an incurable, terminal disease. AIDS has made this a different world for today's adolescent, who needs only to engage in sex to be at risk. With the odds so high, your child needs you to tell the truth about safe sex and about alcohol and drug abuse. There is too much misinformation floating around to allow your child to find out for himself or herself. The same is true for you. If you don't know about AIDS, how it is transmitted and how it can be prevented, find out about it for your kids as well as for yourself.

4. Consistently adher to clearly established rules and limits with the imposition of fair consequences in the event of any violations. Part of your child's misconceptions about the world may stem from your inconsistent behavior with regard to rules. If you can teach your adolescent the meaning and consequences of quid pro

quo, you will teaching a very valuable lesson about life. Your child will watch news broadcasts in which a person charged with a felony is allowed to walk out of court with a slap on the wrist. Your child may then walk into a local convenience store and shoplift a carton of cigarettes or a six-pack of beer. Before your child even realizes what is happening, he or she is sitting handcuffed in the back of a police car, having confessed to a crime, and staring at, at worst, a sentence in a juvenile detention center or at best a humiliating experience in the juvenile court system.

But even as a purely mundane experience, teaching your child that limits and consequences for actions have significance will help him or her to establish social relationships and achieve success in school. This can and should be a positive lesson and not a series of threats.

5. Offer your time and intensity not only in response to your children's calls for attention, but also by attending their performances and sporting events, their projects and special events, and by helping out with activities that they want to be involved in. You should stay in touch with your adolescent children's teachers and guidance counselors, their pastors or youth leaders at the local church or synagogue, and people in the community with whom they come in contact. If your son or daughter is on an athletic team, stay in contact with the coach or faculty advisor. Let your children's teachers, coaches, youth leaders, project organizers, and even their employers know that you are available to talk about your children's work and performance at any time. You're not being a spy; you're being a concerned, *communicating* parent.

As an ACOA who is a parent of an adolescent teenager, you must maintain an awareness of the healthy separation between you and your child. There tend to be no mild disappointments for teenagers. They may feel it is the end of the world because that special boy or girl didn't take notice of them in the hallway at school or say hello. Given the tendency of ACOAs to overreact to events, it is imperative that you separate your emotional baggage from your children's. Your child is going to experience crises and overreact, and needs you to *not* join in this panic. The more you are able to distinguish between your identity questions and self-esteem issues and those of your chidren, the stronger the position you are in to respond positively to their needs and problems.

Perhaps most difficult of all are the beginnings of role reversal that take place when adolescent children act out the personalities of their parents or other role models. You may find yourself arguing with your child's teacher or a role model at school instead of with your child. If that personality condemns something you said or did—adolescents *always* disagree with their parents—your ACOA trip-wire may trigger and your reactions may be way out of proportion to what is being discussed. Since you feel ostracized or even condemned by those people outside the family, hearing through your child the voice of a teacher criticizing something you said or did may be especially painful. Try to look beyond your own background when this happens and deal only with what is on the table. Remember, your child's teacher, guidance counselor, coach, or employer doesn't have a list of all the ACOA parents in the school taped to a bulletin board. No one but you knows your innermost secrets, so there is no conspiracy in the outside world to turn your adolescent children against you because of your past.

Your children's personalities are changing from month to month based on the flow of hormones, outside experiences, or events in the home that may escape your attention. Your background as an ACOA only complicates these events. You, unlike non-ACOA parents, tend not to forgive yourself for past mistakes. Thus, you carry additional burdens into every confrontation or discussion with your children. Try to lay these aside for the majority of the mundane arguments you will have. It does not challenge your very existence to be told that you made a mistake by not showing up on time for a parent/teacher conference. Most non-ACOA parents— perhaps much to your frustration—would simply shrug it off, apologize for inconveniencing anyone, and get on with the conference. You might go home and actually get sick over being exposed as a fraudulent person to the entire school community. You almost certainly *will* overreact. Just try to correct those overreactions by telling yourself that you're not a bad person. In fact, my advice to my clients is to have something of a mantra to keep repeating to yourself when the stresses of dealing with your children build up. Even "I'm OK" is enough to keep you on an even keel in any argument. Just say that to yourself every time you feel challenged or confronted on a gut level, knowing all along that what you sense as gut level is really a casual surface level for your adolescent child.

Forgive yourself for any past mistakes and try to move on. Don't keep chewing on what you perceive as your personality faults and misdeeds. If you feel that you keep getting emotionally hooked and disarmed by your child, consider entering some form of short-term counseling with a mental health professional who is familiar with ACOA issues and, ideally, family therapy techniques as well. Or, if you feel that you can get through it by yourself, just talk to a friend. However, don't minimize potentially serious situations involving your child's possible use of drugs or alcohol, because these can be life-threatening. If you find that your child is constantly overstepping boundaries and displaying the signs of alcohol or drug abuse, don't try to go it alone when you already have so much emotional baggage in that area. Seek out the assistance of:

- Your child's guidance counselor at school.
- The school district psychologist, if there is one, for direct intervention or a referral.
- A mental health professional and family therapist.
- A nonprejudicial and nonjudgmental consultation with the employee assistance counselor at your place of work.
- A frank discussion with your doctor or your child's doctor.
- A confidential telephone conversation with one of the state or local agencies or hotlines listed in the Appendix.
- A consultation with your minister or rabbi or your children's youth pastor. It may be uncomfortable for you and your child to examine family problems in a religious context, but sometimes members of the clergy have a direct approach to problem solving that is particularly

helpful and refreshing. Avail yourself of their offices if you have the opportunity.
- A social worker or juvenile officer at your local police department.

I include the last with some trepidation because your children may feel that you're literally blowing the whistle on them and calling the cops. That's not true. Most local police departments have juvenile officers who seek preventive measures for dealing with illegal substances and alcohol-related behavioral problems. Your local police department is already actively involved in helping your school's antidrug program. You can avail yourself of their sevices as well.

If you still have questions or unresolved doubts, you can confer with a hotline counselor in complete privacy without compromising your own or your children's identities. Be optimistic. Your children's problems will eventually work themselves out, and you will be able to look back on this period as fruitful instead of painful.

Young Adults
Ages 19 to 28

CLARA

I am an adult child of an alcoholic and I know I have enough of the common characteristics. That's why I finally entered therapy and started with the support group. I want to do very well and it's hard for me to feel satisfied with my efforts. I seem to seek out the approval and recognition of other people, but when I get it, the good feeling that comes quickly slips away. I never seem to feel good enough. On the other hand, I did survive growing up with my alcoholic father. I'm proud of the fact that I'm a survivor. My patience helped me to make it out of my family and it has also helped me to deal with my own alcoholic husband. Unfortunately, I have realized that I've used my patience to enable my husband to continue to drink. It's as if I've told him, "Go ahead and drink, I don't really want a mate with whom I can share and discuss my life." And for thirty-one years he did just that; sat in that sunken spot in the middle of the couch watching TV.

I'm afraid for the damage that growing up in this atmosphere has done to Bob, my son. I feel guilty for not doing something sooner. We were both surprised when I demanded last year that his father stop drinking. Bob, Sr., went to treatment and no longer drinks. Unfortunately, he doesn't go to A.A. and he still sits in the middle of the couch having nothing to say. The only thing that's different now is that the beer can is gone. I'm relieved that Bob has decided to go for counseling. I am sure it will help him get his marriage started on the right foot. But now I'm afraid about me.

Bob's moving out when he gets married and finally it will be just me and my husband. I was hoping it would never come to this. I feel ashamed to say that I at times wish he hadn't stopped drinking. Maybe then he would have just died and I wouldn't have to deal with him. But he's alive and still sitting on the couch. I am very nervous about confronting him and it looks like it's going to come down to that. I dread it.

JON

I know my mom loves me. Sometimes it feels like she loves me too much. I am planning on leaving community college in the fall and entering a four-year school. She agrees that it is a good idea, but she only wants me to go to school nearby. She doesn't admit it, but I think she wants me as close as possible . . . and I want to get out before I suffocate.

It's crazy. I feel like I want her approval and she wants mine at the same time . . . and when I don't give it she gets all hurt. Who is the kid here anyway? I know I am insecure and get down on myself too easily, but I wish my mom would work on her problems. We're both ACOAs. My father left when I was real young and hers was crazy throughout her growing up. My stepfather makes me crazy now. Nothing I can do ever seems to please him and he spends so much time trying to control me and her. He's so busy trying to be in charge of me that he never notices the good things I do: I run track, get good grades in college, I'm always studying, and I don't do drugs or alcohol like lots of other kids do.

In a way—it's nothing personal to them—but I want to live on my own away at college. I want to learn to rely on myself. I want to try and see if I can be in charge of my own life, but mom doesn't want me to go. Oh, she says she does, but she's always making excuses why I should go to school nearby. First it was that my grandfather was dying and now it's that they don't have enough money. I've checked into it and the school I want to go to (a couple of states away) costs no more than the one nearby. I know I am a little afraid about going away to school, but I just can't figure out what she's afraid of.

The scenarios related by Clara and Jon are but two of the many that occur in families as teenagers continue into young adulthood. While it is true that each stage of development in your child's life is unique unto itself, the movement into young adulthood holds special importance. This is a time when your child's growth unquestionably alters the family as a system. Granted that the family has been changing throughout your child's life, but now the change is particularly dramatic. A long-standing member of the family is no longer living at home, no longer a child. The young adult is moving on and out.

Clara is concerned about what will be left in the empty nest after her once little bird has flown. She recognizes she has a life to live, but is disconcerted about spending it with her "dry drunk" husband. Jon tells not only of his personal doubts about moving on, but also of the pull he feels from his mother. She seems to experience some conflict between her wish for her son to grow up by going to college and her feelings of loss at the prospect of losing him.

This time in the life of a family has both its blessings and its sorrows. Non-ACOA families do not experience this transition without some conflict and growing pains. For the parent who is an ACOA, however, we would expect an increased number of potential emotional pitfalls. On the plus side, the resilience adult children of alcoholics often develop by virtue of surviving their own childhoods will help them make it through this period of transition. The dilemma comes when their feelings of loss and abandonment, low self-esteem, and/or difficulties with emotional separation come into play. These are old and familiar feelings for most ACOAs. Now, however, they are mixed with hope for their newly independent children and optimism for their future. The balancing of these feelings can be difficult for some ACOAs, especially when issues between the spouses remain unresolved after years of marriage. The reality is that two critical developmental stages are occurring at the same time. The young adult child is charged with having to develop a sense of intimacy and commitment to another person outside the immediate family, while parents are charged with creating a life that is both meaningful and personally satisfying without children while being available to provide guidance if requested by those same young-adult children. With the successful resolution of this stage parents are able to develop a sense of integrity such that they may recognize the failures and successes of their life with a feeling of self-acceptance.

Intimacy Versus Isolation

The developmental period between the ages of about nineteen and twenty-eight has been identified by Erik Erikson as the stage of intimacy versus isolation. It is during this period your child will either learn to form close relationships or come to feel alienated from others and alone.

If your child is in this age group, chances are he or she is very much on the move. Young adult activities are varied and may include involvement in trade, college, or graduate school, participation with friends and colleagues in various social or political activities, entering the military, direct involvement in the world of work, and commitment to a partner. A common denominator among these activities is that they take place outside of the home. And the activity of greatest emotional significance at this stage is commitment to a partner.

As we have discussed already, a child's success in any given stage of development is a function of how well he or she has resolved the crises of the preceding stages. This is of course especially true as your child enters young adulthood and attempts to make healthy connections with others and perhaps commit to a lifelong mate, for in order to make commitments to others, your child must have a reasonably solid sense of self. The young adult who knows who he or she is, is likely to be able to love and care for others.

On the other hand, if your child has yet to develop a firm sense of identity, he or she risks developing unhealthy relationships as a consequence of a growing sense of inadequacy. This is oftentimes how the cycle of addiction perpetuates itself. A child of a dysfunctional alcoholic family is deprived of the emotional nourishment that would enable him or her to trust others, to develop a sense of autonomy, to act on his or her own behalf, and thus to develop a clear and satisfied sense of identity. It then becomes very difficult for the young adult to feel connected with other people, especially those who are emotionally healthy. If low self-esteem is not adequately addressed, this person is likely to be attracted to another "hurt" individual. In this case pain seeks out pain and emotionally similar people will attract one another. By now we are all too familiar with the pattern of young ACOAs marrying alcoholics or drug abusers or becoming such themselves. This is the case with twenty-year-old Donna.

Bobby and I both come from really sick families. I did not even know how bad mine really was until I started to go for counseling. My mother finally divorced my father after years of him being emotionally abusive to all of us. He's still drinking and then she married a man who's just as bad, except that he doesn't drink. And Bobby's family is even worse: lots of drinking, arguments, violence, and real head games. If someone from his family tells you something, you can't tell if they're telling the truth.

So Bobby and I fight a lot. We're both real jealous of each other, even though we don't have any reason to be . . . we're faithful to each other. But we fight and say horrible things . . . and I don't say half of what I want because he gets hurt so easily. I wish he'd go to counseling, but when I ask him about it he says I make too big a deal about the past . . . and meanwhile he goes out of the house (we live together), screaming and slamming the back door. My friends say he's too immature and that I can do better, but I just can't leave him.

Donna is caught in the middle. More and more she is coming to have an increased understanding of her place in her family's dynamic, but she's not yet to the point where she can foster a healthy relationship and demand that Bobby reciprocate. Fortunately, she has chosen to work on herself in counseling. Hopefully she will learn to feel better about herself and in the process develop a clearer sense of identity. Her ability to choose a healthy partner and commit herself to a fulfilling relationship is then likely to follow.

Erikson points out that real intimacy is possible only after a reasonable sense of identity has been developed. Whether the intimacy is with a member of the opposite sex, any other person, or even with oneself, a sense of self-understanding and self-acceptance is first required. In Donna's case we see her being drawn to unhealthy relationships. The second negative consequence is the fostering of distance between oneself and others. While this may conjure up the image of a loner, this is often the case in relationships where two apparently dissatisfied partners have no intention of remedying the situation either by getting help or by dissolving the relationship. The following comments of a client of mine serve as a case in point.

My parents can't stand each other. They do everything out of a sense of obligation or guilt. Nothing is genuine. They're forever complaining about each other and they don't change. I don't think they want to change. It amazes me that they stay together . . . they have absolutely nothing in common.

Oh, quite the contrary, they in fact have a great deal in common. His parents are distancers. While they may not feel fulfilled with themselves or their marriage, they do derive a necessary sense of security in knowing that the other is there. It is sad to hear of this kind of lonely relationship, but the fact is, these partners feel safe. Though each partner doesn't want the other to really go away, he or she certainly doesn't want the other to come any closer. Without a solid sense of identity some partners create distance in order not to "lose" themselves in the other. Nevertheless, a certain emptiness and loneliness result.

I hope that the discussion of these potential pitfalls does not cause upset or despair. There is a good chance that because you have been mindful of providing a healthy environment for your child, he or she has entered young adulthood with an adequate sense of self. Most young adults have been actively searching for themselves throughout the adolescent years and have sometimes almost driven you crazy with their insistence on having an identity separate from yours. Your healthy child is no longer a child. He or she is an adult ready for intimacy. Your child has developed both the capacity to commit to partnerships and the ethical strength to honor such commitments. He or she also has enough sense of self to be able to make sacrifices and even compromises. This young adult is indeed ready to move on, out of the house and into a meaningful relationship.

Letting Go

This time of life, when your child is exiting the family and entering young adulthood, is a period of major transition. The type and degree of involvement you had with your child in the past will never again be quite the same. Your child's need for your involvement has actually been slowly changing and decreasing since he or she entered adolescence. But at about the age of seventeen to nineteen a new era is ushered in. Once your child enters young adulthood you will experience a dramatic shift in involvement—from being a very active participant in your child's life to being much more of a passive, though interested and concerned, observer.

When your child was very young he or she most likely went through a period of following you around the house telling you about all the exciting and interesting things that happened at school. Sometimes it may have felt like too much for you, but you listened. Most of the time you probably truly enjoyed your child's wanting you to know all about his or her world. Most parents still want to hear about the wonderful things their young adult children are doing. They still want some involvement. Yet more often than not they find that their children are too busy to tell them the details. "Not now, I gotta go out"; "Can I borrow the car?" and, "Tom and I are going to the beach for the weekend, see ya later," are some of the usual phrases parents hear. "Don't forget you have a family"; "I'm surprised you remember where you live"; and, "Do I have to make an appointment to see you?" are among the statements parents are likely to utter. This is normal. This is the way of family life in America.

In this scenario parents wish for their adult children to come back and report their happiness and successes. Non-ACOA parents do in fact experience some frustration when they find their children are always on the move and are too busy to include them. There is a general rule of thumb that I think may be helpful for you to keep in mind. I have come to see the following axiom validated time and time again in my psychotherapy practice: If children get what they need from their family, they move on; if they don't, they keep on coming back, either psychologically or physically. It seems to hold true that children who receive appropriate amounts of emotional support tend to develop into healthy adults, no longer dependent on their parents. On the other hand, children of dysfunctional families who have not developed a sense of themselves as fully functioning adults tend to continue to seek what as children they never received.

If your children have received the necessary love and affirmation while growing up, chances are they will be out there involved in the world, rather than needfully continuing to seek your approval. Try to allow this healthy separation to serve as an indication that you have been successful as a parent. It gives you all the more reason to feel good about yourself, considering that as an adult child of an alcoholic, you probably missed getting a full complement of healthy parenting yourself.

It is important for all parents but especially you as an ACOA to be mindful of the emotional conflicts both you and your older child may be experiencing. This awareness may help to forestall some of the potential pratfalls of this life stage. ACOAs may be inclined to experience the independence of their child as a personal defeat. You may feel no longer loved, valued, or appreciated. Again, it is important to remember that you don't have to be an ACOA in order to have these feelings. Many parents do. However, it is important what you do with these feelings. You must remember that your child's moving on and your emotional reaction to it are part of the normal processes of growing up. Your job as parent is both to encourage your child's self-reliance and to begin to create more of a life of your own. Do take note, however, that if you find yourself wallowing in feelings of worthlessness, you should seek professional help. You'll need someone to help you understand what is going on inside you and remedy the depression that is likely to follow.

When Your Child Needs You

Life, however, is not always a bed of roses, for you or your child, so there is a fair chance that at some point he or she will be back for help. Yes, your young adult child who went charging out of your house and your immediate world may be heaped upon your doorstep a figurative, and sometimes even literal, smoking wreck. Your son or daughter is experiencing a crisis and now calls on you for help. The reasons for it could test the expanse of your imagination: problems with drug or alcohol abuse, trouble with the law, disciplinary action taken in college for either academic or behavior problems, pregnancy, or dire need of money, just to name a few. At this point there are two don'ts to keep in mind: (1) don't blame yourself; (2) don't enable your child.

The all too common reaction among both ACOAs and other concerned parents is to quickly panic and blame themselves. You might find yourself having an inner dialogue along these lines: "There it is. I've finally had my worst fear confirmed. My child is messed up and I am to blame. If I wasn't such a failure as a person, this wouldn't have happened. I never should have tried to raise a kid. I've passed the bad seed on."

If you are feeling this way, take note of it and do your job as parent. With your child's return, it's readily apparent that your parenting skills are required. I want to encourage you, in the face of feeling like a failure, to deal with your now adult child in such a way as to help in solving his or her problem. There is also no need for: "I told you so"; "You thought you were so high and mighty," or other backward-looking judgments. If you find that you are either feeling too much resentment or having feelings of failure, try to sort out these emotions on your own; otherwise, they will only get in the way of your effective parenting.

Your child needs to be neither berated nor excessively coddled at this point. Your young adult needs to find a solution to his or her dilemma. It is imperative in the process of helping that you do not enable your child. He or she is a young adult and you can best help by supporting him or her emotionally and sometimes financially as he or she works out the problem. I want to encourage you to make reasonable arrangements for payback should you provide financial help. Don't, however, expect your child to owe you emotionally. Your payback will come from both his or her appreciation of your support and his or her having resumed an independent life. Your feeling of satisfaction as a parent will come from seeing your child solve his or her problem in a responsible manner.

Drugs, Alcohol, and Young Adults

Your baby is no longer a baby and the bottle he or she may be drinking from probably isn't milk. It is my hope that you have discussed the family problem of alcoholism, as I have suggested, on many occasions throughout your child's youth and teenage years. In that discussion you've told your child of the increased risk in your family of becoming an alcoholic or marrying one. Now that the child is a young adult it is important that you still continue this dialogue.

Regardless of whether or not your child seems to be abusing alcohol or other drugs, you must raise the issue. This is especially important in dealing with young adults because their bravado makes them even more susceptible to the denial that accompanies the addiction process. Oftentimes these resilient young people will slough off your concern with statements such as: "I know what I'm doing"; "I'm just having a good time"; "Everybody's doing it"; or, "You worry too much." While they may be right that you as an ACOA worry too much, it is certainly not without reason.

Let's presume that you have provided adequate drug and alcohol education as your child grew up. What do you do now if you suspect he or she is acting in a potentially dysfunctional manner? Certainly, you must watch to make sure you don't overreact. If you do, you might set off the pattern of defensiveness and rebellion that characterized the teenage years. At this point you don't want your child to be any more blinded to the issue of his or her substance use or abuse than he or she may already be. The best way to alert young adults to the possible thin ice they may be walking on is *not* to point an accusatory finger, but rather to *indicate* your concern. Statements such as "I am concerned about the amount you've been drinking"; "I worry about your use of pot"; or, "I know you might think I'm overreacting, but I hope you keep in mind that alcoholism runs in this family." If you share your feelings, you will increase the probability that your child will hear you.

There is a chance that your child may continue the cycle of addiction by developing a substance-abuse problem. If this happens, raise your concerns as stated above, but be sure not to enable. Don't bail your child out of jams, whether they're legal, financial, vocational, or personal, without the condition that he or she enter and follow through with appropriate treatment. Your local community mental health center or Council on Alcoholism is available to help determine an adequate course of treatment. Last but certainly not least, begin regular attendance at Alanon. It is my experience that many parents are initially reluctant and uncomfortable with the idea of Al-Anon, but most return to thank me for making the recommendation. Remember:

1. Bring your concern to the attention of your child.
2. Don't enable.
3. Attend Al-Anon.

The Empty Nest: Subtle Messages and Vicarious Living

Sue has entered college; Debbie moved away after she was married; Jim joined the navy; Bob's job seems to keep him always on the road. No matter how they do it, regardless of their age at the time, the primary job of children is to grow up and move on. The primary job of parents is to help their children acquire the skills it will take to make it on their own. In the aftermath of your success you will find that you are now faced with the empty nest.

Let's presume the child who limped back to you with life in emotional, financial, or legal tatters has pulled him- or herself back together. Chances are he or she is back on course, in pursuit of some of the dreams and hopes that fill young adulthood. The question now is, What are you now going to do with your life?

When you are a parent, you are constantly sending messages to your child. Some of them are overt and direct statements, while others are much more subtle. However, silent though these signals may be, they are nonetheless powerful. No matter how old your child is, he or she is still tuned in to you. It is therefore incumbent upon you, at this time as ever, to take note of the messages you are sending.

Children, even young adults, continue to learn from their parents. As a parent you are also a role model and as such how *you* come to accept your child's growing up and out will teach your young adult how to adjust later in life. You are a model for how older people deal with changes in life. It is important to keep this in mind, especially during these moments when you might want to say, The hell with it all.

Another phenomenon occasionally associated with the empty nest is a parent's attempt to live vicariously through the child. Perhaps the most dramatic example is stage-mother syndrome. Here we have a woman who has devoted her entire life to cultivating her child's acting career. Barbara hails from a family with a rich acting and entertaining tradition as well as a long intergenerational history of alcoholism. She describes her experience with her mother:

Mom did everything for me. She was always there. I knew at the time there was an unsettling quality . . . just below the surface. When I was sixteen I won an important role on a TV soap. Mom was with me all the way and I did pretty well. It was a part they wanted to grow up with me. But then my mom started getting too intense on the set. She'd get all hyper and began yelling at me and the producers, telling them how they should do their jobs. A while after that I got written out of the script. It took me a little growing up before I realized that my mother had absolutely nothing of her own. She didn't even have a life.

Barbara's mother had worked as a page in the studios years before when she was a teenager. She had a strong desire to carry on the family tradition of going into show business. Becoming an accountant or going into another profession wouldn't be good enough for this family—esteem and recognition were given only to thespians. Unfortunately for her, she didn't have the requisite talent and in addition she was an adult child of an alcoholic father. In subsequent years she had a daughter and began to live out her dreams through Barbara.

One of the problems with vicarious living is that there is very little internal control over feelings. Your moods and feelings of self-esteem may rise and fall in reflection of grades on a report card, touchdowns thrown, number of invitations to the prom, or sales made. If your child succeeds, you are a success and if your child fails, you are a failure. Not only are you allowing your emotional well-being to be controlled by external factors, but the whole scenario is not real. Your child's life is not your life and any significant blurring of the two may negatively affect you both.

Sometimes when the child is successful he or she is made to feel guilty by a less successful parent. This may be the result of a subtle competition the parent carries on with the child. Along with the child's success comes resentment and guilt from the parent. This, too, was part of Barbara's experience.

I was one of the prettiest girls in my high school, and with all the clothes my mother bought me, it was easy to look stylish. I had lots of friends and maintained a high grade-point average. More and more, I realized that I hated my mother. I felt guilty for feeling it, because she always did so much for me, but I did. She always wanted me to do well, but when I did, it felt like it wasn't enough. It was as if she didn't like me for it, although she never said anything directly.

Barbara went on to college and continues to be an academic and social success. At this point she is burdened by the anger she still carries for her mother. In counseling, Barbara is increasingly able and ready to acknowledge her resentment for her mother's having "ruined my career" because of the loss of the soap opera job. It had later been verified through friends of the family that the producers had wanted to keep Barbara but the constant presence of her mother made it not worth the effort.

Needing to Be Needed

Earlier in this chapter I touched upon how it is quite healthy to be supportive of your child should he or she return to you after taking a few of life's blows. It is my hope that by now you recognize your potential as an ACOA parent to feel like a failure because your child is in trouble. It is just as likely that you may feel less than adequate if your adult child is doing well. Sheri speaks to this problem:

I went away to college in the East. It was a big deal for my family that I went to college at all, no less if I dared to leave the Midwest. I was the first in my family to go and I think my parents resented me for it. The way my mother rationalized it was to say, "At least you'll be able to teach if your husband died." . . . Anyway, on vacations home from college my mother would load up my suitcase with a supply of Zest soap and Halo shampoo. Enough for the entire college. I explained to her that it made my suitcase much too heavy for me to manage and also that I could always buy my own at school. I also told her that I now use the kind that my roommates use. My mother did not say anything to me then but on the way to the plane she began to talk tearfully about what a bad mother she had been and that how although she tried her best . . . she'd let me down and that I didn't need her. . . . This was the way it was whenever I would leave to go back to college. She'd pack a load of guilt along with the soap and clothes. But she was wrong. I did need her. I wanted to be able to confide in her and tell her my dreams and my fears. But she was so busy feeling inadequate and needy. . . . Oh, how could I lean on her when she was always leaning on me?

Sheri was a competent young woman, a good student, and a person whose personality drew others to her. Unfortunately for Sheri, her mother resented her success and interpreted it as a put-down. Sheri could have used her mother's support and guidance. They might have helped her to avert one failed marriage and conflict in her second. Her mom wanted to be needed but was too focused on herself to really see her young adult daughter. If she had, she might have been able to give both support and guidance while appreciating Sheri's competence and beauty as a person.

If you find yourself wishing your child still needed you in a dependent way, try to remind yourself that this is an opportunity to get to know your child in a new way: as an adult. It is wise, however, to seek professional counseling if you find your longing for the good old days starts to build into melancholy or an excessive neediness or a resentment toward your child.

Parents of all backgrounds have the potential to question, "What's the use in living now that the kids are gone?" Although ACOAs are survivors by their nature, they may be more vulnerable to these feelings of despair. They may have overidentified with the child, so that if the child is no longer around, their life lacks direction. It is your task at this point to find purpose and give new meaning to your life. That you do so is important for you and your child. Hobbies, politics, a new job, school boards, volunteer services, golf, choir, gardening, reading, it doesn't matter *what* you choose, but rather *that* you choose something. Experiment with different activities until you find your niche. If in the face of your doubts you keep on trying, you'll eventually find what fits you best.

You, as an ACOA parent, have taken the time to read this and other books. You have probably also expressed your interest in getting well by attending counseling and support groups. Much of your energy has been directed at breaking the negative patterns of addiction and dysfunction in your family. Chances are you have been reasonably successful. This can be seen in how well your child is doing. Conscientious parents such as you usually produce children who are better able to handle themselves in relationships than you were able to at their age. They didn't grow up under the veil of alcoholism and are much more able to make healthy connections with other young people.

Some ACOAs may be prone to feel that by their child's success, something is in some way being taken away from them. In this situation resentment may build toward the child. You may even ask yourself, "Why are my children successful when I am not?" The answer is twofold: (1) Your children are successful because as a result of the good job you did as a parent, they were able to tap their personal resources and talent; and (2) I'm not so sure you aren't successful. As most ACOAs are competent at the tasks they perform, I suspect that feeling incompetent and unsuccessful is merely a holdover feeling from your past. It is no longer valid.

As a grown ACOA you are in a position to applaud your children's success as non-ACOA parents do. I hope you will allow yourself to applaud yourself as well. You made sure as best you could that your children didn't have to carry on the secret of alcoholism in the family that was once yours.

9

When You're in the Middle

DAVE

I could never reason with Ronnie even when he was younger. But by the time he was sixteen and driving, he was almost out of control. I knew he had begun to drink because I could smell it on his breath. He smoked cigarettes to cover it up, but at night, when I went into his room, the odor of stale beer was thick in the air. I couldn't talk him out of drinking, and because his friends drank as well, he acted as if he were just one of the crew.

I tried to explain that my father, Ronnie's grandfather, had a drinking problem and had almost died from liquor. But Ronnie wouldn't listen. Then my father got into the act. "Lay off the kid," he would tell me while Ronnie was standing right there. "If you had a few beers every once in a while, you'd lighten up." When I would tell my father to mind his own business and stop meddling in mine, then Ronnie would pipe up and tell me off. Before long, the three of us would be standing there screaming at one another. It got so bad a couple of times that we began pushing each other back and forth. And the two of them were ganging up on me.

My wife was so pissed off that she walked out of the house and didn't come back for hours. Then Ronnie stomped out, to go drinking with one of his friends, no doubt, while my father just stood there and told me, "Your wife walked out and now your kid has walked out, too. You can't do anything right. How could I have raised such a loser?" I thought to myself, It's just hopeless, I'll never get out from under.

There are many ways you can find yourself in between your alcoholic parent and your child. It can be an ongoing problem or a situation that crops up at any point during the child's development. But it's almost always painful because as the ACOA, you're the one person who is never allowed to lose control or stop taking care of those around you. You may be involved in a constant running battle with your teenagers while at the same time you are still dealing with your parents or in-laws. You may still have contact with your alcoholic parent, or perhaps both of your parents are dead. Nevertheless, it may seem as if time were standing still and your alcoholic parent, your enabling parent, or both continue to be firmly entrenched dysfunctional mechanisms in your psyche.

If you are fortunate, your alcoholic parent is in recovery and attending Alcoholics Anonymous, while the enabler is an active participant in Al-Anon. On the other end, your children may be functioning as competent and independent young adults or, much to your discomfort, they may be exhibiting signs of substance abuse. It is entirely likely that you are the only person up until this point who has been coping reasonably well. Now the squeeze is on and you are feeling pressure from both parents and children: What do you do?

First of all, you realize that anyone who has living parents and teenaged children will at some time find himself or herself in the middle. This is a typical situation for anyone in a three-generation family, and the pressure will build from both sides no matter what you attempt to do to prevent it. The key to managing the situation successfully is not to avoid the problem but to respond to it reasonably and navigate through it. The tendency for ACOAs, as we know, is usually one of two extremes: to overreact and become too involved in finding an immediate solution or to underreact out of a sense of powerlessness or deep resentment. Either scenario will only exacerbate the situation and increase rather than decrease the building tension.

If you are able to maintain perspective on your parents' and children's problems and not see them as manifestations of your own perceived character flaws, your own natural coping and survival skills will help you through. You will find, as you found throughout your life, that your inner resourcefulness, your success mechanism that turned you into a survivor, will continue to aid you, and by understanding the needs of both your parents and children at moments of crisis, you will be able to develop insights that will help you come up with alternative solutions to the problems. Remember, pressure from both generations is a natural occurrence in all families. You just have to make sure that you don't get squeezed too hard or unfairly by the converging forces.

You should realize also that ACOAs are very much stuck in the middle by the nature of their situation. Because your alcoholic parents acted much like children when you were growing up, you were forced to become a surrogate parent in the household. Now that you are a parent with older parents who continue to act like children and older children who will always act like children toward you, your middleman situation is a virtual certainty.

There are, however, real differences between these two generations that you must appreciate. First, you were raised in a family in which even if only one parent drank, the other parent behaved in such a way so as to enable that parent to drink. Hence the nonalcoholic parent let you down as well because he or she helped perpetuate the other parent's behavior. This is the dynamic of the dysfunctional family.

Your present family is not dysfunctional and stands in stark contrast to your childhood family. You have done your best to break the cycle of alcoholism and have probably helped your children understand the nature of the disease and the problems it causes. In so doing, you have most likely raised self-reliant children who, even though they may have doubts about their abilities from time to time, have the capacity to overcome them and succeed. In other words, you have probably done wonders in raising your children, especially in light of the fact that you were never really shown how to do it right. But now you have to know how to handle it when pressure closes in on you from both generations.

Perpetuating the Bad Seed

Most ACOA parents I have counseled have expressed concern about their children becoming abusers of alcohol or other drugs. Their worries are not without cause. Studies have indicated that ACOAs are three times as likely to manifest alcohol abuse problems as are children from nonalcoholic backgrounds, and there is a commensurate increased risk for children of ACOAs as well. As most researchers have indicated, the two most prevalent causes of alcoholism are learned behavior from parents and genetic predisposition. When both influences are present in a family environment, there is a greater likelihood that alcoholism will manifest itself at some point in the person's life, even if only briefly, than if these factors aren't present.

As a conscientious ACOA parent, you have probably done your best to eliminate the first factor as a predominant force in your children's environment. Accordingly, you may have decided not to have any alcohol in your house. If you drink, you might drink only sparingly and even then only on social occasions. You probably never drink alone or around your children, except when other adults are present. If your alcoholic parent is still drinking, you also might have restricted his or her access to the children. But no matter how carefully you may have watched over the situation to prevent the environment from influencing your children, it is impossible to eliminate the genetic factors. If your children are predisposed genetically, their bodies may be waiting to be set off by an insidious craving that will only be satisfied through indulgence in alcohol or other drugs. It is important, therefore, that *you* react responsibly should that time bomb go off, even though you are not responsible for its having been set.

As the person in the middle, you are both child and parent. You didn't ask to be born into an alcoholic family nor are you responsible for having been put there. Although you may sometimes feel as if it's your fault, you are not paying for any sins in a former life nor are you deliberately spending your purgatory on earth. You have simply been dealt a weak hand and will have to play it out as carefully as possible. Life is not fair, as you already know, but you have to live it nevertheless.

Knowing this, you must not allow yourself to wallow in the guilt for having passed the seed of alcoholism on to your children. Nor can you blame your parents for having passed it on to you. Excessive guilt or anger can only disarm you and render you powerless to make the necessary decisions during family crises. The only real question is how you will react if you find that a child of yours is abusing alcoholic substances.

Dealing with Potentially Substance-Abusing Children

As Bob, one of the members of my ACOA group, reports:

Reflecting back on it now, I can see how easy it was for me to look the other way. Along with the other parents in the community, my wife and I were engaged in a conspiracy of silence. We didn't say it like our kids did, but the message was essentially the same: What's so wrong with drinking if everybody else is doing it?

It first happened back when our twelve-year-old was at summer camp. He and a few of the other kids in his bunk broke into the counselor's liquor locker. They all drank the hard stuff straight and got sick as dogs within hours. Well, it wasn't hard for the head counselor to discover who did it. I guess it was their green faces coming out of the bathroom that gave them away. Looking at it in retrospect, I am even amazed that we took it so lightly. "Boys will be boys," we said, and "All campers go through this. It's part of growing up."

We were all pretty much yuppies—liberal and permissive in a very self-conscious way. We wanted to believe we were were open-minded. So our first reaction was not to react at all. We behaved as if nothing really happened. None of us made either the kids or the camp answer for the incident. And the camp director just reflected our attitude. After all, as far as Gary was concerned, if the parents didn't bitch, he didn't get worried. If only I had done something about it then, maybe Jonathan's drinking and drug use never would have progressed as far as it did.

The Need for Prevention

Bob's first mistake was that he discounted the influence of his behavior and attitude on his son. He and his wife certainly recognized how alcohol abuse had disrupted his childhood family, but in terms of their own immediate family, it was as if they denied its existence. Although they characterized themselves as nondrinkers at home, Bob and Pat occasionally drank when they socialized with friends at parties. Not only was drinking the norm for adults in the community, but the parents sometimes allowed the teenagers to join them and once or twice even provided a keg of beer for the teenagers at neighborhood get-togethers. In retrospect, Bob came to see that his son's drinking behavior should have been expected and dealt with early. After all, Bob's son was only following the pattern set by Bob's parents.

Bob's father was an ACOA from a dysfunctional family and also a recovering alcoholic who had struggled with his problems for years before Bob was born. Bob didn't know any of this until he was a young teenager. Pat had no alcoholism in her background. Jonathan, of course, knew nothing about his family's history of alcoholism because Bob had not seen any reason to bring it up. By neglecting to address the issues of family history and his son's early experimentation with alcohol, Bob had handed Jonathan a loaded weapon with no instructions or explanation. Perhaps Jonathan's drinking could have been prevented had Bob discussed the issue openly, as I have suggested in earlier chapters.

As an ACOA parent, you have a responsibility to explain your family's history to your children. They have to know that they may be predisposed to substance abuse so that they can avoid alcohol and drugs even if they're in a school or neighborhood where drinking and drug use take place. Bob and Pat, for example, not only neglected to provide the family history information that might have helped Jonathan, but also denied problems when they arose and ignored the clear signals of an early abuser.

Watching for the Signs

BOB

I know now that the signs of Jonathan's troubles were all there. But it was hard. Every kid makes mistakes. I didn't want to make a big deal out of his getting drunk. I just figured he'd learn his lesson. Anyway, it's hard to tell if he's on drugs. All the kids were moody at different times as teenagers. Other than catching them red-handed, you just don't know.

ANN

Joey stopped going with his old friends. I knew them and I like them. Come to think of it, he pretty much stopped bringing friends around the house altogether, but I didn't like the looks of some of the new ones that I saw waiting for him in their cars.

Money started to disappear from the cookie jar and my purse. Then, like a fool, I believed him when he took his stereo out to get fixed. The television went, too, and they were never returned. It got so that he even lost his job.

The situation only deteriorated further. My husband and I would leave for work in the morning at eight and Joey would still be in bed, usually until eleven or noon. He was nineteen at the time, out of school, but still living at home. We made him pay room and board because we wanted him to be responsible, but after he lost his job, we didn't have the heart to pressure him for money he didn't have.

It was only after we started family counseling and began going to Alanon that we found out he was drinking and taking drugs. We were devastated.

Unless you actually see your child taking drugs or drinking to excess in your presence, there isn't any one surefire indicator that your preteen, adolescent, or young adult child is a substance abuser. The signs are more subtle, but you don't have to have a videotape of your son or daughter drinking or using drugs in order to call the issue to his or her attention. Remember, you are the parent. And because this is a family discussion and not a court proceeding, your reasonable concern is ample ground for discussion.

You should not make false or hysterical accusations about alcohol or drug abuse. However, if you have suspicions, you should air them as well as your concerns that the child doesn't understand that he or she is playing with fire. Furthermore, the child is probably acting in ways that have you feeling disturbed. Regardless of whether the cause is substance abuse or another problem, the fact is that you have a deep concern and are upset by your child. At the very least your concern needs to be addressed because you are a caring parent.

The Four Warning Signs of Substance Abuse

There are four signs which serve as potential warnings of substance abuse: (1) changes in attitude; (2) changes in activities; (3) low self-esteem and depression; (4) dishonesty.

Changes in Attitude.   You may notice that your child is angry and hostile toward you, teachers, or other authority figures over a long period of time. While some mood swings are part of adolescent experience, sustained negative and uncooperative behavior must be noted.

Changes in Activities.   Adolescence, in particular, is a time of change and experimentation. If changes are too dramatic, there may be cause for concern. Take note of a pattern of decline in academic performance and disinterest in sports, school, or work activities that were previously an integral part of your child's life. Take special notice, as Ann did, if your teenager drops old friends in favor of a new group whose values and integrity you question.

Low Self-Esteem and Depression.   Some teens and young adults begin the cycle of alcohol or drug abuse by becoming withdrawn. They may be feeling bad about themselves and spend an inordinate amount of time in their rooms. They may also seem to be increasingly depressed and sullen and take to sleeping a lot.

Dishonesty.   A son or daughter who has previously followed through with responsibilities may suddenly "forget" and avoid commitments. You might notice a decrease in the contents levels of bottles in your liquor cabinet. There might also be a series of unexplained losses of money from your purse or wallet or complaints by younger siblings of money missing from their piggy banks or even, as in Ann's case, instances of expensive items disappearing from the house.

A child who has substance-abuse problems needn't have all the signs. On the other hand, a child who returns home from a party in a drunken condition may not be an alcoholic. However, if the event is part of a pattern, or if a pattern of drunken behavior starts to emerge, you must take action. The first step is to face reality.

Intervention

The question for all parents is when to intervene in order to get treatment started. As Bob explained:

Sooner or later we had to face it and all of a sudden it was much sooner than we thought and much worse than we could have imagined. There he was, face down on the bathroom floor vomiting his brains out. At first he said he was sick with the flu. But the smell of rank liquor was so intense in the bathroom that only a person deliberately lying to himself would not have admitted the truth. Jonathan was not only dead drunk, he was suffering from alcohol poisoning.

Initially, he fought off any attempts to help him to his feet. Then he kept passing out. We didn't want to call the first aid squad because that would have been tantamount to posting a notice on a public bulletin board. Everybody knew the kids had been down at the river drinking and partying.

We called the doctor, who told us to meet him at the hospital that evening after the vomiting stopped. Jonathan slept for a while and then tried to resist us again when we took him to the hospital. We knew, as we loaded him into the car, that what we wished would neven happen had finally happened. We knew that we had to get him help and that we also needed help in dealing with him.

You may have only a sneaking suspicion that your son or daughter is abusing him- or herself with alcohol and/or other substances. Perhaps, like Bob and Pat, you might find a prone child serving as a ghastly reminder of your own alcoholic parent as seen through your, then, very young eyes. In any event, this is not the time to panic, but to take action. What you have on your hands is not merely a misbehaving child. You must face the fact that he or she may be a drunk or at least a very troubled child with a serious substance-abuse problem.

First, accept the reality that your child is not misbehaving, rather, that he or she is in need of medical attention. Recognizing this, you should seek immediate help for yourself as well as the child. Remember, having a child with a substance-abuse problem is reason enough for most parents to seek help. However, because you are an ACOA, you must allow yourself to recognize that your guilt, self-doubts, and feelings of failure are natural and to be expected. Parents from non-alcoholic families would feel like failures in this situation also. Therefore, don't deny your feelings just because they are all too familiar.

Next, you must educate yourself. You will come to understand that addiction is usually more of a dynamic family-system problem than a static problem of your child in isolation. Therefore, I recommend the following three-tiered approach to self-education:

1. Information

You need to get a quick, yet thorough, education about what alcohol and other drugs are, their biological and psychological effects, the symptoms associated with their use, and the treatment for addiction. You also need to learn about the family dynamics of addiction, including the roles of the enabler (the person who enables the victim to pursue an addictive behavior pattern), the victim, the provocateur (the person who precipitates the behavior), and the child of the alcoholic. You can find much of the basic information you need in your library or from your county office of the Council on Alcoholism.

2. The Experiences of Others

Some of the most powerful information comes in the form of testimony of others. By attending Families Anonymous or

Al-Anon you will hear from other parents in your position and also from those who are further along in the process of recovery. You can find the nearest meeting simply by looking for the organizations in your local telephone directory, or by calling the county office of the Council on Alcoholism, or a local community health center, or emotional-help hotline. There is absolutely no requirement that you say a word at these meetings, although you are welcomed to do so and encouraged to share any problems with the group.

Listening to others, however, is many times helpful enough to families who feel alone and isolated. It will also be helpful for you to acquire and read the Twelve Steps and Twelve Traditions of Alcoholics Anonymous before you attend any meetings. Reading these will also help you understand the treatment process that you and your child are about to undergo. At the same time, because you are an ACOA, it will also put you in touch with your parents' problem and help treat you as a child of an alcoholic as well as a parent of an alcoholic.

3. Personal Consultation

Along with educating yourself and listening to the experiences of others, it is important that you get help tailored specifically to your unique situation. Your child has a medical problem as well as an emotional one; therefore, you should seek professional help. Remember, when your child was younger and came down with a virus, you called the doctor without hesitation. If your child fell off a bike, broke a wrist, or had an accident of any sort, your first act was to call the doctor. Abusing alcohol and drugs, becoming antisocial or even violent, and upsetting the lives of family and friends are no less a medical problem than getting the flu or catching chicken pox. You wouldn't try to cure a broken wrist by yourself; you shouldn't approach substance-abuse problems by yourself either. Just because you are an ACOA, you should not let your guilt, fear, and personal anger get in the way of helping your child recover from substance abuse. Non-ACOA parents call a doctor; so should you.

I recommend that you have several consultation sessions with a mental health practitioner who specializes in working with adolescents and substance-abuse problems. The ideal professional is a psychologist or social worker who is also certified as an alcohol or substance-abuse counselor. This person is in a position to provide an objective outside perspective and thus can determine the proper treatment components for you, your family, and your child. This professional will also be able to advise you on whether a course of outpatient treatment comprised, for instance, of family and individual therapy along with support group involvement is sufficient or if intensive residential treatment is in order. Try to allow yourself to trust and confide in your counselor.

You might find yourself wondering how you can find a professional who is really worthy of your trust and confidence. By all means, shop around, but do it quickly. You can start with your local phone directory under the headings "Physicians" and "Psychologists." You can also look under the "Alcoholism Information," "Family Counseling," and "Social Worker" headings as well. In your conversations with them, determine whether they are chemical dependency specialists. Your county office on alcoholism or drug abuse will have listings of the local counselors and clinical facilities as well as any community outreach programs or health centers. If you are a student, avail yourself of the counseling programs at your college or university. You can also ask your child's guidance counselor at school for help or referrals.

You can also wait until you've attended one or two Alanon meetings so you can ask the group members whose values seem closest to yours who they might recommend. Above all, remember that the mental health care professional you select absolutely must have a background in alcohol or substance-abuse problems. There are many psychologists and counselors who are perfectly competent in their individual fields but who are entirely ignorant of alcohol or substance-abuse problems. Just because a person has a practice does not mean that he or she can automatically help you with your unique family situations. Ask around and look specifically for specialists in your particular problem area.

Make sure that you inform the counselor in the very first intake session about your family's history of alcoholism and identify yourself as an ACOA. That will help the counselor develop a treatment program with your child. Also share whatever concerns, anxieties, and guilt you feel as an ACOA because your history and personal dynamics will be an important part of your child's treatment program.

In the event that your child is very much in denial or he or she is a young adult living outside your home, discuss with your counselor the possibilty of conducting an intervention. An intervention is a special approach to treatment used when the substance abuser is especially resistant to acknowledging the presence of the problem and is thus unwilling to change. Briefly stated, the entire family (but not the abuser), along with other special people in your child's life (teachers, clergy, friends, or a favorite relative), are helped to examine how the child's abuse has affected them. After several training sessions, the larger "family," along with the counselor, then meet with the abuser and share their pain and concern (not their guilt or anger). If the intervention is conducted effectively, your child is then likely to accept an offer for treatment. The intervention is a powerful tool. Therefore, as you shop for a counselor, you might want "experience in conducting interventions" as one of your essential criteria.

Remember, your best efforts to either prevent or address a substance-abuse problem in your child will amount to nothing unless you first examine your behavior and attitudes toward alcohol and other drugs. Also keep in mind that even if your child is not chemically dependent, you still have reason to be concerned about his or her well-being on the basis of his or her actions. Consultation with a counselor may help to address that concern and your child's possible problems in coping with the pressures to take drugs or start drinking.

The Return of the Alcoholic Parent

It may have been twenty, thirty, or forty years since you had to worry about the problems of living at home with your alcoholic parent. You may feel by now that you've gotten your past well behind you. You may be satisfied that now, at age thirty-five or forty-five, you've put your life together. You have managed a good career, are succeeding at your job, have a loving and supportive spouse and wonderful children, own a lovely home, belong to an upscale or affluent community, and, despite the fears that still haunt you from your childhood years, you can say that you've succeeded. Even your childhood friends who know where you came from might agree that you've done all right for a child of a dysfunctional alcoholic.

It has been many years since the tirades in your childhood family, the constant elevated level of anger and frustration, and the crushing disappointment every time you let yourself believe that things would be different or better. Through the intervening years, you have done your best to heal yourself, either on your own, with your spouse, or with a counselor. You may be among the many ACOAs who haven't seen their alcoholic parents since they were children. Then it happens. Just when you thought it was safe after all these years of balancing to put your other foot down, you hear an ominous knock on the door of your life. Your alcoholic parent wants back in.

The scenario may take many forms. Your parent may be in recovery, he or she may be very old and sick and just want to set things right before going away for the last time, or, like a piece of loose cargo in the hold of a tossing freighter, your parent may still be actively drinking and crashing into the one thing he or she hasn't been able to destroy: your life. Whatever the scenario, it is as if your worst childhood nightmares burst out of the darkness and into the present. Your blazing migraine will not go away, you are violently ill, you begin to lose touch with your job and those around you, accusatory voices that you thought had long been quieted now arise inside your head in a common chorus. You've been exposed for the fraud you've been your entire life, and now it will all unravel. An all-knowing Karl Malden steps out of your television screen into your real-life living room: "What will you do?"

SUSAN

I got a call from my mother the other night, just like a call from the grave. She and my father have been divorced for twelve years, almost. I hadn't seen either of them in over twenty. She had found out from the sister of someone who'd lived with him five years ago that my father, my crazy, alcoholic father, wasn't keeping the house up any more. He was just an old man holed up in the bedroom. She wanted me to go down and help.

This was the house I grew up in. Other than being terrorized by the man occasionally, I actually have some pretty good memories of the place. When I was young, it was a beautiful Victorian farmhouse with large-paned leaded-glass windows, plenty of frills and gingerbreading, and a long wraparound front porch with a big old swing on it. Inside were high ceilings with trim work like the icing on a wedding cake. Now the slate roof's leaking really bad, and because of the incessant rain, the plaster ceilings are crumbling. All the rooms need cleaning too. It's a real mess!

We went over to fix the place up, my sister and I, and I can't tell you what it did to my life. I had monster fights with my husband, began hitting out at my son, and almost lost my teaching job in a district where I'd spent over fifteen years and was about to become an assistant principal. All this after the second weekend. After four weekends, I was almost a vegetable. And then I finally figured out why. You'd think that after saving his property and helping the old man out, my father would at least be appreciative. He was just as surly and as angry as ever, almost throwing me out because I drank one of his lousy beers. They were the only things in the fridge. Finally, I just left. I cried a lot afterwards and I wanted to crawl back to him just for one kind word. But mostly I just balled up in a corner of my bathroom, locked the door, and cried.

Susan had had her share of doubts and apprehensions about bailing out her father's years of flagrant neglect of his house. But she and her sister and their spouses took on the task anyway. Even though part of her truly wanted to help out her father, she also seemed to do it for herself. It was if restoring the old house would enable her to preserve at least some of the good memories from her childhood. Her father's abusive attitude, however, brought too many of the painful remembrances of the past directly into her present. As a result, she found herself trapped in the middle of her father's alcoholic behavior, the requirements of her job, and the needs of her family. She collapsed under the weight and reemerged only after a period of counseling in which she was finally able to confront the wants that had built up in her over the years.

DONALD

Donald's natural father is also still actively drinking. His mother left his father when Donald was five after years of neglect and drunkenness. She remarried a few years later, and it is his stepfather that Donald still refers to as dad. Like dad, Donald became a police officer, and it is in that capacity that he still occasionally encounters his natural father.

I still see my father sometimes when he comes into town. I get disgusted so quickly when I see him that all I can do is say, "You're nothing but a drunk, you know that?" Still, he wants me to call him "dad" and says I'm being disrespectful when I don't. I tell him that in my mind, he hasn't earned that respect. I refuse to call him dad, but I still talk to him. As angry as I am at him for who he is, for what he did, and for trying to get money off me now, I still talk to him. I was an alcoholic, too, but I've been recovering for the past two years. So when he says, "Like father like son. We should be friends," I tell him to go to hell. There's no way I'm letting him back in my life or even close to my kids. It amazes me sometimes that I still keep on talking to him. And he's right about one thing: my two boys look just like him. He doesn't know that I feel guilty as hell about not letting him see the kids.

Donald's father has nothing to offer, yet it seems that Donald feels drawn into accepting his invitations for contact. He does, however, have a clear sense of how far he is willing to go with his natural father, and he understands the dangers inherent in letting the man have access to his grandchildren. The fact that his father is still an active alcoholic makes Donald's decisions easier to live with. But considering the guilt that Donald must bear, it is clearly not a decision he likes. It is much more difficult when an estranged alcoholic parent returns after a period of absence as a recovering individual. Then, the choices are far more painful because the ACOA feels as if he or she is punishing a recovered and vulnerable parent.

BILL

Things were going really well for me. I was proud of my children and my wife's career. I had recently completed work on a merger that would put my political and economic future within the company on a very solid footing. I had begun to shop for used BMWs very casually, just to get the feeling of what it would be like and to reward myself. Then I got the call.

I hadn't even seen my father's face in literally fifteen years when his new wife called. It seemed that he had stopped drinking for several years before he started experiencing problems with his stomach. Now he had cancer and was seeking my help through his wife. As it turned out, he was short of the money and wherewithal to manage his way through treatment. If it had been any other family member, I would have been more generous. As it was, however, I felt like someone had walked into my office and dropped a basket of snakes into my lap.

It turned out that Bill was also very angry. The man who had taken far more from Bill's childhood than he ever gave back had returned and now, again, was asking for more. Bill's anger was also tainted by guilt. Although his father had ill-provided for Bill and his siblings, a part of Bill felt as if he should do something for the man. However, Bill had made himself successful on his own and now resented his father's imposition. For an ACOA who relied on external markers and signposts to guide him along in his career, here was a situation in which Bill could only go with his gut instinct. But when he looked inside, he could not identify any guiding emotion because they were all too tangled up with anger, frustration, and guilt.

TRACY

Still another scenario which may present itself to you concerns a recovering alcoholic parent who is not infirm or sick but who seeks contact after a prolonged period of absence. Although the return of a missing parent who wants to reestablish some form of communication with a child is entirely normal, for the ACOA it presents a host of emotional conflicts. If you feel as if you survived your childhood rather than enjoyed it, the telephone call from the estranged recovering alcoholic parent presents you with the same basic decision: Will you let the person back into your life? That was the question Tracy had to answer when she was confronted with her mother after years of absence.

My mother had been a fall-down drunk for the entire first twelve years of my life. How I hated her for all the disappointments and embarrassing times she put me through. One of the only redeeming things she did was to stay in her bed all shit-faced most of the time. That way I was able to have friends over without running into her and those ratty slippers she wore all the time.

My mother has been sober for fifteen years now. In fact, she works as an alcoholism counselor. And now she wants to be involved with my family. She's always wanted access to her grandchildren, but I've always resisted. Now I'm wondering what's best for my kids.

I grew up entirely on my own, finished graduate school without anybody's help, and got married. Steve and I have a pretty nice life and the kids are great. What do I need her for now?

Tracy ended up agreeing to come to a family therapy session along with her brother and mother. You could have cut the tension in that room with a knife when the three of them sat there staring at one another from across the years. I remember her saying to me in front of her mother, "My mother wants me to love her but I don't have the feelings." Tracy's anger boiled over with every interaction during the discussion, yet she still returned for a few more sessions. Later, in fact, she actually invited her mother to her house to spend Passover with her husband and children. Ultimately, she decided that there was more to gain by having contact with her mother than by shutting her and the past out. Moreover, because she was perceptive as well as intelligent, she was able to admit, after over twenty years, that the cool, aloof attitude she presented to the world was an old defense. She knew also that to continue to act this way when the dragon didn't live in the cave anymore would only inhibit her personal growth. It is apparent that Tracy agreed to let her mother back into her life for her sake as well as for her mother's.

Deciding on Whether to Deal with Aged Alcoholic Parents

JOAN

I just sat there in silence as the voice said, "Joan, Daddy." I had nothing to say. After all the years of silence, there was his voice. "Did you get the package?" Sure I did, but I didn't open it. I rewrapped it and gave it away. "Are you on vacation or something? Do you have time to drive down?" Again silence. Couldn't he take the hint? "I might be up in your area in a week or so with Jeannie." I could feel the migraine welling up behind my eyes. It was like the boulder that chased Indiana Jones out of the cave. It just kept getting bigger and bigger and no matter how much I said no and tried to run away from it, it kept getting closer. There was no getting around this one; I was going to be as sick as a dog in a matter of minutes. "Maybe we could stop in if you can't get down," he said.

I mumbled something incomprehensible as the first wave of nausea came over me. Then I hung up the phone and ran to the bathroom, where I wretched and wretched until my insides were dry as a desert and my headache blazed in fury like the fiery sun on the Day of Judgment.

And all he had to say was one kind word. Just one. One phrase like "I love you" and it would all be right again, just like when I was a little girl before the drinking started. If I could hear that from him, my whole life would start right over again.

There is no clear and simple way to handle a situation in which your alcoholic parent, recovering or active, reenters your life after a period of prolonged absence. Susan, Donald, Bill, and Tracy were charged, as are you, with the task of finding a solution that is right. Although Tracy was apprehensive, she was interested in extending herself to her mother just enough to test the waters. Finding that she could deal with the hostility after all the years, she extended herself further. Finally, she decided to open her life to her parent and resolve long-buried feelings of conflict in her personality. Tracy didn't have to accept her mother, just as you don't. Simply because a parent is recovering doesn't mean that you have to welcome him or her back with open arms. Tracy decided that it was right for her to try. If faced with a similar situation, you may very well decide not to permit your mother or father to have contact with your children at all or perhaps only during short visits supervised by your spouse.

This does not mean that you are a heartless, unforgiving, spiteful, or bad person. It may only mean that you are not ready for this kind of involvement with your alcoholic parent. There is simply no single right or wrong way of determining in advance the correct thing to do. You have to examine your emotions and motives, determine how much pain you will endure if you open communication with your parent, and decide whether you have the strength or ability to handle it. If you don't, it is better to admit it at the outset rather than making yourself into the martyr that your enabling parent was. Above all, you don't have to feel guilty, although for you as an ACOA it is reasonable to experience guilt feelings as you weigh your parent's request. Allow yourself to acknowledge the presence of the guilt along with the resentment and anger, but remember, you do not have to let these feelings direct or dictate all of your actions.

What Are Your Choices?

You have essentially three choices when you receive a request for help or involvement from a parent who still may be dysfunctional: (1) cut off the dead wood, (2) martyrdom, or (3) trust your feelings. The first two are at polar extremes and may represent a "quick-fix defense" mentality.

Cut Off the Dead Wood.   Simply put, this is to absolutely and without question, further input, or extended dialogue cut off entirely from the parent. This option recognizes that there are plenty of ACOAs who have been tragically wronged by their alcoholic parents. These ACOAs have very legitimate reasons to "just say no" to their parents. The problem with the cutting-off-the-dead-wood approach is the degree of rigidity involved with it. I am not suggesting that you owe your parent anything; rather, it is you who are owed. Additionally, the stone-wall stance that cutting off requires might require more strength than you admit to having.

You may feel like placing your hands over your ears as you hear, "Help me!" or, "I want to enjoy my grandchildren just once or twice before I die." You might even be forced to react to: "I'm your father and I'm dying. I want to see you to make it right." You may also have to deal with your parent's claim that he or she is fully recovered: "I'm all right now, and I'm sorry. I always loved you."

You may choose to deny the parent's request, but by simply cutting off you are also preventing the free flow of feelings that may be helpful to your own healing and personal growth. I know you don't want to feel upset or relive the old anger or disappointments. No one would blame you, including your parent. Nor would I or anyone else suggest that you stir up old feelings of pain. You should, however, acknowledge to yourself what is still there from your past before you decide to close the door. And if your parent is dying, it is a door you will close for the rest of your life.

One common motivation for cutting off feelings among ACOAs whom I've worked with is the reluctance to raise the hope that, "Finally I have the father I've always wanted." Rather than relive old disappointments, a rigidly defensive posture is assumed and maintained in the face of all requests, no matter how emotional they become. The reality is that unless there is a real threat, there is no need to be defensive. Please consider, should you find yourself feeling this way, that perhaps you are feeling as you did when you were a child. Consider also that your rigidity suggests you are not yet done with your healing process. Even that is OK. There is no need for either perfection or shame. Remind yourself, also, that because you are no longer a child, you are in a much stronger position to choose, whatever your decision may be.

Martyrdom. In this case you may feel compelled, even in the face of impending disaster, to come to the aid of your parent. The ACOA choosing this course isn't really choosing, but playing out an old pattern of behavior common to many children of alcoholics. There is, in fact, little sense of choice, but rather a feeling of guilt and obligation.

On the basis of my experience, it seems to me that if you are inclined to martyr yourself you should consider that you haven't yet finished working through your ACOA issues. All too often I have counseled ACOAs who grit their teeth as they bear yet another burden for their alcoholic parents. These are the same people who end up lying in bed with a migraine afterward. If in your heart you know you are reluctant to take on the medical expenses, share your house or children, or even entertain the possibility of reestablishing a relationship, decide at first not to decide. Tell your parent that you have to think about it and talk it over with your spouse. Then, when you are ready, inform your parent of your decision.

Trust Your Feelings.　If you can develop trust in yourself and give your feelings validity, you'll probably make some pretty healthy choices when the time comes. Trusting feelings is perhaps one of the most difficult tasks for you as an ACOA. Most ACOAs have been given sufficiently confusing signals about their feelings as children so that they've often had to learn how to operate in the world without listening to their feelings. That's not unlike a pilot attempting to land in the fog without the aid of his or her instruments. The double messages you were given taught you to discount your intuitions and your feelings. Now, as an ACOA in between your aging parents and your growing teenagers, you need them more than ever in deciding whether or not you will include your returning alcoholic parent in your life.

You must first give yourself permission to say no. The returning parent was not there for you as a child and there is little reciprocity required. Perhaps the contact was kept to a minimum over the years or maybe there were long periods of absence. If you find that the quality of your relationship with your alcoholic parent warrants no further involvement, then allow yourself to move on. Whether or not the parent is in recovery, if you feel on the basis of history that you have no more room for him or her in your life, you should take that stand. If perhaps you do not want your children exposed to your parent's presence, I also urge you to give yourself permission to say no.

On the other hand, even if you give yourself the option to refuse the request, you don't have to say no if you don't want to. You may feel strong enough to explore the gradual inclusion of the estranged alcoholic parent in your life. This is exactly what Tracy did. She had her doubts, but was willing to see if having contact was workable.

You may also chose to help your parent even if you know you can't do very much. In this case the parent either may still be drinking or may be either physically or emotionally deteriorated. You must acknowledge your real feelings, trust in their validity, and act upon them rather than second-guessing yourself or making compromises with your guilt. It is better for you to offer help out of a genuine willingness than out of a sense of hopelessness. If you feel obligated and guilty, try to talk the feelings out with a friend or a counselor. If you listen, you will probably find a wise inner voice that will guide you.

Again, as in the case of "martyrdom," should you have too many doubts, set well-defined limits within which your parent may operate with you and your family. You can also indicate that you are unwilling to have any further contact at this time until you have thought through your position. In the event that you feel capable enough to monitor your relationship with your parent, especially in regard to your children, it would be reasonable to have a warming-up of your relationship. Let's be clear, however; you are not saying yes because you want to be a nice, loving child. Rather, you have examined your parent's motivations and determined the potential plusses and minuses. On the basis of your assessment of how much you are willing to handle, an affirmative decision may then be made.

Involvement with Your Alcoholic Parent

You may have agreed to allow the previously absent alcoholic parent to be involved with your family, or he or she may have been there in the background all along. In either event, you are in the middle and must regulate your parent's involvement with your children and also educate your children about your parent, about the disease of alcoholism, and about the role that alcoholism has played in your family history.

I have already stressed the importance of telling your children about alcoholism, your family's involvement with it, and your child's potential predisposition to alcohol or chemical abuse. This discussion with your child must not be minimized, especially if one of your parents is around and still actively involved with alcohol. In your discussion, you must be as honest and forthright as possible. Compensating for the age of your children, tell the details. Don't just gloss over them as your enabling parent did for you when you were your child's age. Your children need to understand that their grandparent loves them and *also* has an illness.

In Kim's family it was decided by a conspiracy of silence that since her grandfather was dead, there was no need to tell her about his alcoholism.

We lived in the duplex right next to my grandmother. It seemed that we were always over there. We'd eat there and celebrate holidays there. I guess I thought on some level it was strange how barren our house was compared to my grandmother's. My grandmother's house was filled with furniture, much of it from the 1940s and '50s. My parents' stuff, however, was still in cardboard boxes from when they had first moved in before I was born. They had never even unpacked and had no furniture. My mother didn't even attempt to fix up our house. The feeling was real eerie, and I had it for as long as I could remember. My own bedroom was just like a doll's house, but the rest of the place was like a cavern with lots of boxes all around. I just felt like something was wrong.

Indeed there was a great deal wrong. In addition to the grandfather's alcoholism being ignored, so too was the inadequacy of Kim's mother. She was an ACOA who was still very much a child, protected by her mother. The never-furnished house stood in stark contrast to the decorations and care lavished on the house next door. Kim's house reflected the emptiness her mother felt inside. Unfortunately for Kim, the shroud of silence perpetuated her own self-doubts that later led her to enter counseling. Only then was she able to piece together the puzzle. And when she gained enough insight, she saw the secret for what it was: a family disease. It would have helped her in growing up to have been able to place her feelings of uneasiness within a context. If a responsible aunt or uncle had helped Kim's mother explain to her how alcohol had affected her family, she might have grown up without such a pervasive feeling of unworthiness.

You will find that if you provide sufficient information about alcoholism in general, as well its impact on your family in particular, your children will demonstrate a healthy understanding appropriate to their ages. Instead of developing self-doubts as a consequence of carrying a secret they don't even understand, your children may openly participate in how "we're handling granddad's problem."

Perhaps, at age thirty-one, you find that your father is still actively alcoholic yet adored by your six-year-old daughter. He may forever be bringing her presents and always have a loving twinkle in his eye for her. While you value the healthy caring that your daughter receives, you are also rightfully discontented at his habit of walking leisurely past the bar with her as he takes his daily stroll for the newspaper. You may also feel that it's only a matter of time before the walk past the bar turns into a visit to the bar. If you stand back and do nothing, you are creating a potentially devastating situation for your child.

Children, even as young as six, are fully capable of understanding about alcoholism if it is explained to them on their level. Without an adequate explanation, your daughter may feel you are unfairly punishing her, that there is something wrong with her, or perhaps that there is some vague, secret problem in the family if you restrict her contact with her grandfather. Honest discussion will both help children to understand that your decision has nothing to do with how you feel about them and help them learn appropriate guidelines in dealing with the alcoholic grandparent.

If, for example, your father attempted to form a secret alliance with your daughter by sneaking her into the bar, she would be able to say, "You know Mom doesn't allow me to go in there with you and I wish you wouldn't go in their either, because it's bad for you." You may have already role-played this scenario with your daughter as a way to help her be assertive. Ideally, you have also let her know that she has permission to talk with you about anything and that she doesn't have to keep any secrets from you no matter what anybody tells her. Neither she nor the person she talks to will be punished, and her confidence in you won't be breached. In these days of increased recognition of the problems of child abuse, clearly laying out the ground rules for parent-child communication is especially important.

On the other hand, if you allow your alcoholic parent access to your children, it is absolutely imperative you set and monitor clear guidelines concerning the wheres, whats, and whens. This is of obvious concern when the grandparent is still drinking. In the example we have just cited, you would have to lay out in advance with your parent clear and specific parameters regarding his or her involvement with your child. Along with the restrictions, you must tell him or her the consequences for breaking the rules. There could be, for example, no more unsupervised time with either grandparent if one or the other violates the rules. This is a major role reversal because you are setting the limits for your parent much as you would for a child. But then again, as an ACOA, you know a great deal about role reversal.

Sometimes, paradoxically, ACOAs experience a greater inner conflict when setting limits on an alcoholic parent who is no longer drinking. Regardless of whether it is a matter of establishing guidelines for activities with your children or even letting the parent into your family at all, a recovering alcoholic parent may evoke an enormous amount of guilt in his or her adult child.

Consider the scenario in which you have not had much contact with your alcoholic parent for years. Suddenly you find him or her on your doorstep, asking for your forgiveness. If your parent is truly in recovery and not just dry drunk, he or she may be actively working through the program of Alcoholics Anonymous. You may hear your recovering parent say that he or she made a "searching and fearless moral inventory" (Fourth Step) and "made a list of all persons I have harmed and became willing to make amends to them all" (Eighth Step). Therefore, your parent wants access to you and your family in order to make up for the past.

If this happens to you, it is helpful to consider the feelings you may still carry as an adult child of an alcoholic. Underneath the anger and disappointment, you may find yourself still craving the love and acceptance which you never received from your alcoholic parent. You may find yourself tempted to welcome him or her back with open arms as if you were still a child. Be very cautious! As an adult, you are more than capable of discovering the motivations of others. Just because it may be good for the recovering alcoholic to work the steps of AA doesn't mean that you must let him or her do it with you and your family. In fact, the latter portion of the Ninth Step speaks directly to this: "Make direct amends to such people wherever possible, except when to do so could injure them or others."

You can't pretend that everything is wonderful if it isn't. If the damage done is irreparable, then you have every right in the world to say no to the returning parent. If you choose to try, then slowly check out the new relationship as Tracy did and make your way gradually through the pain that has built up over the years. Remember, your response, whatever it is, is tied directly to the needs of your own children. Whether the returning parent is still actively drinking or in recovery is only one issue. If he or she had emotionally, physically, or sexually abused you when you were a child, that is an entirely different issue. Exercise extreme caution, therefore, in entertaining any involvement with the person, especially if access to your children is one of the parent's stated wants. Your response will then be tempered by the need to protect your children.

Regardless of the decision you make and the safeguards you build in, if you allow contact with the grandchildren you probably will come under the scrutiny of others. Your in-laws might say, "You're not going to let *him* in, are you, not after all he's done?" Or, if they see themselves as forgiving people, they might say just the opposite: "You're not letting him in? After all, all he wants is to make everything up to you. Give him a chance."

Face the fact now that you might be perceived as a heartless villain in someone's eyes no matter what you do. That's the way it is, and you have to make your choice in spite of it. Therefore, since you already know you are going to be blamed by someone, why not choose what's right for you and your children instead of trying to please the world.

It is especially important for ACOAs to understand that they can never win if they look outside of themselves for direction, however much they are tempted. If you are trying to avoid conflict or seek approval rather than satisfying your own personal needs, you will always be disappointed. You probably have already experienced this. The problem ACOAs face is that when they were growing up, they learned that it was not OK to make mistakes. They oftentimes used their fear of failure as a way of avoiding the hard choices. In so doing they missed the opportunity to learn new information or experience the challenge of trying something different. You may be in this position yourself. Because you were afraid of being labeled a failure, you perhaps found yourself either avoiding important decisions or looking for others to make them for you. This is dysfunctional behavior that only inhibits your success. However, when confronted with the return of your alcoholic parent, you cannot avoid the decision forever. In this situation, you and you alone are the best judge of what's right for you and your family. You must decide what to do with your returning parent.

In functional families, a sense of self-reliance is built into the upbringing of the children. Even if a parent or child makes a mistake, he or she is allowed to recoup or try again. Because, in functional families, there is less pressure to be perfect, there is much more latitude given in choosing among different alternatives. Try to allow yourself this positive parenting. Pretend, just for a moment, that you are functional and that there is no need to be perfect. Close your eyes, visualize what you would do if you didn't have to worry about failure, and come up with the decision as if all things were equal. Now apply this decision to your everyday present existence. Did you come up with a different option? If you did, then the chances are that you were worrying too much about being right and not enough about doing what is right.

No doubt you have plenty of good reasons to deny your alcoholic parent access to your family. But if you do permit contact, make sure you build in checks and safeguards. You have the absolute right and responsibility to evaluate how it is going. If you feel that the sustained contact does more harm than good to you, your spouse, or your children, you can alter the agreement or stop the contact altogether. Because these decisions are admittedly confusing, consider talking it over with your spouse, an objective friend, or your counselor.

Above all remember, when you're in the middle between your children who are abusing alcohol or drugs and your returning alcoholic parent, the choices you make will never be easy. They may be self-evident, but admitting the obvious may be more difficult than lying to yourself and doing what you think will please others. Your children and your parents each have their own sets of needs and wants. Each individual in your family will act on his or her needs. If you don't act on your needs, you will wind up at the bottom of the pecking order. They will take care of themselves first, not you. Therefore, please understand that unless you take care of yourself, your needs simply won't be met. You already know from childhood how painful that is. You don't want to experience it again as an adult parent.

Dealing with your returning parent may be one of the most important decisions you make regarding your own life. Dealing with your children and their substance abuse will certainly be one of the most important decisions you make regarding their lives. Be aware of the consequences and don't take the job lightly. If you are honest about your feelings, you can save a lot of lives in the process, the most important one being your own.

10

Changes

CAROL

It was Bud's family that was the "official" family for the kids. His parents were the grandparents. On Christmas and Thanksgiving, we always went there for dinner and they always put up the tree. When we gave out the presents on Christmas morning, we gave them out at their house. Summers meant that the kids would go to their place at the shore for two months while Bud and I took our vacations. My parents meant nothing. Even as far as the kids were concerned, my parents were invisible. And I guess I would have been invisible, too, if it weren't for Bud.

Bud's mother hated me and my background. She always felt that Bud had married beneath him. After we divorced—it didn't matter that he had slept with every cocktail waitress between here and Philadelphia—it was my fault. His mother wasn't even surprised when Bud didn't want any part of a custody battle. She felt that the man shouldn't have to raise the children. That was woman's work. If she could have taken custody she would have.

What happened was worse. Every time the kids visited Bud's parents—mainly because Bud didn't want to watch them—his mother would wring her hands and apologize to the kids about my not being a good mother but because of the courts and the law, there was nothing she could do. "You poor kids," she would cry. "You have to be raised in that home by that woman." By the time she had finished her weekend's work, I had to put the kids into a decompression chamber just to get them ready for school the next morning.

You know what? It's fifteen years later and those kids still treat me like a second-class citizen. Bud's parents are dead now, but that doesn't matter. Any female that he chooses to live with for two weeks becomes the kids' soul mate in absentia while they live out their court-imposed sentences with me. And then my father has the gall to ask me why the kids don't ever want to see him. I don't even want to see him.

On the surface, Carol's divorce was much like the tens of thousands of divorces that take place every month in the United States. Carol had a job, Bud had a job, and each only wanted to escape the other. However, Carol was an ACOA who had shunned her family from the moment she reached high school. Bud was her escape from the humiliations that punctuated her adolescence: her father's screaming out the open window, the police car that had to take him to the hospital one night when he threatened to jump off the roof, the bruises that Carol occasionally wore on her face on Monday mornings, and the patches her mother would sew into her school uniform because her family couldn't afford clothing. Her nickname all throughout her school years was "Patches." It wasn't until she won the scholarship to the University of Pennsylvania that she was able to meet people who didn't treat her as a leper. That was when she met Bud, and married him after she became pregnant in her sophomore year. However, as she finally realized, even that relationship was doomed to failure because she had never come to a reconciliation with her own past and her reasons for needing Bud's family as much as she did.

It wasn't even Bud that I wanted to marry. It was his family. You only had to see that Christmas tree and listen to the men guffawing in the den over their after-dinner drinks to want to be a member of that group. I believed that if I could bring a set of children into that family, I would wipe away all of my past, I would have the last laugh on my father. I had the best intentions, I thought at the time. But if I did everything right, why do I feel so rotten about it fifteen years later?

PATRICK

When my mother asked me why I gave up custody to my mother-in-law after my wife died, how could I tell her that I never really had custody? But it was true. When I was married, my wife's family was legitimate and mine was worthless. That was the party line and I went along with it. Even though my wife's father was an alcoholic, it didn't matter. Her mother brushed it under the rug so effectively that to criticize him was like criticizing "Leave It to Beaver" or something. But my family was dysfunctional, and I told myself that my in-laws had all the validity. I knew it was a wrong decision at the time, but it didn't matter. It just wasn't worth the fight or the discussion. And today, I see my two very mediocre children from time to time, and they have about as much distaste for me as any two human beings can have for a natural parent. It hurts, but not as much as you'd think.

Like Carol, Patrick married into a family that promised him legitimacy and offered to confer upon his children the childhood bliss that he never experienced. He overlooked the obvious dysfunctions of his wife's family and let his mother-in-law have custody of the children because he told himself that it would be best for them. Having been raised in a dysfunctional family, Patrick grew up with a sense of illegitimacy, an assumption that he didn't have the same rights as did people who grew up in functional families, and a belief that anyone who came from a family that he perceived as normal was more worthy than he. Accordingly, he felt his children belonged in his wife's family, and willingly gave up custody after she was killed in an automobile accident.

Changes in the Family

Even the most successful parents—those who claim to know where they are going—have trouble coping with changes in the family environment. For ACOAs who have worked hard during their child-raising years at buttressing their families against the chaos that change can bring about, the concept of change is a threatening one. Remember, any change— positive or negative—will be unsettling for those ACOAs whose lives have been a struggle to stabilize their environment and prevent change from disrupting their world.

You yourself may have weathered your toddler's terrible twos and coped with your adolescent's flirtation with alcohol and substance abuse and know firsthand that dramatic change is something that you can't plan for. You can only try to understand that time does indeed provide a measure of healing and that all change eventually becomes amalgamated into your present reality, even the most painful of changes.

The changes that will most certainly confront you at some point are the deaths of your parents and your spouse's parents. Less likely but possibly even more painful are the deaths of any of your children. Then there are the changes in your immediate family that result from the birth of younger children, divorce, or separation. Unfortunately, with about half of all marriages ending in divorce, separation and divorce are very likely changes.

When you realize just how much change your family will have to accept during the course of your child-raising years, you will begin to understand why families have to be resilient units that grow as a result of change rather than shrink from it in fear. If you are an ACOA, your reactions to change will be more critical simply because you will help establish the mechanisms which will enable your children to cope. If after a divorce you become mistrustful, bitter, and even violent, your children will fear being around you, even if you were not the spouse "at fault" in the separation. If you can honestly acknowledge your loss while at the same time assuring your children that you will care for them, they will respect you more after the immediacy of change has passed.

The Birth of Additional Children

Technically, this is a happy event, the reaffirmation of your family and your relationship with your spouse. You can expect tensions to arise among your older children, particularly if you have an only child who feels that he or she will be replaced in your affection. Surprisingly, though, tensions will also arise between spouses who will feel the additional burdens of coping with new financial demands, additional constraints on their time, and the increased emotional responsibility of caring for the new child. If tensions have been increasing already beneath the surface of your marriage, these, too, may be exacerbated by the arrival of a new child.

For Jeff, himself a recovering alcoholic as well as the son of an alcoholic father, the arrival of his second child completely upset the equilibrium he had established with his wife.

I had three strikes against me from the start. My father was a drunk all the time that I knew him. After he died, my mother married John, who was good to me, but, I found out later, was also an alcoholic. I was pretty wild when I was a teenager. . . . I drank very heavily, but was able to control it. I became a cop, married young, and my wife, whose father was also an alcoholic, took care of things in the family while I continued to drink.

I finally woke up two years ago, entered an ACOA program and began to recover. It was like I'd been Rip van Winkle, asleep for thirty years. I began to make friends, understand what people expected from me, and I began to meet women who didn't know me as the drunk at the bar who would come on to them instead of just trying to make friends. Then I realized that I didn't love my wife anymore. She had just coped with me for ten years; she didn't love me either.

The last straw was when she told me was going to have another baby. I'm sorry! She's better off with someone who'll love her for her, not someone who's hanging around out of gratitude. I want to experience life on my own now. I've seen the world, and I want some of it.

Jeff's flight reaction is unfortunately typical of most people whose substance-abuse problem has kept them out of the world for substantial periods of time. As Jeff reports, just like Rip van Winkle, or Miranda in *The Tempest*, he awakened from twenty years of drinking to find a new world, and the birth of his second child was his trigger to begin exploring it. His actions may or may not be appropriate, but they nonetheless reveal a very typical response in the lives of most ACOAs—an overreaction to change.

As an ACOA, you have spent a considerable amount of energy coping with changes in your environment. You may have looked upon change as a threat, something to be managed quickly and quietly. When you got married, your worldview changed. It grew to encompass the needs and responsibilities of a relationship. When you had your first child, your worldview changed again and you achieved a new state of equilibrium. As your child grew, you worked hard at reestablishing that equilibrium, always reacting to his or her changing behavior while at the same time trying to figure out what your child would be up to next. Now, however, with the appearance of a second child, you may feel that your whole balance has been upset. You must understand that this is a normal reaction, given your background and circumstances, and that you will adapt to it as efficiently as you've adapted to all the other changes that have taken place in your life.

Raising a second or third child is not as hard as it initially seems. There are greater financial demands, to be sure, but in terms of emotional responsibility, nothing will happen now that has not happened before. You've already been through the drill with your first child; your second child will be easy by comparison. You can make it even easier still by trying to gain the cooperation of your older child before the new baby arrives.

Ask for the child's help around the house and with caring for the infant. Explain that he or she will have an added responsibility now as well because the oldest child always occupies a special place. Your oldest will now have to be the big brother or big sister, protecting the younger sibling and helping to lay down the rules of the family. Explain that there will be times when your older child will wish that a new baby hadn't arrived to demand mom and dad's attention and wake everybody up in the middle of the night by crying, but that the family will be happier because there will be more people to love. Taking steps now, before the baby arrives, will not only make your job as parent easier but will ease many of the tensions that are bound to surface between you and your child.

Coping with Separation and Divorce

The number of single-parent families has become so large that at least half of all children in American public school systems have spent some time as members of single-parent families. In many communities, the number of children in families that have gone through a divorce outnumber the children in families in which there has never been a divorce. And this social phenomenon has taken only thirty-five years to establish itself. This means that you should not have to wear a scarlet letter if you find yourself contemplating, negotiating, living through, or recovering from a divorce, no matter how painful that uncoupling may be.

As an ACOA, you will have the added burden of dealing with the past as you try to sort out your future. If you are from a dysfunctional family, your divorce may bring with it the stigma of the bad child who is doomed to failure in any relationship because of a basic character flaw. You have to acknowledge that you may feel this way, that you may have a crippling sense of guilt that your parent's alcohol problem was "your fault," and that you may be flying completely blind as a parent because you have no role models, but you have to get beyond that acknowledgment into active parenting. In other words, just because you feel crippled by your divorce doesn't mean that you should abandon your role as parent and caregiver for your children.

When I was the most miserable during the divorce, I would cry into Beth's baby cereal that I was warming up on the stove. And in a flash, I was a little girl all over again. Maybe it was the aroma of the baby food or the burden of caring for this kid while I was being torn up on the inside. Maybe it was my mother, who kept on calling and calling and calling. Or maybe it was my lawyer bugging me for the check, but I just turned and screamed at Beth, "Why did you do this to me?" And she looked up at me with those blue eyes frozen in a kind of terror and then screwed her face up into a million wrinkles before crying a baby cry that split the whole kitchen. And we stood there, day after day, just crying at one another while the cereal boiled all over the stove.

If you have little children, they will look to you for strength. They need to know that even though daddy or mommy may be leaving the family nest, it doesn't mean that they are abandoned. You have to provide them with as much continuity as possible to help their scars heal over quickly. Reinforce their natural resiliency by telling them that feeling sad and guilty about their parents' breakup is completely natural but that *it's not their fault*. I can't stress this too strongly. You will have to rise above all of your childhood feelings of guilt and bitterness. You will have to assume a responsibility—even if it is totally manufactured for the occasion—that lifts from your children the burden of guilt and causality.

They will now feel very much the same feelings that you experienced as a child in your dysfunctional family. You, because of your background, will find it easy and convenient to replay the tape of your own childhood because it's a comfortable feeling of misery—only this time your children will be standing in the way of your feelings. Therefore, even though you will tend to want to replace their feelings with yours, you must work some kind of self-preserving logic into your anger. This won't be easy and you will almost certainly fail before you succeed, but it is important that you keep on trying.

One way to help maintain stability even before the actual separation takes place is to establish family rituals which will provide for continuity when times get rough. By taking one night for fast food and another night for the movies or an amusement park in warm weather and a third to visit a relative or even your in-laws, you will create a pattern that you and your children will come to rely on. You can also set up patterns around the house for doing the laundry, taking baths, or doing crossword puzzles. The trick is not what you do, but that you do something to pull the family closer together in the face of great change.

You should also develop personal mechanisms for dealing with the loss of control you will feel as you experience the pain and loneliness of divorce and separation. Here is one such technique that some of my clients have adopted successfully. At the moment when you feel your control about to slip away, when you are about to unleash your most deep-seated childhood-based fears upon your own children, make believe you can turn the mirror on yourself instead of on them. Try to see yourself for what you are at that very moment: a lost child just like them. They can't solve your problem for you, but they can give you the unconditional love that you desperately need at that moment. Take their love. Hold them to you as tight as you can and sponge up all the love they have. It will make you feel better, it will keep you from treating them as objects of your misery, and it lets them know that they are still at the center of your universe. They have to know that despite all that is going on you are still on their side.

Divorce and Older Children

I used to watch from the upstairs window when Janet would take Charlie and Darah away for her weekend with the kids. Bennett would always show up too because he had a big car and the kids liked to bounce around in the back. Sometimes he would bring his son, Bennett, Jr. And when they came back there would be the obligatory 48 hours of decontamination before I could show the kids to my parents. The levels of hatefulness were unbearable. "Bennett did this" and "Bennett did that." To be honest, I didn't know who I hated more, Janet, Bennett, or the kids. When they would drive away, I wished, way down deep in the darkest, most forbidden part of myself, they they would hit a tree and be vaporized in an instant. They would all go to heaven, of course, and I would be left to rot here on earth. But at least I wouldn't have to put up with the kids coming back and hating my very existence.

Divorce is generally easier on younger children than on older ones. Your kids will almost certainly have behavior problems as they get shuttled back and forth between their respective families and stepfamilies. Jealousies will be compounded on all sides and neither you nor your ex-spouse will be able to be completely objective and without emotions or loyalties. This is natural and to be expected. Unfortunately, kids do bear the brunt of the divorce because they are the emissaries of the past, reminding us of our failures and exposing our shortcomings to the new families of our ex-spouses. Your role, even if your ex-spouse chooses to undermine it rather than support it, is to confront the negative behavior without destroying the child in the process. As hateful as a child may behave upon returning from your ex-spouse and the new girlfriend or boyfriend—and it will only get worse before it gets better—you have to lay down the law, tell the kid as firmly as possible that you will not tolerate being humiliated or held up to ridicule, but at the same time let your child know that you understand exactly how painful the entire experience is for him or her to bear.

You have to understand that your children are not having a picnic even though "the bimbo" has taken them shopping or "the geek" has gotten them backstage passes to a Bruce Springsteen concert. They will return to you feeling as guilty as can be, and they will punish you for it. Understand that your children, no matter how mature they seem, have no mechanism for balancing conflicting feelings of guilt and happiness. They are happy to be with their other parent. But they are guilty about feeling happy because they are not with you. At the same time, they sense that you will feel a level of resentment toward their happiness, and they are guilty over that as well. Because they can't rationalize their feelings of guilt and happiness and shame, they tend to express them through sullenness, ill-temper, and a nasty disposition in the period immediately following their return. This is completely natural and expected. You don't have to like it, and you don't have to be a victim, but you should understand it and let them know that it does not diminish your love for them.

It is in ACOA families that personal feelings are more intense and the emotional trip-wires much closer to the surface. First of all, your own levels of guilt over the divorce will be much higher. If you sensed everything was your fault when you were a child and did not know better, you absolutely *know* it is your fault now because you walked into this situation with both eyes wide open. Even if it isn't your fault, you will say that it is because you feel as if you need to bear the guilt. Second, your sensitivities to rejection and pain will be much higher. You learned as a child how to feel pain in places where no child should suffer. Those scars are still very tender and exposed. Therefore, when your ex-spouse turns on you and your children become his or her weapons, what they say and do penetrates your defenses like bullets through chicken wire.

How should you react? You can begin by realizing that it is as hard on your children as it is on you. You should also realize, although this may be a tiny consolation, that your spouse is getting the same nasty treatment that you are. Children give equal opportunity when it comes to displaying negative reactions and will dole out their sullenness and intransigence in like measure to both parties. Above all, you should look on your children's behavior as their immature attempts to deal with real adult problems. If you can assume the role of adult, you can rise above the insults and the barbs and help your children reconcile the emotions at war within them. Look at it selfishly if you want to. Use this as your opportunity to grow by helping them resolve conflicts that you never could when you were their age.

Dealing with Stepparents

As hard as it seems to deal with the divorce, dealing with a new dad or new mom will be that much harder. Your children will make comparisons: "Charlene lets us stay up later"; "Fred lets us park his Corvette in the driveway"; "Michael is going to take me to the firehouse on Saturday and let me work the siren on his chief's car"; "Donna said I could be on her TV show." Face it, if your ex-spouse is dating someone exotic or even mildly different from you, you are going to come out second best no matter what you do. You must squelch the very natural urge to put down the other party in front of your kids. That's what you have friends and confidants for. In fact, if your children's behavior is especially bad and they seem too entranced with your ex's new love, you should seek out someone you can trust and let your venom spill all over the rug. There's nothing wrong with that.

You must understand that your children are being required to reconcile new levels of guilt and shame. They want to love and respect whomever their parent chooses to love. They want to welcome the new stepparent into their lives. However, there is also a natural reluctance to replace one parent with another. Children feel a sense of guilt and shame at their own disloyalty. They will look for flaws in you to make it easier for themselves. They will also try to trigger your temper to make it easier for them to say, "She's mean to us and I like my new mom better." Don't make it easy in a negative way; do it in a positive way by showing your children how they can welcome a new person into their lives without being disloyal to either of their parents.

For ACOAs, the presence of a new parent figure cuts right to the heart of feelings of abandonment and illegitimacy. "They were the legitimate family," Patrick kept repeating throughout his ex-wife's engagement and eventual marriage to her second husband.

I would always tell myself that every time I watched them drive away on weekends. "They belong together. Why don't I just disappear. Make it easy for all of them to form up as a family. I don't belong. Never did." And so one day I just took off and never saw my kids again.

After years of compensating for the sense of abandonment that characterized your childhood, you may suddenly feel that it was all for naught. You may see your children with another mother or father and surrender all of your parental rights in an instant because you were never taught to be a part of a family. Even if you were sure of yourself, it would be difficult. But as a person who is unsure, the presence of a rival for your children's affection trips a set of reactions that threatens to destroy the balance you so painfully achieved.

The first trap you should avoid is direct comparison. There is nothing inherently inferior about you that would make you come out second in a competition with a stepparent. The second trap to avoid is to see competition where there is none. Understand that you are already the children's parent. You have been their parent since birth and they have no other biological father or mother. Simply stated, you can't be replaced by a stepparent no matter how hard your ex-spouse, his or her lawyer, or some family court judge might try. Knowing that you can't be replaced should provide you with the confidence to be yourself at your best and it should allow you to love your children with no strings attached. They don't have to profess their loyalty to you every day you're together. Unless you take active steps to drive them away, they'll remain loyal to you throughout the process of divorce and the establishment of stepfamilies.

Therefore, don't make it any harder on them or yourself. Accept the reality of the divorce and your ex-spouse's need to form a new family. Accept that your children will find the stepparent a bit more exotic than you. And, finally, accept that just as you are your parents' child for the rest of your life, so will your own children remain yours for the rest of their lives as well. Your ACOA background, although it has weakened your ability to deal with many domestic adversities, has also given you many strengths. Because you felt abandonment and sadness as a child, you are easily able to relate to those feelings in others and respond to them. You will have a natural empathy for your children's deepest fears during this period. If you allow yourself to tap into it, you can be a more effective parent than one who has not experienced what you did in your childhood.

Death in the Family

The first few hours after Stephen died, I was mentally lost. The realization didn't sink in until the next day, really, but for those hours after the doctors told me he was gone, I felt totally alone. Then someone said, "Who'll tell the children?" and that's when I remembered I had kids.

When someone we love dies, there is an immediate sense of aloneness. How long that lasts and how quickly one is able to reach out and share the grief with others vary from person to person. In the case of your parents, you will probably have already prepared yourself for the end because of advancing age or illness. In the case of a spouse, unless the person is in a high-risk job or is the victim of a serious illness, the death will usually be unexpected. In the case of one of your children, even the onset of serious illness is often unexpected.

How you cope with grief and how much you let others share in that grief will often determine how quickly you heal. Except in the rare instances where a person loses an entire family and must begin life all over again, most people try to pick up the pieces of their lives and continue on the courses they have set. What you do, however, is not as important as how you do it.

Death of a Parent

When my wife told me that my sister wanted me to go down to the hospital in Philly to arrange transportation for my mother back to Jersey, I took it as just another chore. I was always doing that sort of thing for my brothers and sisters. So I drove down to Philly without giving it another thought. But when I arrived at the hospital, they told me she was dead. Just like that. Died during the night. I was in a state of shock. She was a recovering alcoholic and had had kidney problems for years, but just to die so suddenly was almost not possible.

I called my wife and sister and told them to prepare my dad. Then, still pretty teary, I drove home to talk with dad. I didn't even stop at my house. I just drove straight to Trenton to see my dad.

There was no answer when I rang the doorbell. . . . I tried knocking. Still no answer. Then I went around back to the kitchen, something I didn't want to do because he gets frightened whenever he hears footsteps on the back porch. I knocked—really pounded— but there was still no answer. I used my key.

He was upstairs, lying face down beside the bed in a puddle of clotted blood. His left hand was still gripping the bedspread as if he had tried to break his fall by yanking on it. I knew he was dead from the moment I saw him there. I stayed there just long enough to make phone calls to my wife, sister, the police, and the rescue squad and then went downstairs. By the time the rest of the family arrived and the ambulance had taken my father's body to the hospital, I was ready to leave.

I went into his neighborhood bar, started drinking there, and worked my way halfway across the county before going home. I've been a drunk ever since.

For an ACOA, the death of either the alcoholic parent or the enabler is a form of release at the same time that it is a confrontation with the years of unresolved guilt. Your over-whelming temptation, and indeed your need as an ACOA, will be to meet the death of your parent as an intensely personal event, a private catharsis that takes place at the core of your being. This is as it should be, and you should not feel a secondary sense of guilt at shutting out your spouse or children. You cannot help them if you are unable to reconcile your own feelings at this moment of personal loss.

You may experience wildly conflicting emotions. You hated your alcoholic parent on the surface, yet you loved him or her deep inside. Your needs as a newborn for affection, touching, and parental love never vanished. Therefore, if you never got them from your parent, his or her death will leave those needs forever unresolved. You may cherish the memory, experience a mid-life crisis, or burn with fury at the lousy hand dealt you by fortune, but you will have to come to grips with the fact that what your living parent didn't give to you your dead parent never will.

It's OK to wrap yourself up in a shroud of grief and deal with your private demons after your parent has died. Your spouse should support you in this and help you return to the family emotional circle to reconnect with your children. At the same time, you have to be the preserver of your parent's history, because it is that history which will inform your own children's futures in one way or another. This is why you should seek counseling or therapy, if necessary, and promise yourself that you will confront all of the issues with your children if and when they are old enough.

What you must not do is even consider medicating yourself with alcohol or drugs. If you feel the need to do that, even before you fight any personal battles over the compulsion, seek counseling at once. One of the lies that you will tell yourself is that when you have resolved the conflicts surrounding your parent's death or pigeon-holed the emotions into a safe place, you will get off the drug or stop drinking and get back to reality. After all, you may say, you're not an alcoholic, you're not your parent. You handled the problem for thirty or so years, and you can handle it now. These are the same illusions that tempted your alcoholic parent two generations earlier. Don't you fall for them now.

Reentering Your Family Circle.   At some point you must return from the fears that haunted your past and bring them into the present. The death of your parents presents you with the watershed opportunity to accomplish this. First of all, you know that you have a lot of explaining to do to your children. If they are old enough to understand what alcoholism is and what your parent was, they are old enough to understand some of your emotions. If your in-laws cannot help you, don't turn to them. Let your spouse know that the last thing you need at a moment of personal crisis is a judgmental attitude that denigrates the memory of your parent into a form of good riddance. Expect that your spouse will understand this. After all, you've been there for your spouse during these years.

Now you have to deal with your children's grief. If your parents were a part of your family life, expect that your children will experience a dramatic sense of loss. If little children, they may not understand death or why their grandparent won't be coming over on Sundays anymore. If they are older children, let them go through a private sense of grief and reconcile their own memories. This is part of their growing-up process and it should not be short-circuited. Above all, encourage your children—whether young or older —to cry with you and participate in a period of family mourning. Teach your children to stand up for their grandparents and to shoulder the responsibility that the living must bear for the memory of their dead loved ones. They should be at the funeral and should welcome the other mourners who come to visit. By grieving over the death of your parents, they will celebrate their lives and amalgamate what has been passed on to them from your family. In the long run, they will benefit from being asked to bear this responsibility.

Death of a Child

We all knew that Tommy would have a short life after he was diagnosed with childhood leukemia. I quit my job, pulled him out of day care, and just circled the wagons while I waited for the end. The problem was that I made the circle too small. I didn't let anyone else in. My husband couldn't even get near Tommy during those last months before he went into the hospital. And the older children, Tommy's sisters, they just sat on their beds and watched. When it was finally over and Tommy had been buried next to my dad, I thought that returning to the family would be just like coming home. Except that home was no longer there. My husband and the girls wound up blaming me for keeping Tommy from them, and they were right.

Christine considered herself fortunate in therapy because she was able to prepare for her youngest child's death. She also found that in the very act of grieving for Tommy, her family drew themselves around her and eventually became stronger. Other parents, those who lose older children to accidents or crime, don't have any time to prepare themselves: they are confronted with the loss and have to acknowledge it before grieving over it.

When I saw Jason laid out in that coffin, his white shirt and jacket cleaner than any of his clothes had ever been in life, the acceptance of what happened finally crashed in on me. They had to carry me home from the funeral parlor. When I found out about the motorcycle accident I was working. Two guys on my shift walked up to me, told me to take off my goggles and go with them to the shop steward's table because there was a problem that only I could solve. Then I noticed that the shift manager was there and that nobody was smiling. I figured I was getting laid off. When they told me there'd been an accident, I thought about Wendy first and my next thoughts were how I would take care of the kids. Then when they said Jason I just put my head down.

I had managed to go through my whole life up to now without hurting nobody. I had gotten away from my father in one piece, and he shouting after me that I would always be a me-first son of a bitch like the people who laid him off for drinking on the shift. I cursed him when he was alive and cursed him after he died. And when my kid started drinking I cursed him, too. Now, when Jason lay there in his suit, I knew that I had no one.

I still drive by the spot where he went into his skid and slid into the tree. And the hole inside of me is bigger than the bike that killed him.

For an ACOA parent who has put all of his or her effort into raising a child, the death of that child, whether from sickness or accident, almost always carries the potential for life-shattering consequences. You have to account for the years you spent parenting that child and find meaning in them. You have to deal with your spouse and, of course, the other children in the family. And you have to deal with your own guilt. Did you buy the child the motorcycle that killed him? Did you let your daughter go to the store with her friend even though you had lazy misgivings that something might happen? Did you get all the medical opinions you should have before committing to one course of treatment?

You can ask yourself these questions for a lifetime without ever resolving them. The voices that haunted you throughout your life may grow even louder now and threaten to overwhelm you. Certainly, upon the death of one of your children, counseling or therapy is in order. Even the most normal of parents requires some form of help to cope with the crisis. Stable marriage partners have a tendency to blame themselves and one another for the death. Siblings are sometimes blamed—not for contributing to the child's death but simply for remaining alive.

If you are an ACOA, every one of these problems will be compounded by the sense of guilt and tragedy that you already feel. Moreover, ACOAs have grown up in families that, as a general rule, denied reality, the truth, and their own feelings. Remember, your alcoholic parent wasn't drunk, he or she was just "sick," and the world outside of the family could never understand that. This sense of denial prevented you from acknowledging your feelings at first, and then from feeling altogether. This ACOA tendency will dovetail with perfectly normal feelings of denial that arise after the death of a child. Every parent will have an initial reaction of "It can't be true," and "Tommy is still in his room waiting for us." That sense of denial may last only a few days or as long as a few months. It is one way the mind buffers itself from feelings of catastrophic grief. Ultimately, the parent must fully accept what has happened and begin to mourn privately. However, because you are an ACOA who has practiced denial of reality as an ongoing activity, you may become frightened that the reality of your child's death hasn't penetrated yet. Don't blame yourself for this or cause yourself even greater pain. All that's happening is a natural, normal feeling of denial that everybody experiences when a close family member has died.

Eventually you must accept the reality of what has happened. Accept it in the abstract in the beginning, if that helps, but at least acknowledge that after a child has died there is nothing you can do to bring him or her back. Torturing yourself won't help the child, and it will almost certainly cause pain for your other children. The answer to how you will cope lies in your ability to see your responsibility to your spouse and other children. If you allow yourself to burn out from the combined forces of stress and guilt, you will simply become another family casualty. If your family's resources are so strained after coping with the loss of the child that they can't compensate for you, or, worse, if the family has been relying on you to keep things together, your loss amounts to a double casualty.

The course of emotional and family stability after the loss of one of your children lies, first, in the acknowledgment of what really happened. Next, there is the binding together of the children, the encircling of the family grief around the siblings so they can share their parents' tragedy and find a meaning in their own sadness. This is where you and your spouse must become larger than life. You must guide your children through the process of grief and reconstruction. You must not allow them to keep their grief internal until it explodes into violence or antisocial behavior. This will only cause greater pain.

One of the unhappy facts you will discover in this circumstance is that most teachers and doctors do not know how to deal with someone else's grief. They avoid it and make it worse. If your other children are in school, you will almost certainly have to intercede for them and force the school psychologist and principal to understand what your family is going through. Be brutal with them if you have to, but do not let their platitudes take the place of assurance that they stand ready to help your children. After all, you're paying them. They must understand that your children are angry at the turn of events. Their true sadness is masked by a feeling of guilt that they are still alive while the sibling is dead. It is also masked by a jealousy which becomes no more apparent than in the schoolyard when their classmates are playing. "Why should the rest of the world be happy when I am sad?"

they might ask. "Why are the lives of my friends uninterrupted by what I feel? Why am I the outsider?"

At the same time, you may notice that your friends in the neighborhood will withhold their children from playing with yours after tragedy strikes. If you are an ACOA it is easy to interpret this reaction as a form of scarlet letter, a public announcement of your sin of trying to fit in where you don't belong. The death of your child, you may feel, is a form of chastisement for all the world to see. You are flawed and you brought forth flawed children. Now one of them has died, and your other children will pay the price in shame and humiliation.

Of course, none of this could be further from the truth. The facts are that typically when a child has died in a neighborhood, the other parents feel skittish. It's almost as if death has visited the community and might be looking for more victims. If their children are around your house, death may return and claim them as well. As silly as that sounds, it's a superstition that goes back to the Middle Ages when the black plague was ravaging Europe. You should realize, however, what the real truth is. It is normal for other families to deny what happened to your child by shunning you and your other children. By denying you, they deny the truth of death and combat the very real fear that it will happen to them as well.

You can mitigate the negative reactions from your neighbors by calling upon them for help and support. They might distance themselves from you at first, but a healthy reaction from someone who considers him- or herself to be an upstanding member of the community is to confront friends in the neighborhood directly. You might begin by a phone call and ask the person over for coffee or dessert and conversation after dinner. Explain to your neighbor that you know what everyone's natural reaction will be and that you understand it. Your children might not understand it, however, and that is why you would like your friend to help you explain it to your children. Stress the importance of friends and the role they can play in forming a community. If parents and children can pull together in the face of tragedy, the whole community will be the stronger for it. If your neighbor agrees in wanting to raise his or her kids to be participating members of a community, he or she will help you. If your neighbor avoids you, he or she will be the weaker for it. In either case, you win because you are behaving like a strong adult. Remember, ACOAs are unsure about their feelings and emotions as a rule and will especially be so now.

Dealing with Your Family and In-Laws After Your Child Has Died.   Everyone's first reaction will be to offer verbal support. If you feel overburdened with guilt and have no one on either side of the family you can talk to, you will have to rely on your spouse to intercede with your in-laws, even though he or she is as grief-stricken and guilt-ridden as you are. You will need each other's support during this period, even though there may be an undertow of tensions pulling you apart because, secretly, each may blame the other—a very natural defense mechanism.

Your in-laws will naturally assume that their help is expected and required. They are the grandparents and will be as grieved over the death of your child as any grandparent would be. Therefore, let your comforting include them as well as your spouse and children. Don't relegate yourself to a second-class position, but don't shut out members of your larger family just because you may fear their reprobation at a later date. Assignment of blame and judgment is standard drill when people are trying to cope with the loss of a loved child, and should be expected even if feared. If, during your period of mourning, you let your in-laws know that you understand if they blame you in some way and do not hold it against them, the healing process will be faster and more complete.

Your own parents might be a different matter, especially if you've deliberately kept them out of your family life. Perhaps you feel that there is precious little your parents can offer you in the way of comfort. After all, they didn't comfort you when you were a child; why should they be any different now that you are an adult? If you were able to see beyond your immediate situation, you would understand that by offering comfort to someone else, one allows oneself to grieve more meaningfully and reach an emotional catharsis sooner. Catharses are important because they are the cleansing mechanisms of the human spirit. They help people to come to terms with the inherent sadness of living. If your parents have lived their lives selfishly and have allowed alcohol to interfere with your life, they will seek to become a part of your grieving process. By shutting them out, you perpetuate the sadness for yourself as well as them. Let them in, even though it might be painful for you initially. Let them in because the death of your child should not be used as a club to hurt others; it should be a bonding experience for all those who are alive. In other words, celebrate your child's memory by committing to life rather than by continuing to curse the darkness of your own past childhood.

Dealing with the Death of Your Spouse

Telling a child that his or her parent has died is an experience that no one wants to go through, least of all the other parent. In the midst of your own grief, and anger that your spouse has left you alone, you must assure the children that you can do the job of both parents while assuring them that their own existence is as certain as it ever was. Again, the younger the children, generally the easier the job is. If your children are older teenagers who have begun to establish their separate existences, the job is hard, but you can rely on their support in your need. If, however, your children are between the ages of seven and sixteen, the event can become a gut-wrenching period of agony that can last many, many months.

I didn't tell the kids at first that Stephen had died because I couldn't say it without becoming hysterical. I told them, "Daddy's going to be away for a while" or "Daddy's had an accident and can't come home tonight," something like that. It was getting serious because the children kept asking for him and I kept dodging their questions between periods of running to the bathroom and trying to sob as quietly as I could. I was afraid the kids would blame me if they knew Stephen was dead. I was afraid they'd tell me that the only reason they were staying with me in the first place was because of Stephen. That sounds stupid, I know, because the kids were only four and six, but that's how I felt. Any minute, I believed that Stephen's mother would show up at the door and say, "That's it, I'm the new mother and you have two hours to pack your bags and get out. "You see,

Stephen was my link to the world. Without Stephen I didn't deserve to have the kids or live in the house or anything.

It was Stephen's parents who finally forced Cheryl to tell her children that their father was dead.

Stephen's dad was amazing. He was a full-bird colonel in Korea and had this ramrod-straight bearing about him. Real West Point stuff. He just walked into the living room, his eyes were red and puffy, sat the kids down and said, "You boys are gonna have to become men now because your dad has been hurt real bad and can't look after your mom anymore. I'm gonna stick around to make sure that you're all right, but you're gonna have to grow up and be the two men your father knows you can be." The kids just sat there with their eyes as wide as plates. Then they started crying. I cried. Stephen's father cried, too, and told them that crying was a good thing and it was OK for men to let it all out. But when the crying stopped, he told them, they had to good soldiers on account of their dad. Stephen's mom kept on hugging me and telling me that she wouldn't let anything bad happen to me. We would all be a family.

Then Stephen's parents looked me right in the eye and told me to come over and sit on the couch. They watched and listened while I told the boys that their father was dead, killed when the car he was in jumped the median barrier over on the Interstate. I felt like a weight had been lifted, even though I knew that the toughest times were still ahead.

Cheryl's road back began with an honest acknowledgment to her children about their situation. Her husband's parents had forced her into accepting the reality of death, and, consequently, she was able to work out of her problems sooner rather than later.

Not all ACOAs can be as fortunate as Cheryl was in that situation. Most are left to their own devices without the intervention of competent family members to smooth the way. If you face the death of your spouse and feel overwhelmed by the prospect of, first, breaking the news to the children and, next, finding a way to manage your own grief while helping your children through their immediate pain, you should seek some form of counseling as quickly as possible. Counseling—and that does not necessarily mean psychotherapy—can take the form of honest conversations with members of the clergy, frank discussions with a close friend or relative of your spouse, or occasional professional advice from your doctor or someone he or she refers you to. Remember, the death of a loved one is considered a catastrophic occurrence by most professional psychologists. Catastrophes generally require serious repair work and a significant period of reconstruction before the person can set out again. Even then, the person usually never completely recovers from a catastrophe but simply learns to live with the scars.

So it is with the death of an intimate. You will never forget your spouse. He or she will remain a part of your life even if you remarry and move to a new city. Similarly, unless your children are very young, their deceased parent will remain in their memories as well. They will idealize their dead parent—and grandparent as well—regardless of whether he or she was a loving parent, an alcoholic, or completely dysfunctional. Therefore, it is important that you allow your children to indulge in fantasies about their dead parent. It will help them to heal and to preserve whatever was good in their relationship with the person. You can help your children at a later date gain a better perspective of their parent or your parent by sharing your relevant memories with them. However, give them the appropriate time to place the entire event within a meaningful context before challenging their memories of the person.

Recognizing how children will idealize the dead and hold on to their memories, it is vital that you help your children amalgamate the past into their future and begin the process of healing. Rely on whatever friends you can and those family members who offer to help. You shouldn't even attempt to navigate this period alone. Funeral arrangements will have to be made and your children will have to participate in them. Call upon all your resources and the resources of your spouse. Remember, the celebration of someone's life is a family function and the family should be brought into it.

As an ACOA, you won't find that task an easy one. Your spouse's death may serve to reinforce the sense of abandonment that you've felt since childhood. His or her death also reinforces your sense that you can't make it on your own.

This is a normal feeling for non-ACOAs as well. However, it may be especially hard on you because you are an ACOA. Remember, feeling grief and a sense of great loss means that the relationship was and continues to be important for you. It *proves* that you were worthwhile. If you believed that you were lucky enough to find and marry the one-in-a-million person who could understand and love you, the suddenness and inevitability of that person's death may bring back a thousand demons to stir up your worst fears of worthlessness. To make matters worse, you also have children to worry about, so you can't simply retreat into a corner and steel yourself against the world. You have to make their lives easier while you are fighting your own internal battles. If you were worthwhile during the relationship you are worthwhile now, and you can help your children and yourself through this period of grief.

Surprisingly, being a parent may make dealing with the grief and loss easier. Unless you are so ravaged that you feel out of control and on the edge of violence—in which case immediate medical care and professional therapy are required—the need to help your children through this period forces you out of your cocoon. Your kids have to eat, they have to go to school, they have to reconnect with the outside world, and their lives have to continue even though you are still feeling intense pain. You have not stopped being a parent. Therefore, use the daily drill of caring for the children as the routine which works you back into your schedule. Don't deny the pain you are feeling, but at the same time you should try to let your responsibilities to your family soak up some of the anxiety.

Above all, keep repeating to yourself over and over again, "It's not my fault." You may feel guilty that your spouse is dead and you're still alive, but that's a natural reaction. However, because you felt that the dysfunction that crippled your alcoholic family was somehow your fault, you are particularly sensitive to those feelings again. If you are aware of the likelihood of their recurrence after the death of your spouse, you will be better able to work through them.

The feelings that it's your fault may never go away, just as they've never gone away since childhood. However, your continual reassertion of the facts—it really wasn't your fault—helps you more than it seems to on the surface. At the very least, when you are feeling overwhelmed by the world, your own voice of reason, however hollow it may sound against the chorus of the past, can be a lifeline out of depression. And knowing that you have to care for your children helps you control the guilt that may dog your actions from day to day. Eventually, the pain will begin to ease somewhat and you will be able to laugh again. You will reconnect with the world, and your fears that the entire community is pointing fingers of accusation at you will subside. You will recover—the passing of time will see to that—and you will find solace in having helped your children shoulder their grief.

Reacting to Change

ACOAs sometimes nurture a childhood belief that the whole world can be a kind of benevolent magic kingdom completely under control. If someone is unhappy in the magic kingdom, the ACOA can fix the problem and restore happiness. Translated into a family situation, this means that a hypervigilant ACOA parent is always on the alert for the grumblings or complaints that signal dissatisfaction with the way things are. Then the ACOA parent can try to remedy the situation, even if the person has not asked for a remedy, to make things all right again in the environment. The problem is that not all complaints need to be remedied and sometimes situations are better off left alone. But worse, sometimes the unhappy event looms so large that even the ACOA is overwhelmed by the magnitude of what has to be corrected. Faced with the impossibility of the situation, the person simply surrenders and assumes that it is his or her fault that people around him or her are unhappy.

In instances of catastrophic change such as divorce, accidents, or the death of loved ones, many times there can be no meaningful assignment of blame. The situation simply is what it is and needs to be dealt with realistically rather than magically. But because ACOAs may be unable to allow for the existence of negative events without sponging up the responsibility and guilt, the situation itself is never dealt with, only the ACOA's inability to have prevented it from happening. As you can see, if you perceive things this way, it interferes with remedy and healing because there are too many personal levels of explanation and justification for you to go through before you see the event for what it is.

The answer is to recognize that many times you are going to react to any type of unhappy change as if it's all your fault; that if you could have somehow seen the future and fine-tuned all of the forces crossing your path, the future would have turned out differently. That is simply not the case. And to make matters even more complicated, there are those events for which you can assign blame, but doing so only keeps you from remedying them. On the other hand, there are types of unhappy events that can be remedied only by recognizing where the blame lies and addressing fault before you repair the damage. The trick is to recognize which is which. But if you have a knee-jerk reaction in assuming that it's always your fault, you won't be able to tell one type of event from another.

In dealing with the catastrophic changes that affect our lives, we have to develop adult reactions based on realistic assessments. For the ACOA as parent, this means that the perceptions and reactions that got you through childhood usually won't work anymore because you have to augment your thinking to cover your children as well as yourself. You can't be a loner once you are a parent. Thus, if there is a general set of rules for ACOA parents to help them deal with catastrophic change, the first rule might be to automatically silence the voice which accuses you of blame. Wallowing in guilt will not help. The second rule is to determine who is most in need of immediate help and attention. Once the situation itself has been stabilized, you can then try to determine causality—if that is important—and see whether you can prevent the situation from reoccurring in the future. Then you can assess the long-term damage.

Make no mistake about it, catastrophic change often involves work on your part to set things right or effect some form of remedy. However, you only make your job more difficult by spinning a web of guilt and self-recrimination around yourself. If you can focus some of the objectivity you developed as a parent in normal times directly on the change that's disrupted the lives in your family, you will almost certainly find that the event, although painful, may not be as hopeless as it seemed when it first occurred. Major change sometimes brings with it solutions to problems that we never even perceived as problems because we were unable to see the big picture until the catastrophe occurred. Now that we can see it, maybe we can address it.

11

The ACOA as Grandparent

JEAN

Look, Michael chose to have the kids and they're his responsibility. It's not my job to keep them from getting pregnant or from using drugs. I've already put in my time. Now it's his turn.

On the surface, Jean seemed as if she could remain detached from the problems of her grandchildren. At times, she almost seemed cold toward them. However, that was just an illusion because in reality Jean was like an egg. If you hold an egg longways and squeeze, it's impossible for the shell to crack. But if you hold it sideways, the shell that seemed so rock solid just a few minutes earlier quickly becomes fragile and shatters. Jean, like the egg, was strong and fragile at the same time.

I relied on no one else in my whole life. Just me. When I had to survive, I was the only person I could count on. My parents didn't amount to nothing.

She was the product of a harsh and demanding mother and a passive alcoholic father. She learned early to rely on only herself because neither parent was capable of raising her. She used both her will and her wits to escape from her childhood in a dysfunctional household and then later to bounce back from two disappointing and unhappy marriages. The first marriage was to a passive and dependent man who died in his early thirties, and the second was to an active alcoholic who was involved in romantic liaisons with other women throughout his marriage to Jean. Jean's only child was her son, who completed college, pursued his career in midlevel management in an electronics firm, and now had a family of his own. Thus she personified the image of the ACOA as survivor.

However, even as a grandparent, all of the anger and frustration at seeing a cycle of addiction reemerge in the third generation of her family kept bubbling to the surface. Though she remained aloof and outwardly kept her distance from her son's family, inside she was seething as she saw his children experiment with drugs and liquor and watched their father take no extraordinary methods to stop it.

All right, all right, of course I'm worried about them. I feel like I have to hold myself back from running over to Michael's house, pushing him out of the way, and straightening out his kids. It's like, if I can be in charge of how they are raised, I can fix them. Not that they are hopeless or bad kids or that Susie or he can't handle them by themselves, but I worry. I'm always worrying.

As an ACOA grandparent, she is in an awkward position as she observes the insidious cycle of alcohol addiction and drug abuse repeat itself in her grandchildren. It was frightening for her to watch it happen to her parents when she was a child, but then she was capable of running away. It is frightening and frustrating to watch it happen to your own grandchildren because you know you can fix it, but you're only a grandparent and not the one in charge.

Look Before You Leap

Perhaps nothing can be worse than to realize that your grandchildren are abusing themselves with alcohol or other drugs. You may be overwhelmed with a feeling of devastation when you discover that all your best efforts in parenting your own children have not prevented your family's pattern of addiction from repeating itself in your grandchild. If you are faced with the unfortunate circumstance of this happening in your life, be forewarned of the possible reemergence of the nagging feelings of inadequacy and failure so common in adult children of alcoholics. But first do your best to be sure there is a problem before you allow your state of alarm to kick off these feelings.

Despite the differences in style, the stages of psychological and social development remain remarkably consistent from generation to generation. This is something you won't see for yourself until you are a parent in your parent's position. Perhaps you notice that you have some of your parent's personality traits now, but even more will emerge when you assume the role of parent. Because there is such a consistency in personality and behavioral traits, try not to be fooled into thinking that the rebellion and moodiness in your grandchild are an automatic indicator that the child has gone wrong or that your child has botched the job of parenting. It may well be the same struggle for a sense of purpose and identity you watched your own child go through. However, that rebellion may take different forms for this new generation.

Through the eyes of a grandchild of an ACOA, the grandparent may seem like the only voice of stability during years of adolescent crises. As Jonathan, a twenty-year-old grandchild of an ACOA grandmother, describes it:

I never knew that grandmom was a child of an alcoholic. My parents and our family was always so straight—no booze, no joints, no pills—that addiction was never even discussed. I did go through hell growing up because my mother was such an obsessive that everything had to be done exactly right or not at all. My grandmother, however, seemed laid back. I never knew that she was the one who was the stickler when mom was growing up; that she turned my mother into a prison guard. My mother told me that when I was born, my grandmother became very mellow and my mother became the stickler.

To look at Jonathan today—he has a short haircut, collegiate dress, and the concerned, almost intense, bearing of a premed—one would never guess that just four years earlier he had dressed and acted like a punk-rocker. He wore his deep brown hair in spikes with the ends tipped in pink dye, a black

leather biker's jacket with the logo of his favorite rock band
sewn across the back, and spiked bracelets on both wrists. He
spoke of searching for the meaning of life, wallowed in the
hopelessness of middle-class American teendom, and sat for
hours in a darkened room reading Kafka and Dostoyevsky.
His mother thought he might have been secretly using drugs
or was suicidal, but none of that was true. In fact, he was
perfectly straight and became distressed at those of his
friends who used drugs or even drank. He was also quite
responsible, and earned money by coordinating the local
bookings for several punk-rock bands in his high school. He
also served as the editor of a statewide newsletter about rock
music and the local appearances of touring music groups.

He expressed the same misgivings about becoming an adult
that all teenagers express; however, for Jonathan there was a
big difference. Because his grandmother had squeaked out
her survival in a badly dysfunctional alcoholic family, she
had developed within herself powerful survival skills. Those
skills so shaped the lives of her children that her youngest
daughter, Jonathan's mother, reacted to them with rebellion.
And as Jonathan rebelled against his mother, he found a soul
mate in his seventy-year-old grandmother. She served as an
island of support, acceptance, and caring amidst the excessive demands and judgments of his mother.

I could never describe what it was like growing up in my mother's
house. It wasn't just that you had to do everything she wanted, it
was that you had to do it exactly and precisely in the way she
wanted you to do it. If she said, "Take out the garbage and then wash
the dishes," she didn't mean wash the dishes and take out the
garbage. It had to be done in the right order, even if it didn't matter.
And heaven help you if you mixed up the order. But when grandmom walked into the room, even mom shut up. My grandmother is
made of iron, and even today the waters just seem to part whenever
she wants to walk through them.

His grandmother's ability to see behind the spiked hair and
punk outfits helped Jonathan enormously. Had she disap-
proved of him the way his mother did, it would have increased the likelihood of his rebelling to far greater extremes.
Her clarity and patience also relieved her of needless feelings

of worry and guilt—typical in an ACOA with older children—
and they prevented her from becoming alienated from her
grandson. It may be hard for a grandparent to see the child
behind the mask, but it is worth every effort to do so.

The immediate temptation to step in and correct the
mistakes of your grown children has to be resisted at every
turn. You are not the parent. You have raised your children to
lead productive and successful lives. You have to have the
confidence that even though you had neither bench marks nor
role models when you were raising your family, you did at
least an adequate job. Now as the parent of adult children
and a grandparent to their children, you have to observe from
a distance and let your efforts work themselves through the
hands of your children. If you raised them with love and
educated them about your parents and alcohol addiction, you
must expect them to act on their own behalf. Be there for your
children and grandchildren when they seek support, but
don't intrude on their lives.

Looking Inside

It is, of course, possible that much to your chagrin you find
that your suspicions are well-founded. You have checked out
the situation and have determined that there is some dysfunction being manifested in the life of your grandchild. She
may have gotten pregnant out of wedlock or while still a
teenager; he may have been arrested for driving while intoxi-
cated, or she may have been picked up for possession of drugs.
Their performance in school may have tailed off or one or
both of them may be hanging around with bad elements in
the neighborhood that you may know for a fact or strongly
suspect have involvement with drugs or alcohol. You may see
the big picture forming and feel the need to charge into their
lives, confront your own adult child, and announce that
you're taking over. No matter how much you feel this way,
stop and make sure of your facts first. Do not launch your own
crisis intervention unless specifically asked to do so by your
adult children, your grandchildren's school, or the juvenile
authorities. First, examine your emotional reaction to what
you believe to be true.

One of the most common initial reactions you as an ACOA can expect is a pervasive feeling of anger. It may well up inside of you and seem to envelope you like an exploding mushroom cloud of fury. The problem with this feeling is that it may obscure your awareness of what else you may be feeling. You know you are angry, but at whom and for what?

At first swipe, it may seem as if your grandchild is the sole recipient of your anger. He or she has broken the code of behavior that you adopted when you were a child. The child has gone beyond the boundaries of reasonable social expectations, and anger will likely be one of the first feelings provoked in you. Try, however, to let yourself see if there is a spilling over of some self-directed anger onto your grandchild. There is a good chance that you may actually be angry at yourself for having perpetuated the bad seed. As such, you may have been looking to your grandchild to verify your self-worth by demonstrating successful behavior which may be presumed to come only when a child is reared in a good family. If you have indirectly asked your grandchild to carry the mantle of responsibility and perpetuate the myth that there is "nothing wrong in this family," then your anger can be easily understood. It is not justified, only understood, and you have to separate the two concepts. To say "We had such high hopes for you, and you let us down" does not address the problem. It is a misleading statement because you also had high hopes for yourself, and these expectations may never have been met. It is both unfair and unrealistic to base your feelings of self-worth and those of your entire progeny upon the shoulders of a grandchild, however much of a star he or she may be in your life. If you find your inner dialogue sounding like "As long as Johnny does well in school and stays off drugs, then I'm a successful person"; or, "I'm counting on Johnny to hold up the family banner that will tell the world that this family and I are OK," then you probably have not adequately resolved your own personal problem of self-esteem that stems from your alcoholic childhood family. Remember, you are never too old to work through these feelings. You might find that clarifying them in a personal journal or counseling may be helpful.

On the other hand, don't jump to the conclusion that if you are disappointed, there is something wrong with you. You may be legitimately disappointed not so much in the behavior of your grandchild but *for your grandchild*. This is a very important feeling because it relates directly to your caring and worry for your grandchild's best interests and not to your childhood feelings of inadequacy. It is likely that you, like most grandparents, have a special twinkle in your eye for your grandchildren. You love them and wish only the best for them. The undisputed propensity for grandchildren to be lovingly spoiled at the hands of a grandparent is well known. Grandparents also tend to serve as the people who will really listen to the grandchild when his or her mother or father can't or won't. When through reasons of abuse of alcohol or drugs, that special connection across the generations is damaged, strained, or even broken, you truly have reason to be concerned. The question is what to do next.

Taking Action

As a consequence of your childhood spent in a dysfunctional alcoholic family, you are a natural survivor. As an ACOA parent who has raised a family and prevented the cycle of addiction from reaching into your children's generation, you evidenced concern and caring. Those attributes will not desert you now that you are a grandparent. You will still have the concern and vigilance that helped you raise your own healthy children. There is a good chance that you will want to take some sort of action if you feel that your grandchildren are in trouble, and it is likely that your desire to take action will be construed as helpful and positive. But it might also be overzealous, and this requires caution.

You are one of the most experienced persons in your extended family. You may even be the oldest. You have weathered the storms of your own childhood and did the best you could in your child rearing. Perhaps from the perspective that the passing of time gives, you wish that you had done some things differently. But hindsight is always 20/20, and it's too late to worry much about that now. The fact is that you know a lot more now than you did then and want to use your life's experience to help your troubled grandchild and his or her frustrated parents. As you choose how you are going to intervene, try to be aware of your impassioned tendency to want to fix the entire problem by yourself. However, because it is not exclusively *your* problem but rather a problem shared by your extended family, it is best if the solution is a joint venture. To this end, it is important that you distinguish as best you can between, on the one hand, what you know and want to share lovingly with your family and, on the other, your tendency as an ACOA to possibly overreact so as to maintain control. Wish as you may, you are not in a position to control either your adult child or your grandchild. Sometimes merely becoming aware of these old familiar feelings is enough to allow you to regain your sense of calm and perspective. You have a wealth of insight and experience that may be priceless if channeled wisely and prudently.

Therefore, ask yourself honestly how you can get your child and grandchild to listen to you. The key may be to first listen to them. Let them sound off. When you listen, you will probably find out the particular problems they are concerned about and you will come to understand what they're feeling. It is imperative in your discussions with them that you convey this understanding and willingness to hear them out. The chances are that they will be more open to you if you do so—although, depending on your grandchild's degree of involvement with chemical substances, it is quite possible that your words may fall on deaf ears. Regardless, it is important that you express your concern and a patient willingness to listen because you may be one of the only people in your family who is not thoroughly caught up in the throes of the drama or the immediacy of the conflict.

It is both a clinical and personal observation and a scientific fact that self-disclosure and openness usually elicit a similar response in the other person. It is likely that your child and grandchild will respond to you as openly as they can at this time in reaction to your nonjudgmental listening. You are now in a position to offer your guidance and insight. Your words may or may not be heeded, but don't underestimate their value. At this time, it is likely that you are the patriarch or matriarch of the family who, in most families, is granted a special status. Use it well. You may, for instance, enter the situation much like an arbitrator of a dispute between labor and management. In that case, both sides are listened to and a reasoned compromise is offered as a basis for continued negotiations. Both sides are likely to listen because you are trusted.

You will find yourself in a position to offer a variety of suggestions. You could offer to serve as a mediator in a direct conversation between parent and child. You could suggest to the grandchild who "has nothing to hide" to go and get an evaluation for drug or alcohol problems in order to "get your parents off your back." This can be conducted at the local Council on Alcoholism or community mental health center. You could also suggest that perhaps it would be best if the entire family enter some form of family therapy either on a short-term or an extended basis if the problems have been long in the making. Your grandchild may be more willing to do so because you are not pointing the finger of accusation at anyone, but are upset that the members of your family are not getting along with one another. If, however, your grandchild is emotionally dysfunctional as a result of alcohol or other drug use, it is entirely reasonable that you discuss with your adult child the use of a structured intervention. This is an effective approach to getting an individual who is in denial into treatment. You can find a mental health professional who specializes in this technique by contacting any of the county or state agencies on alcohol or substance abuse in your area or through a social service agency affiliated with your church or synagogue. A private and confidential talk between you and your pastor might start the entire process without embarrassing anyone.

It may, however, be your unfortunate circumstance to find that neither your child nor your grandchild is interested at this time in addressing the problem. Both may be in denial. Your grandchild may not have hit bottom yet and his or her parents may not be ready to acknowledge the extent of the problem and take action. No doubt you are worried, angry, and upset, but it is time for you to lovingly detach. You must recognize that your direct intervention will only alienate you from all parties and make the situation that much worse. Your decision, therefore, has nothing to do with not caring, but rather with an acceptance of the limits of intervention and your ability to change the lives of those you love. Your position as an intermediary will be compromised if you intervene prematurely and may prevent you from ever being able to give advice or help solve the problem at a later date. Accept the fact that your hands may be tied and return to Alanon as a means to cope and gain support in your struggle. By no means should you let their problems cause you to go into a crisis at this stage of your life or feel that all your efforts have been fruitless.

As any successful problem solver will tell you, knowing *when* to intervene is just as important as knowing *how* to intervene. Diplomats who engage in "shuttle" negotiations between warring countries know that if they begin their efforts before the parties are ready to admit that their actions no longer work, they will be unsuccessful and might actually exacerbate the problems. They wait, therefore, knowing that the damage caused by waiting is less destructive than the damage that will be caused if they are unable to help because they jumped in too soon. You, like any diplomat, must put time on your side by remaining confident and available to help. Put your good offices at their disposal. Let your telephone be the conduit for your child and grandchild to communicate with one another indirectly for a period. Let them vent their anger and frustration to you so you can recast them in terms the other party can understand. Be ready to listen, but be wary of telling your child and grandchild what to do. Play the role of the passive therapist who knows that advice given too quickly and too forcefully will drive the other person away.

Remember that you are trusted and revered, even if your child and grandchild never express it directly. Remember also that just as you wanted praise from your alcoholic parent when you were growing up, so your child and grandchild need praise and encouragement from you. And above all, do not let your children's failures become your failures. They are not extensions of your personality. They are now adults making their way in the world with their own families. You may have raised them and have inculcated your values into them, but they are running their own lives. Like the overwhelming majority of ACOAs from dysfunctional childhood families, you may feel that you don't really know how successful you were in raising your children. Perhaps you never will. But once your children are gone, you can't let your doubts about the past dictate your future.

If doubts continue to plague you, you can hang on to these sure things: (1) Your primary objectives in growing up in a dysfunctional alcoholic family of origin were first to survive and then to succeed. You achieved these goals. (2) Once you decided to raise a family of your own, your primary objectives were to raise healthy children and to prevent the cycle of alcoholism and addictive behavior from penetrating into your children's generation. If you achieved these objectives, then you succeeded as a parent.

You don't have to prove yourself any longer. There is no bad seed. You broke the cycle; now it's your adult child's job to raise healthy children just as you raised yours. If he or she can't do it, it's no more your fault than was your parent's addiction or dysfunctional behavior. Recognizing that some events are out of your control is one of the signs of a mature and healthy personality. Accepting this axiom about people and the ways they behave is the first step in being able to help them when they ask for it. You will be able to help. But your child and grandchild will have to ask you for it in their own way and in their own time and be ready to accept. You only have to keep your eyes and ears open.

Appendix: Resources and Supplementary Information

In this section we have listed sources and resources that can offer you help and guidance should your own family situation threaten to get out of control. Some of these telephone numbers provide you with immediate access to a counselor or trained professional who can give you advice over the telephone. Other telephone numbers will enable you to obtain more detailed information specifically for your particular problem. At the very least the hotlines and referral services cited here will provide you with a helpful, nonjudgmental, supportive voice no matter what time of the day you call. These organizations exist precisely because you may have a problem that requires an additional set of eyes and ears before a solution can be found. We have also included some important books that may give you a more detailed insight into some of the problems we have addressed in this book. Resources are organized according to the following categories:

- Addiction and Alcoholism
- Adult Children of Alcoholics
- Parenting
- Personal Growth
- Relationships
- Your Parents

Addiction and Alcoholism

Organizations
Addiction Research Foundation
33 Russell St.
Toronto, Ontario, Canada M5S 251
(416) 595-6144

Al-Anon/Al-Ateen Family Group Headquarters, Inc.
1372 Broadway
New York, NY 10018
(212) 302-7240

Alcoholics Anonymous World Services, Inc.
468 Park Ave. S.
New York, NY 10016
(212) 686-1100

American Council on Alcoholism
8501 LaSalle Rd., Ste. 301
Towson, MD 21205
(301) 296-5555

Narcotics Anonymous
P.O. Box 9999
Van Nuys, CA 91409
(818) 780-3951

National Clearinghouse for Alcohol and Drug Information
P.O. Box 2345
Rockville, MD 20850
(301) 468-2600

National Council on Alcoholism
12 W. Twenty-first St., Ste. 700
New York, NY 10010
(212) 206-6770

National Council on Alcohol Abuse and Alcoholism
5600 Fishers Ln.
Rockville, MD 20857
(301) 443-2403

National Institute of Drug Abuse
11400 Rockville Pike
Rockville, MD 20857
(301) 443-6500

Rutgers Center of Alcohol Studies
P.O. Box 969
Piscataway, NJ 08854
(201) 932-2190

In addition to these organizations you will find your state divisions on alcoholism and drug abuse listed under the state department of health in your telephone directory's white pages. You also can look under the white pages listings for your county or municipal government to find a local office on alcohol and/or drug addiction.

HOTLINES AND HELPLINES

	Area Covered	Telephone
Al-Anon Family Group Headquarters	United States (except New York)	1-800-356-9996
Alcohol and Drug Helpline	United States	1-800-821-4357
Cocaine Hotline	Connecticut, Delaware, Massachusetts, Maryland, New Jersey, Rhode Island, Washington, D.C.	1-800-262-2463
Dial-A-Sober Thought	United States (except Pennsylvania)	1-800-457-6237
Drug Abuse Information and Referral Hotline, National Institute of Drug Abuse	United States	1-800-662-4357
Hazeldon Foundation Educational Materials	United States (except Minnesota)	1-800-328-9000
Narconon International	United States (except California)	1-800-331-5659
Narcotics Education	United States (except Washington, D.C.)	1-800-548-8700
National Federation of Parents for Drug-Free Youth	United States	1-800-554-5437
Pride/National Parents Resource for Drug Education	United States	1-800-241-7946

Bibliography

Books

Beattie, Melody. *Codependent No More*. New York: Hazeldon/Harper & Row, 1987.

Black, Claudia. *My Dad Loves Me, My Dad Has a Disease*. Denver: M.A.C., 1974.

Brecher, Edward. *Licit and Illicit Drugs*. Boston: Little, Brown, 1972.

Cane, Pricilla. *Going Home!: Life After Treatment*. Center City, Minn: Hazeldon, 1987.

Chatlos, Calvin. *Crack*. New York: Perigee, 1987.

Gold, Mark. *The Facts About Drugs and Alcohol*. New York: Bantam, 1986.

Marshall, Shelly. *Young, Sober, and Free*. Center City, Minn: Hazeldon/Harper & Row, 1978.

Radcliffe, Anthony, Peter Rush, Carol Forror Sites, and Joe Cruse. *The Pharmer's Almanac: Pharmacology of Drugs*. Denver: M.A.C., 1985.

Schaef, Anne Wilson. *Co-Dependence: Misunderstood and Mistreated*. San Francisco: Harper & Row, 1987.

_____. *When Society Becomes an Addict*. San Francisco: Harper & Row, 1987.

Wallace, John. *Alcoholism: New Light on the Disease*. Newport, R.I.: Edgehill, 1985.

Weil, Andrew, and Winifred Rosen. *Chocolate to Morphine: Understanding Mind-Active Drugs*. Boston: Houghton Mifflin, 1983.

Periodicals

Alcoholism and Addiction Magazine

The U.S. Journal of Drug and Alcohol Dependence

Adult Children of Alcoholics

Organizations

Children of Alcoholics Foundation, Inc.
200 Park Ave., 31 Fl.
New York, NY 10166
(212) 351-2680

National Association for Children of Alcoholics
31582 Coast Hwy., Ste. B
South Laguna, CA 92677
(714) 499-3889

Bibliography

Books

Ackerman, Robert. *Children of Alcoholics*. Holmes Beach, Fla.: Learning Publishers, 1979.

Black, Claudia. *Repeat After Me*. Denver: M.A.C., 1985.

_____. *It Will Never Happen to Me!* Denver, M.A.C., 1981.

Marlin, Emily. *Hope*. New York: Harper & Row, 1987.

McConnell, Patty. *A Workbook for Healing: Adult Children of Alcoholics*. San Francisco: Harper & Row, 1986.

Seixas, Judith, and Geraldine Youcha. *Children of Alcoholism: A Survivor's Manual*. New York: Harper & Row, 1985.

Woititz, Janet. *Adult Children of Alcoholics*. Pompano Beach, Fla.: Health Communications, 1983.

Periodicals

Changes: For and About Adult Children of Alcoholics

Parenting

Organizations

Parents for Parents, Inc.
125 Northmore Dr.
Yorktown Heights, NY 10598
(914) 962-3326

Parents' Resources, Inc.
P.O. Box 107
Planetarium Station
New York, NY 10024
(212) 866-4776

The Mother's Connection
468 Rosedale Ave.
White Plains, NY 10605
(914) 946-5757

The National Parent Center
1314 Fourteenth St., N.W., Ste. 6
Washington, DC 20005
(202) 483-8822

Mothers At Home
P.O. Box 2208
Merrifield, VA 22116
(703) 352-2292

Children Are People, Inc.
1599 Selby Ave.
St. Paul, MN 55104
(612) 227-4031

Parents Anonymous
6733 S. Sepulveda Blvd., Ste. 270
Los Angeles, CA 90048
1-800-421-0353

Community Intervention, Inc.
220 S. Tenth St.
Minneapolis, MN 55403
(612) 332-6537

Tough Love
P.O. Box 1069
Doylestown, PA 18901
(215) 348-7090

Families Anonymous
P.O. Box 528
Van Nuys, CA 91408
(818) 989-7841

HOTLINES AND HELPLINES

	Area Covered	Telephone
Agency Information and Referral Service/Intervention for Adolescents	United States	1-800-621-3860
Parents Anonymous	United States (except California)	1-800-421-0353
Child Abuse Hotline	United States	1-800-422-4453
Parents Without Partners, Inc.	United States (except Maryland)	1-800-632-8078

Bibliography

Books

Ackerman, P., and M. Kappleman. *Signals: What Your Child Is Really Telling You.* New York: New American Library, 1980.

Ackerman, Robert. *Children of Alcoholics: A Guidebook for Educating Therapists and Parents.* Holmes Beach, Fla.: Learning Publications, 1974.

Caplan, Frank. *The First Twelve Months of Life: Your Baby's Growth Month by Month.* New York: Bantam, 1971.

Caplan, Frank, and Theresa Caplan. *The Second Twelve Months of Life: Your Baby's Growth Month by Month.* New York: Bantam, 1977.

Cross, Wilbur. *Kids and Booze: What You Must Know to Help Them.* New York: Dutton, 1979.

Dobson, James. *Hide or Seek: How to Build Self-Esteem in Your Child.* Old Tappan, N.J.: Revell, 1974.

Elkind, David. *The Hurried Child: Growing Up Too Fast Too Soon.* Reading, Mass.: Addison-Wesley, 1981.

Erikson, Erik. *Childhood and Society.* New York: Norton, 1963.

_____. *Identity and the Life Cycle.* New York: Norton, 1980.

_____. *Identity, Youth and Crisis.* New York: Norton, 1968.

Ewy, Donna. *Preparation for Parenthood: How to Create a Nurturing Family.* New York: Signet, 1986.

Eyre, Linda, and Richard Eyre. *Teaching Children Joy.* Salt Lake City, Utah: Shadow Mountain, 1980.

Galinsky, Ellen. *The Six Stages of Parenthood.* Reading, Mass.: Addison-Wesley, 1981.

Ginott, Haim. *Between Parent and Teenager.* New York: Avon, 1969.

_____. *Between Parent and Child.* New York: Avon, 1956.

Leboyer, Frederick. *Birth Without Violence.* New York: Knopf, 1975.

_____. *Loving Hands.* New York: Knopf, 1976.

Marzollo, Jean. *Supertot: Creative Learning Activities for Children from One to Three and Sympathetic Advice for Their Parents.* New York: Harper & Row, 1977.

Milgram, Gail Gleason. *What, When, and How to Talk to Children About Alcohol and Other Drugs.* Center City, Minn.: Hazeldon, 1983.

O'Gorman, Patricia, and Philip Oliver-Diaz. *Breaking the Cycle of Addiction: A Parenting Guide to Raising Healthy Kids.* Pompano Beach, Fla.: Health Communications, 1987.

Salk, Lee. *What Every Child Would Like His Parents to Know (To Help Him with the Emotional Problems of His Everyday Life).* New York: Simon & Schuster, 1984.

Spock, Benjamin, and Michael Rothenberg. *Dr. Spock's Baby and Child Care.* New York: Simon & Schuster, 1945.

Personal Growth

Organizations

Personal growth by its nature is an individual and internal journey. Sometimes, however, the counsel of others is helpful. Consider your priest or minister or mental health center as a source of information.

You can also try to find help through a referral service provided by your state or county psychological association or office of social services.

Bibliography

Books

Alberti, Robert and Michael Emmons. *Your Perfect Right*. San Luis Obispo, Calif: Impact, 1970.

Bland, Jeffrey. *Your Health Under Siege: Using Nutrition to Fight Back*. Brattleboro, Vt.: Stephen Green Press, 1981.

Bloomfield, Harold. *Making Peace with Yourself*. New York: Bloomfield Press, 1985.

Dyer, Wayne. *Pulling Your Own Strings*. New York: Avon, 1978.

Goldberg, Herb. *The Hazards of Being Male*. New York: Signet, 1977.

Harris, Thomas. *I'm O.K.—You're O.K.* New York: Harper & Row, 1967.

Lazarus, Arnold, and Allen Fay. *I Can If I Want To*, New York: Warner Books, 1975.

Lerner, Rockelle. *Daily Affirmations*. Pompano Beach, Fla.: Health Communications, 1985.

Peck, M. Scott. *The Road Less Traveled*. New York: Simon & Schuster, 1980.

Pelletier, Kenneth. *Mind as Healer, Mind as Slayer*. New York: Dell, 1977.

Phelps, Stanlee, and Nancy Austin. *The Assertive Woman: A New Look*. San Luis Obispo, Calif.: Impact, 1987.

Presnall, Lewis. *First Aid for Depression*. Minneapolis: Hazeldon, 1985.

Rogers, Carl. *On Becoming a Person*. Boston: Houghton Mifflin, 1961.

Rosewater, Lynne Brovo. *Changing Through Therapy: Understanding the Therapeutic Experience*. New York: Dodd, Mead, 1987.

Travis, John, and Regina Sara Ryan. *Wellness Workbook*. San Francisco: Ten Speed Press, 1986.

Vickery, Donald, and James Fries. *Take Care of Yourself: A Consumer's Guide to Medical Care*. Reading, Mass.: Addison-Wesley, 1976.

Wilbur, Ken. *No Boundary*. New York: New Science Library/ Bantam, 1981.

Relationships

Organizations

Remarried Parents, Inc.
102-20 Sixty-seventh Dr.
Forest Hills, NY 11375
(718) 459-2011

Worldwide Marriage Encounter
1908 E. Highland
San Bernardino, CA 92404
(714) 881-3456

Marriage Anonymous
P.O. Box 690
Chambersburg, PA 17201
(717) 532-2800

Bibliography

Books

Bach, George. *Stop, You're Driving Me Crazy.* New York: Avon, 1971.

Campbell, Susan. *Beyond the Power Struggle.* San Luis Obispo, Calif.: Impact, 1986.

_____. *The Couple's Journey: Intimacy as a Path to Wholeness.* San Luis Obispo, Calif.: Impact, 1986.

Cole, Jim. *The Controllers: A View of Our Responsibility.* Mill Valley, Calif.: Growing Images, 1971.

_____. *The Facade: A View of Our Behavior.* Mill Valley, Calif.: Jim Cole, 1970.

_____. *Filtering People.* Mill Valley, Calif.: Growing Images, 1987.

_____. *The Helpers: A View of Our Helpfulness.* Mill Valley, Calif.: Jim Cole, 1973.

_____. *The Holder: A View of Our Relationship.* Mill Valley, Calif.: Jim Cole, 1973.

_____. *Thwarting Anger.* Mill Valley, Calif.: Growing Images, 1985.

McCann, Eileen. *The Two Step.* New York: Grove, 1985.

Periodicals

Focus: On Chemically Dependent Families

Your Parents

Organizations

Gray Panthers
311 S. Juniper St., Ste. 601
Philadelphia, PA 19107
(215) 545-6555

Older Women's League
730 Eleventh St., N.W.
Washington, DC 20001
(202) 783-6686

Phoenix Society
Box 351
Cheshire, CT 06410
(203) 387-6913

American Association of Retired Persons
1909 K St., N.W.
Washington, DC 20049
(202) 872-4700

Concerned Relatives of Nursing Home Patients
P.O. Box 18820
Cleveland, OH 44118
(216) 321-0403

Friends and Relatives of Institutionalized Aged, Inc.
425 E. Twenty-fifth St.
New York, NY 10010
(212) 481-4422

Children of Aging Parents
2761 Trenton Rd.
Levittown, PA 19056
(215) 945-6900

Nursing Home Information Service
c/o National Council of Senior Citizens
925 W. Fifteenth St., N.W.
Washington, DC 20005
(202) 347-8800

HOTLINES AND HELPLINES

	Area Covered	Telephone
Alzheimer's Disease and Related Disorders Association	United States (except Illinois)	1-800-621-0379

For specific information regarding services for your aging or infirm parent, or for information on resources available to you and your family, contact your state office on aging or any county or municipal offices on aging in your area. The telephone numbers and addresses of these bureaus will be listed under the state offices section of your telephone directory and/or under the county offices or municipal offices listings. Generally you can also find information specific to your state or area by calling your state's or city's department of social services information number. The operator will usually be able to direct you to the offices authorized to handle your specific requests.

Bibliography

Books

Bloomfield, Harold, and Leonard Felder. *Making Peace with Your Parents.* New York: Random House, 1983.

Erikson, Erik, and Joan Erikson. *Vital Involvement in Old Age.* New York: Norton, 1986.

Friday, Nancy. *My Mother, Myself.* New York: Delacorte, 1987.

Halpern, Howard. *Cutting Loose: An Adult Guide to Coming to Terms with Your Parents.* New York: Bantam, 1978.

Index